A Primer of Conservation Biology

A Primer of Conservation Biology

Richard B. Primack
Boston University

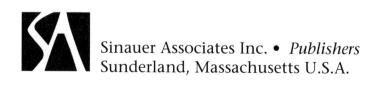

Sinauer Associates Inc. • *Publishers*
Sunderland, Massachusetts U.S.A.

The Cover

Red-and-green macaws (*Ara chloroptera*) gather at clay cliffs in the tropical forests of Peru. Many species of macaws are endangered in the wild; the case study on pages 2–5 discusses their situation. Photograph © Frans Lanting/Minden Pictures.

A Primer of Conservation Biology

Library of Congress Cataloging-in-Publication Data
Primack, Richard B., 1950–
    A primer of conservation biology / Richard B. Primack.
            p.   cm.
    Includes bibliographical references and index.
    ISBN 0-87893-730-7 (paper)
    1. Conservation biology.   I. Title.
QH75.P7525   1995
333.95′16—dc20   95-13972
                                                               CIP

Printed in U.S.A.

5   4   3   2   1

This book is dedicated to my children, Daniel and William, in the hope that they will experience the undiminished richness of nature.

Contents

Preface

Conservation biology has emerged during the last ten years as a major new discipline addressing the alarming loss of biological diversity throughout the world. This biodiversity crisis has attracted increasing scientific, governmental, and popular attention. Conservation biology represents a fusion of theory, research, applied projects, and public policy that is evolving at a rapid pace. Evidence of the explosive increase of interest in this new scientific field is shown by the rapidly increasing membership of the Society for Conservation Biology, the great intellectual excitement displayed in many journals and newsletters, and the large number of new edited books and advanced texts that appear almost weekly.

University students have enrolled enthusiastically and in large numbers in introductory conservation biology courses. The publication of my previous book, *Essentials of Conservation Biology* (1993), and *Principles of Conservation Biology* (1994) by Gary K. Meffe and C. Ronald Carroll provided students with textbooks that synthesize the many subjects included in conservation biology. Nevertheless, a need still exists for a "quick" guide to the field for those who want basic familiarity with conservation biology. The *Primer* attempts to provide a brief but thorough introduction to the major concepts and problems of the field. It is designed for use in short courses in conservation biology; it can also be used as a supplemental text for general biology, ecology, wildlife biology, and environmental policy courses. The *Primer* is also intended to be a concise guide for professionals who require a background in the subject, yet who have no need for the in-depth case studies and discussions presented in the other two books.

I hope readers of this book will want to find out more about the extinction crisis facing species and biological communities, and what can be done to halt it. If they gain a greater appreciation for the goals, methods, and importance of conservation biology, this primer will have served its purpose.

Acknowledgments

Special thanks are due to the many people acknowledged in *Essentials of Conservation Biology*, from which much of the material in *A Primer of Conservation Biology* was drawn. Their assistance was invaluable in the writing of the original book, and the *Primer* would not have been possible without it. Portions of the *Primer* manuscript were reviewed by Janis Alcorn, Katrina Brandon, Cutler Cleveland, Nicholas Gotelli, Joel Heinen, Eric Menges, Charles Munn, Margaret Primack, Mark Primack, Kent Redford, John Silander, Daniel Simberloff, Barry Spergel, Phil Tabas, and John Terborgh. April Allgaier Stern assisted in the editing and provided much valuable commentary on draft chapters. Elizabeth Platt was the principal research assistant and manuscript editor for the original book, and much of her work is reflected in the *Primer*. I would also like to express my thanks to Boston University for the excellent facilities and environment that made this project and its predecessor possible. Thanks are also due to Andy Sinauer, Carol Wigg, and Norma Roche at Sinauer Associates for their assistance and advice in this project.

CHAPTER 1

Conservation Biology and Biological Diversity

AROUND THE GLOBE, biological communities that took millions of years to develop are being devastated by human actions. The list of transformations of natural systems that are directly related to human activities is long. Vast numbers of species have declined rapidly, some to the point of extinction, as a result of excessive hunting, habitat destruction, and an onslaught of introduced predators and competitors. Natural hydrologic and chemical cycles have been disrupted by the clearing of land, which causes billions of tons of topsoil to erode and wash into rivers, lakes, and oceans each year. Genetic diversity has decreased, even among species with otherwise healthy populations. The very climate of the planet may have been disrupted by a combination of atmospheric pollution and deforestation. The present threats to biological diversity are unprecedented: never before in the history of life have so many species been threatened with extinction in so short a period of time. These threats to biological diversity are accelerating due to the demands of a rapidly increasing human population and its continuing advances in technology. This dire situation is exacerbated by the unequal distribution of the world's wealth and the crushing poverty of many of the tropical countries that have an abundance of species. Moreover, many of the threats to biological diversity are synergistic; that is, several independent factors, such as acid rain, logging, and overhunting, combine multiplicatively to make a situation even worse (Myers 1987). What is bad for biological diversity will almost certainly be bad for human populations because humans are dependent on the natural environment for air and water, raw materials, food, medicines, and other goods and services.

Some people feel discouraged by the avalanche of species extinctions occurring in the world today, but it is also possible to feel challenged by the need to do something to stop the destruction. The next few decades will determine how many of the world's species will survive. The efforts now being made to save species, establish new conservation areas, and protect existing national parks will determine which of the world's species are preserved for the future. **Conservation biology** is the scientific discipline that has developed out of these efforts. It brings together people and knowledge from many different fields to address the biodiversity crisis. In the future, people may look back on these closing years of the twentieth century as a time when a relative handful of determined people saved numerous species and biological communities from extinction.

Interdisciplinary Conservation Methods: A Case Study

Macaws are familiar to most people as large, brightly colored parrots with a mischievous, amiable intelligence that makes them the clowns of the bird world. Yet for all their popularity as pets and performers, macaws are in trouble in the wild. Nine of the sixteen species of macaws that reside in the tropical forests of South America are endangered, with at least one species, the Spix's macaw, in imminent danger of extinction. Throughout their range, all species have declined dramatically in numbers as a result of a combination of factors: the systematic collection of wild birds for pets, hunting by local people, and forest destruction. Given the variety of factors contributing to the macaws' decline, it is perhaps not surprising that a multifaceted approach is required for the conservation of these birds. The efforts to protect macaw species serve as a powerful illustration of the interdisciplinary nature of conservation biology.

In spite of their popularity as pets, very little was known about macaws in the wild until recently, in part because they are abundant only in remote regions of tropical forests. One such area is the rain forest of southeastern Peru, where wildlife biologists from the Wildlife Conservation Society (WCS) have been conducting research since 1984 on eight species of macaws (Munn 1992, 1994). At first, these scientists concentrated on learning the species' basic biology: their dietary requirements, reproductive habits, and other basic needs. In the course of the study, however, a previously reported, unique aspect of macaw behavior quickly became evident: large numbers of macaws congregate at isolated clay cliff faces to eat clay (see cover photograph). A biochemical investigation of this puzzling behavior suggested two possibilities: first, macaws may need the trace minerals in the clay to supplement their diet of seeds and fruits, and second, the clay may detoxify poisonous chemicals contained in the seeds the birds eat. In either case, the clay licks represent a vital, possibly irreplaceable resource for the macaws that visit them.

Even before this discovery, biologists were aware that urgent action was needed to halt the decline of the macaws. Mining and timber companies are encroaching on the macaws' habitat. Hunting of macaws for food and collecting for the pet trade by local Indians and more recent settlers are also contributing to the decline in the species' populations. Though political lobbying by wildlife advocacy organizations is leading toward a ban on international trade in macaws by most tropical American countries and imports of macaws by the United States, the combination of internal markets, loopholes in the laws, and a growing black market continue to put pressure on wild macaw populations. Active efforts to protect macaw habitat and discourage collecting and hunting are still needed. The discovery of the macaws' dependence on clay licks emphasizes the fact that any protected areas established for the birds must include key resources to assure the macaws' continued prosperity. Moreover, the macaws' tendency to congregate in specific locations to acquire these resources makes them vulnerable to hunters and collectors. Conservation biologists thus are seeking ways to discourage the collection of wild birds for pets and the hunting of birds for meat.

As a result of the research by the WCS biologists and other scientists working in the area, several steps are being taken to protect macaws and their habitat, including the clay licks. New and proposed national parks in Peru, such as Manu National Park and the 1.5 million hectare* Tambopata–Candamo Reserved Zone, deliberately include many of the macaw clay licks and surrounding forest habitat. Management of the parks is being designed to permit a degree of sustainable development in order to provide employment for local people and to support the parks economically. Key elements in this proposed strategy are sustainable harvesting of Brazil nuts, establishment of commercial zones at the parks' periphery for small-scale streambed gold mining, and ecotourism centered on the macaw clay licks. With assistance from the wildlife biologists, tourist lodges are being built in the parks and on the park borders, many of which are owned, operated, and staffed by local people. Local people are also being trained as field guides, research assistants, and park employees. Information from the ongoing research program is being incorporated into the nature tours and educational materials. Some local people already see that the macaws are the key to their economic future rather than just their next meal, and as a result they are taking an active role in maintaining the beauty and environmental quality of the parks. Wildlife biologists working in the area are also helping these people to gain legal title to their traditional lands so that they are able to have a say in the long-term de-

*For an explanation of the term *hectare* and other measurements, see Table 1.1.

Table 1.1

Some useful units of measurement

LENGTH	
1 meter (m)	1 m = 39.4 inches
1 kilometer (km)	1 km = 1000 m = 0.62 miles
1 centimeter (cm)	1 cm = 1/100 m = 0.39 inches
1 millimeter (mm)	1 mm = 1/1000 m = 0.039 inches
AREA	
square meter (m^2)	Area encompassed by a square, each side of which is 1 meter
1 hectare (ha)	1 ha = 10,000 m^2 = 2.47 acres; 100 ha = 1 square kilometer (km^2)
MASS	
1 kilogram (kg)	1 kg = 2.2 pounds
1 gram (g)	1 g = 1/1000 kg = 0.035 ounce
TEMPERATURE	
degree Celsius (°C)	0°C = 32° Fahrenheit (melting point of ice) 100°C = 212° Fahrenheit (boiling point of water) 23°C = 72° Fahrenheit ("room temperature")

velopment of the region and become players in the highly profitable ecotourism industry. These programs involving local people in park development are not without controversy; other biologists working in the region have proposed excluding all people from the national parks in order to maintain them as wilderness areas with minimal human impact.

The establishment of protected areas for macaws has been a boon to conservation activities and may ultimately turn the tide for the birds. Two recent discoveries about macaw reproductive behavior may prove useful in rebuilding macaw populations. First, ornithologists working elsewhere in South America have discovered that macaws have exacting requirements for nest sites, which are usually cavities in the trunks of large trees. Suitable cavities are apparently few and far between, and if none are available, pairs will not breed. To overcome the scarcity of nesting sites, a Peruvian architect working with the WCS project designed a plastic nest box that can be attached to tree trunks. One species, the scarlet macaw, has shown a willingness to accept these boxes as nests. Distribution of the nest boxes through the parks may not only help to increase the population density of the species but may also allow macaws to breed in logged forests from which large trees have been removed. Second, researchers have determined that although macaws often lay two eggs per nest, only the older nestling typically survives. The researchers found that they can remove the younger nestling and raise it by hand. Once these captive-fostered juveniles fledge, they join the wild flock at the clay licks.

These and other techniques that have grown out of the ongoing research are being incorporated into conservation efforts in Bolivia and Brazil, where macaw species are highly endangered. The most significant outcome of the project for conservation biology as a whole, however, lies in the interdisciplinary element at work in this endeavor. Active, dedicated scientists with a long-term commitment to investigating and protecting an important but poorly known group of species recognized the need to become politically active in order to establish legally protected areas, control international trade in the species, and develop a sustainable economic alternative for local people. By incorporating their research results into a flexible management plan, in this case involving artificial nest construction and captive rearing of nestlings, the researchers were able to make progress toward their goal. Furthermore, by publicizing their results in highly visible publications such as *National Geographic* and in videos produced for international television, the researchers made it possible for the techniques developed by this project to be transferred to conservation efforts in other countries, enhancing the value of their outstanding work. The lessons for conservation biology are clear: by attacking a problem from several different angles, researchers can address the underlying biological, economic, sociological, and management problems that threaten species.

What Is Conservation Biology?

Conservation biology is a multidisciplinary science that has developed in response to the crisis confronting biological diversity today (Soulé 1985). Conservation biology has two goals: first, to understand the effects of human activities on species, communities, and ecosystems, and second, to develop practical approaches to preventing the extinctions of species and, if possible, to reintegrate endangered species into a properly functioning ecosystem.

Conservation biology arose because none of the traditional applied disciplines are comprehensive enough by themselves to address the critical threats to biological diversity. Agriculture, forestry, wildlife management, and fisheries biology have been concerned primarily with developing methods for managing a small range of species for the marketplace and for recreation. These disciplines generally have not addressed the protection of the full range of species found in biological communities, or have regarded it as a secondary issue. Conservation biology complements the applied disciplines by providing a more general theoretical approach to the protection of biological diversity; it differs from those disciplines in having the long-term preservation of entire biological communities as its primary consideration, with economic factors often secondary.

The academic disciplines of population biology, taxonomy, ecology, and genetics constitute the core of conservation biology, and many conservation biologists have been drawn from these ranks. In addition, many

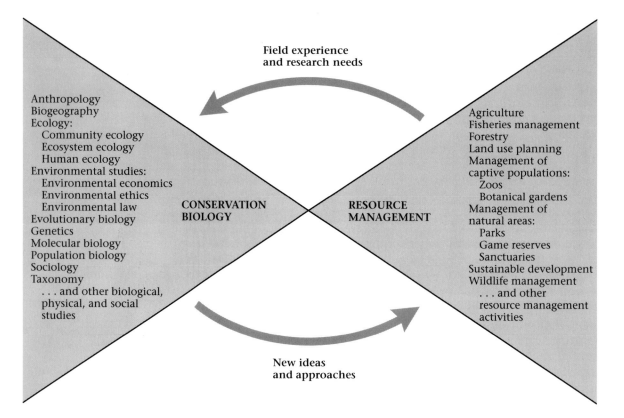

Field experience
and research needs

Anthropology
Biogeography
Ecology:
    Community ecology
    Ecosystem ecology
    Human ecology
Environmental studies:
    Environmental economics
    Environmental ethics
    Environmental law
Evolutionary biology
Genetics
Molecular biology
Population biology
Sociology
Taxonomy
    . . . and other biological,
    physical, and social
    studies

**CONSERVATION
BIOLOGY**

**RESOURCE
MANAGEMENT**

Agriculture
Fisheries management
Forestry
Land use planning
Management of
captive populations:
    Zoos
    Botanical gardens
Management of
natural areas:
    Parks
    Game reserves
    Sanctuaries
Sustainable development
Wildlife management
    . . . and other
    resource management
    activities

New ideas
and approaches

1.1 Conservation biology represents a new synthesis of many academic disciplines (left) that provide principles and new approaches for the applied fields of resource management (right). Experience gained in the field in turn influences the direction of the academic sciences. (After Temple 1991.)

leaders in conservation biology have come from zoos and botanical gardens, bringing with them experience in maintaining and propagating species in captivity. Because much of the biodiversity crisis arises from human pressures, conservation biology also incorporates ideas and expertise from a broad range of fields outside of biology (Figure 1.1). For example, environmental law and policy provides the basis for government protection of rare and endangered species and critical habitats. Environmental ethics provides a rationale for preserving species. Social sciences such as anthropology, sociology, and geography provide insight into how people can be encouraged and educated to protect the species found in their immediate environment. Environmental economists provide analyses of the economic value of biological diversity to support arguments for preservation. Ecosystem ecologists and climatologists monitor the biological and physical characteristics of the environment and develop models to predict environmental responses to disturbance.

In many ways, conservation biology is a crisis discipline. Decisions on conservation issues are being made every day, often with limited information and under severe time pressure. Conservation biology tries to provide answers to specific questions applicable to actual situations. Such questions are raised in the process of determining the best strategies for protecting rare species, designing nature reserves, initiating breeding programs to maintain genetic variation in small populations, and reconciling conservation concerns with the needs of local people and governments. Conservation biologists and scientists in related fields are well suited to provide the advice that governments, businesses, and the general public need to make crucial decisions. Although some conservation biologists would hesitate to make recommendations without detailed knowledge of the specifics of a case, the urgency of many situations necessitates informed decisions based on certain fundamental principles of biology. This book describes those principles and gives examples of how they may be factored into policy making.

The background of conservation biology

Awareness of the need for conservation of biological diversity has existed for decades, even centuries, in North America, Europe, and other regions of the world. Religious and philosophical beliefs concerning the value of protecting species and wilderness are found in many cultures worldwide (Hargrove 1986; Callicott 1994). Many religions emphasize the need for people to live in harmony with nature and to protect the living world because it is a divine creation. In the United States, philosophers such as Ralph Waldo Emerson and Henry David Thoreau espoused nature as an important element in human moral and spiritual development (Callicott 1990). Wilderness advocates such as John Muir and Aldo Leopold argued for preserving natural landscapes and maintaining the health of natural ecosystems. Another, related perspective is the **Gaia hypothesis**, which views the Earth as having the properties of a "superorganism" whose biological, physical, and chemical components interact to regulate characteristics of the atmosphere and climate (Lovelock 1988). Proponents of this idea often advocate reduction or complete cessation of practices and industries that disrupt the normal interaction of the Earth's components.

Paralleling these preservationist and ecological orientations, an influential forester, Gifford Pinchot (1865–1946), developed the idea that qualities found in nature, including timber, fodder, clean water, wildlife, species diversity, and even beautiful landscapes, can be considered **natural resources** and that the goal of management is to use these natural resources for the greatest good of the greatest number of people for the longest time. These ideas have been extended by the concept of **ecosystem management**, which places the highest management priority on the health of ecosystems and wild species (Grumbine 1994b; Noss and Cooperrider 1994). The current paradigm of **sustainable development** also advocates an approach similar to Pinchot's: developing natural resources to meet present human needs in a way that does not harm biological communities and considers the needs of future generations as well (Lubchenco et al. 1991; IUCN/UNEP/WWF 1991).

The modern discipline of conservation biology rests on several underlying assumptions that are generally agreed upon by members of the discipline (Soulé 1985). These assumptions represent a set of ethical and ideological statements that suggest research approaches and practical applications. Although not all of these statements are accepted unequivocally, the acceptance of one or two is sufficient rationale for conservation efforts.

1. *The diversity of organisms is good.* In general, people enjoy biological diversity. The hundreds of millions of visitors each year to zoos, national parks, botanical gardens, and aquariums are testimony to the general public's interest in biological diversity. Genetic variation within species also has popular appeal, as shown by dog shows, cat shows, agricultural expositions, and flower exhibitions. It has even been speculated that humans have a genetic predisposition to like biological diversity, called **biophilia** (Wilson 1984; Kellert and Wilson 1993). Biophilia would have been advantageous for the hunting-and-gathering lifestyle that humans led for hundreds of thousands of years before the invention of agriculture. High biological diversity would have provided them with a variety of foods and other resources, buffering them against environmental catastrophes and starvation.

2. *The untimely extinction of populations and species is bad.* The extinction of species and populations as a result of natural processes is a natural event. Through the millennia of geological time, extinctions of species have generally been balanced by the evolution of new species. Likewise, the local loss of a population is usually offset by the establishment of a new population through dispersal. However, human activity has increased the rate of extinction a thousandfold. In the twentieth century, virtually all of the hundreds of known extinctions of vertebrate species, as well as the presumed thousands of extinctions of invertebrate species, have been caused by humans.

3. *Ecological complexity is good.* Many of the most interesting properties of biological diversity are expressed only in natural environments. For example, complex coevolutionary and ecological relationships exist among tropical flowers, hummingbirds, and mites that live in the flowers. The mites use the hummingbirds' beaks as a "bus" to go from flower to flower (Colwell 1986). Such relationships would never be suspected if the animals and plants were housed in isolation in zoos and botanical gardens. The fascinating behaviors used by desert animals to obtain water would not be apparent if the animals were living in cages and supplied with water to drink at will. While it might be possible to preserve the biological diversity of species in zoos and gardens, the ecological complexity that exists in natural communities would be largely lost.

4. *Evolution is good.* Evolutionary adaptation is the process that eventually leads to new species and increased biological diversity. Therefore, allowing populations to evolve in nature is good. Human activities that limit the ability of populations to evolve, such as severely reducing a species' population size through overharvesting, are bad.

5. *Biological diversity has intrinsic value.* Species have a value all their own, regardless of their material value to human society. This value is conferred by their evolutionary history and unique ecological roles, and also by their very existence.

What Is Biological Diversity?

Although protection of biological diversity is central to conservation biology, the phrase "biological diversity" has different meanings to different people. The definition given by the Worldwide Fund for Nature (1989) is, "the wealth of life on earth, the millions of plants, animals, and microorganisms, the genes they contain, and the intricate ecosystems they help build into the living environment." Thus biological diversity needs to be considered at three levels. Biological diversity at the **species** level includes the full range of organisms on Earth, from bacteria and protists through the multicellular kingdoms of plants, animals, and fungi. On a finer scale, biological diversity includes the **genetic variation** within species, both among geographically separated populations and among individuals within single populations. Biological diversity also includes variation in the biological **communities** in which species live, the **ecosystems** in which communities exist, and the interactions among these levels (Figure 1.2).

All levels of biological diversity are necessary for the continued survival of species and natural communities, and all are important to people. Species diversity represents the range of evolutionary and ecological adaptations of species to particular environments. The diversity of species provides people with resources and resource alternatives; for example, a tropical rain forest with many species produces a wide variety of plant and animal products that can be used for food, shelter, and medicine. Genetic diversity is needed by any species in order to maintain reproductive vitality, resistance to disease, and the ability to adapt to changing conditions. Genetic diversity in domestic plants and animals is of particular value to people in the breeding programs necessary to sustain and improve modern agricultural species. Community-level diversity represents the collective response of species to different environmental conditions. Biological communities found in deserts, grasslands, wetlands, and forests support the continuity of proper ecosystem functioning, providing beneficial services such as flood control, protection from soil erosion, and filtering of air and water.

Genetic diversity in a rabbit population

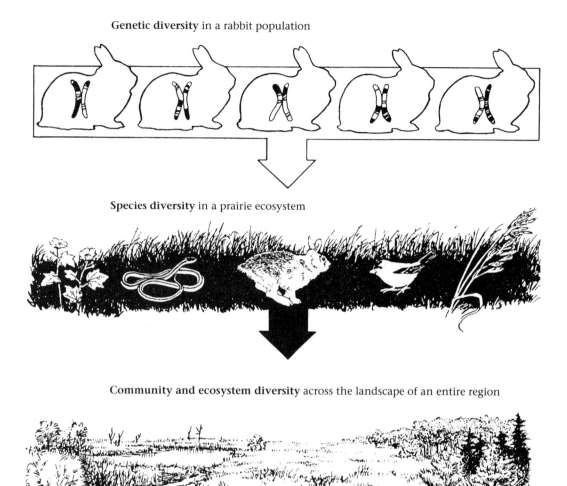

Species diversity in a prairie ecosystem

Community and ecosystem diversity across the landscape of an entire region

1.2 Biological diversity includes genetic diversity (the genetic variation found within each species), species diversity (the range of species in a given ecosystem), and community/ecosystem diversity (the variety of habitat types and ecosystem processes extending over a given region). (After Temple 1991; drawings by Tamara Sayre.)

Species diversity

At each level of biological diversity—species, genetic, and community—conservation biologists study the mechanisms that alter or maintain diversity. Species diversity includes the entire range of species found on

Earth. A species is generally defined in one of two ways. First, a species can be defined as a group of individuals that is morphologically, physiologically, or biochemically distinct from other groups in some characteristic (the **morphological definition of species**). Increasingly, differences in DNA sequences are being used to distinguish species that look almost identical, such as bacteria. Second, a species can be distinguished as a group of individuals that can potentially breed among themselves and do not breed with individuals of other groups (the **biological definition of species**).

The morphological definition of species is the one most commonly used by taxonomists, biologists who specialize in the identification of unknown specimens and the classification of species. The biological definition of species is the one most commonly used by evolutionary biologists because it is based on measurable genetic relationships rather than on somewhat subjective physical features. In practice, however, the biological definition of species is hard to use because it requires knowledge of which individuals are actually capable of breeding with one another—information that is rarely available. As a result, practicing field biologists learn to tell species apart by how they look, sometimes calling them "morpho-species" or other such terms until taxonomists can give them official, Latin names (Box 1.1).

Problems in distinguishing and identifying species are more common than many people realize (Rojas 1992; Standley 1992). For example, a single species may have several varieties that have observable morphological differences, yet the varieties may be similar enough that they are still considered members of a single biological species. Different breeds of dogs, such as German shepherds, collies, dachshunds, and beagles, all belong to one species and readily interbreed despite the conspicuous differences among them. In contrast, there are closely related "sibling species" that are very similar in morphology or physiology, yet are still biologically separate and do not interbreed. In practice, biologists often have difficulty distinguishing variation within a single species from variation between closely related species. Further complicating matters, what are otherwise distinct species may occasionally mate and produce **hybrids**, intermediate forms that blur the distinction between species. Hybridization is particularly common among plant species in disturbed habitats. Finally, for many groups of species, the taxonomic studies needed to determine species and identify specimens have not yet been done.

The inability to clearly distinguish one species from another, whether due to similarities of characteristics or to confusion over the correct scientific name, often slows down efforts at species protection. It is difficult to write precise, effective laws to protect a species if it is not certain what name should be used. A lot more work is needed to catalogue and classify the world's species. Taxonomists have described only 10%–30% of the world's species, and many species are going extinct before they can be de-

Box 1.1   How Do Species Get Their Names?

Taxonomy is the science of classifying living things. The goal of modern taxonomy is to create a system of classification that reflects the evolution of groups of species from their ancestors. By identifying the relationships among species, taxonomists help conservation biologists identify species or groups that may be evolutionarily unique or particularly worthy of conservation efforts. In modern classification,

Similar **species** are grouped into a **genus**: the Blackburnian warbler (*Dendroica fusca*) and many similar warbler species belong to the genus *Dendroica*.

Similar **genera** are grouped into a **family**: all wood warbler genera belong to the family Parulidae.

Similar **families** are grouped into an **order**: all songbird families belong to the order Passeriformes.

Similar **orders** are grouped into a **class**: all bird orders belong to the class Aves.

Similar **classes** are grouped into a **phylum**: all vertebrate classes belong to the phylum Chordata.

Similar **phyla** are grouped into a **kingdom**: all animal classes belong to the kingdom Animalia.

Most modern biologists recognize five kingdoms in the living world: plants, animals, fungi, monerans (single-celled species without a nucleus, such as bacteria), and protists (more complex single-celled species with a nucleus). Although diversity exists at all taxonomic levels, in practice conservation efforts are generally focused at the species level.

Biologists throughout the world have agreed to use a standard set of names, often called scientific names or Latin names, when discussing species. This naming system, known as **binomial nomenclature**, was developed in the eighteenth century by the Swedish biologist Carolus Linnaeus. The use of scientific names avoids the confusion that can occur when the common names found in everyday language are used. Only the scientific name is standard across countries and languages. Scientific species names consist of two words. In the scientific name for the Blackburnian warbler, *Dendroica fusca, Dendroica* is the genus name and *fusca* is the specific name. The genus name is somewhat like a person's family name in that many closely related people can have the same family name (Sullivan), while the specific name is like a person's given name (Jonathan) within their family.

Scientific names are written in a standard way. The first letter of the genus name is always capitalized, whereas the species name is almost always lowercased. Scientific names are either italicized or underlined. Sometimes scientific names are followed by a scientist's name, as in *Homo sapiens* Linnaeus, indicating that Linnaeus was the person who first proposed the scientific name given to the human species. When many species in a single genus are being discussed, or if the identity of a species within a genus is uncertain, the abbreviations spp. or sp., respectively, are sometimes used (e.g., *Dendroica* spp.). If a species has no close relatives, it may be the only species in its own genus. Similarly, a genus that is unrelated to any other genera may form its own family.

scribed. The key to solving this problem is to train more taxonomists, particularly for work in the species-rich tropics (Raven and Wilson 1992).

Genetic diversity

Genetic diversity within a species is often affected by the reproductive behavior of individuals within populations. A **population** is a group of individuals that mate with one another and produce offspring; a species

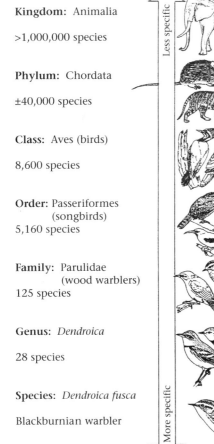

Kingdom: Animalia

>1,000,000 species

Phylum: Chordata

±40,000 species

Class: Aves (birds)

8,600 species

Order: Passeriformes
(songbirds)
5,160 species

Family: Parulidae
(wood warblers)
125 species

Genus: *Dendroica*

28 species

Species: *Dendroica fusca*

Blackburnian warbler

The Blackburnian warbler (*Dendroica fusca*) can be grouped with more and more other animals at successively higher levels of taxonomic organization.

may include one or more separate populations. A population may consist of only a few individuals or millions of individuals.

Individuals within a population usually are genetically different from one another. Genetic variation arises because individuals have slightly different **genes**, the units of the chromosomes that code for specific proteins. The different forms of a gene are known as **alleles**, and the differences arise through **mutations**—changes that occur in the deoxyribonucleic

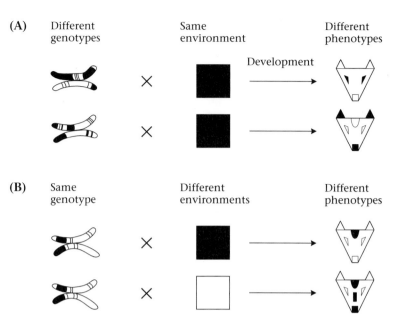

1.3 The physical, physiological, and biochemical characteristics of an individual—its phenotype—are determined by its genotype and by its environment. (A) Genetically different individuals may have different phenotypes even if they develop in the same environment. (B) Genetically similar individuals may have different phenotypes if they develop in different environments (e.g., hot vs. cold climate; abundant vs. scarce food). (After Alcock 1993.)

acid (DNA) that constitutes an individual's chromosomes. The various alleles of a gene may affect the development and physiology of the individual organism differently. Crop breeders and animal breeders take advantage of this genetic variation to breed higher-yielding, pest-resistant strains of domesticated species such as wheat, corn, cattle, and poultry.

Genetic variation increases when offspring receive unique combinations of genes and chromosomes from their parents via the **recombination** of genes that occurs during sexual reproduction. Genes are exchanged between chromosomes during meiosis, and new combinations are created when chromosomes from two parents combine to form a genetically unique offspring. Although mutations provide the basic material for genetic variation, the ability of sexually reproducing species to randomly rearrange alleles in different combinations dramatically increases their potential for genetic variation.

The total array of genes and alleles in a population is referred to as its **gene pool**, while the particular combination of alleles that any individual possesses is referred to as its **genotype**. The **phenotype** of an individual represents the morphological, physiological, and biochemical characteristics that result from the expression of its genotype in a particular environment (Figure 1.3). Some characteristics of humans, such as the amount of body fat and tooth decay, are strikingly influenced by the environment, while other characteristics, such as eye color and blood type, are determined predominantly by an individual's genotype.

The amount of genetic variability in a population is determined both by the number of genes in its gene pool that have more than one allele (referred to as **polymorphic genes**) and by the number of alleles for each polymorphic gene. The existence of a polymorphic gene allows individuals in the population to be **heterozygous** for the gene, that is, to receive a different allele of the gene from each parent. Genetic variability allows species to adapt to a changing environment. In general, it has been found that rare species have less genetic variation than widespread species and consequently are more vulnerable to extinction when environmental conditions change.

Community and ecosystem diversity

A **biological community** is defined by the species that occupy a particular locality and the interactions among those species. A biological community together with its associated physical environment is termed an **ecosystem.** Within an ecosystem, water evaporates from biological communities and the Earth's surface to fall again as rain or snow and replenish terrestrial and aquatic environments. Soil is built up out of particles of parent rock material and decaying organic matter. Photosynthetic plants absorb light energy, which is used in the plants' growth. This energy is captured by animals that eat the plants, or is released as heat, both during the organisms' life cycles and after they die and decompose. Plants absorb carbon dioxide and release oxygen during photosynthesis, while animals and fungi absorb oxygen and release carbon dioxide during respiration. Mineral nutrients, such as nitrogen and phosphorus, cycle between the living and the nonliving compartments of the ecosystem.

The physical environment, especially the annual cycle of temperature and precipitation, affects the structure and characteristics of a biological community, determining whether a particular site will be a forest, a grassland, a desert, or a wetland. The biological community can also alter the physical characteristics of an ecosystem. In a terrestrial ecosystem, for example, wind speed, humidity, temperature, and soil characteristics at a given location can all be affected by the plants and animals present there. In aquatic ecosystems, such physical characteristics as water turbulence and clarity, water chemistry, and water depth affect the characteristics of the associated biota, but communities such as kelp forests and coral reefs can in turn affect the physical environment.

Within a biological community each species utilizes a unique set of resources that constitute its **niche.** The niche for a plant species might consist of the type of soil on which it is found, the amount of sunlight and moisture it requires, the type of pollination system it has, and its mechanism of seed dispersal. The niche for an animal might include the type of habitat it occupies, its thermal tolerances, its dietary requirements, its home range or territory, and its water requirements. Any component of the niche may become a **limiting resource** when it restricts population size. For example, populations of bat species that have specialized roosting requirements, forming colonies only in limestone caves, will be restricted by the number of caves with the proper conditions for roosting sites.

The niche often includes the stage of succession that the species occupies. **Succession** is the gradual process of change in species composition, community structure, and physical characteristics that occurs following natural or human-caused disturbance to a biological community. Certain species are often associated with particular successional stages. For example, sun-loving butterflies and annual plants most commonly are found early in succession, in the months immediately after a gap opens in an old-growth forest. Other species, including shade-tolerant wildflowers and birds that nest in holes in dead trees, are found in late-successional stages, among mature trees in an old-growth forest. Human management patterns often upset the natural pattern of succession; grasslands that are overgrazed by cattle and forests from which all the large trees have been cut for timber typically no longer have their rare late-successional species.

The composition of communities is often affected by competition and predation (Terborgh 1992a; Ricklefs 1993). Predators often dramatically reduce the numbers of their prey species and may eliminate some species from certain habitats. Predators may indirectly increase biological diversity in a community by keeping the densities of some prey species so low that competition for resources does not occur. The number of individuals of a particular species that the resources of an environment can support is termed the **carrying capacity.** A population's numbers are often well below the carrying capacity when it is held in check by predators. If the predators are removed, the population may increase to a point at which it reaches the carrying capacity, or may even increase beyond the carrying capacity to a point at which crucial resources are overtaxed and the population crashes.

Community composition is also affected by **mutualistic relationships,** in which two species benefit each other. Mutualistic species reach higher densities when they occur together than when only one of the species is present. Common examples of such mutualisms are plants with fleshy fruits and fruit-eating birds that disperse their seeds; flower-pollinating insects and flowering plants; the fungi and algae that together form lichens; plants that provide homes for ants that supply them with nutrients (Figure 1.4); and corals and the algae that live inside them (Howe 1984; Bawa 1990). At the extreme of mutualism, two species are always found together and apparently cannot survive without each other. For example, the deaths of certain types of coral-inhabiting algae may be followed by the weakening and subsequent death of their associated coral species.

Trophic levels. Species in a biological community can be classified according to how they obtain energy from the environment (Figure 1.5). The first of these classes, called **trophic levels,** comprises the **photosynthetic species** (also known as **primary producers**), which obtain energy directly from the sun to build the organic molecules they need to live and grow. In

(A)

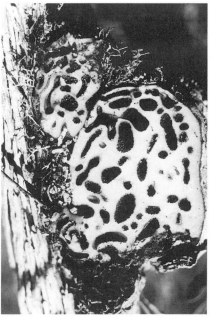

(B)

1.4 A mutualistic relationship. (A) This *Myrmecodia* in Borneo is an epiphyte—a plant that grows on the surface of another plant. *Myrmecodia* produces a tuber at its base that is filled with hollow chambers, as seen in (B). The chambers are occupied by ant colonies, which use some chambers as nesting sites and some as "dumps" for wastes and dead ants. The epiphyte absorbs the mineral nutrients it needs for growth from these "dumps," while the ants obtain a safe nest. In the epiphyte–tree relationship shown in (A), the epiphyte benefits while the tree it grows on is neither benefited nor harmed. (Photographs by R. Primack.)

terrestrial environments, higher plants such as flowering plants, gymnosperms, and ferns are responsible for most photosynthesis, while in aquatic environments, seaweeds, single-celled algae, and cyanobacteria (blue-green algae) are the most important primary producers. **Herbivores** (also known as **primary consumers**) eat photosynthetic species. **Carnivores** (also known as **secondary consumers** or **predators**) eat other animals. **Primary carnivores** (such as foxes) eat herbivores (such as rabbits), while **secondary carnivores** (such as bass) eat other carnivores (such as frogs). Carnivores usually are predators, though some combine direct predation with scavenging behavior, and others, known as **omnivores**, include a substantial proportion of plant foods in their diets. In general, predators are larger and stronger than the species they prey on, but they usually occur at lower densities than their prey.

Parasites form an important subclass of predators. Parasites, such as mosquitoes, ticks, intestinal worms, and disease-causing microparasites such as bacteria and protozoans, are typically smaller than their prey, known as **hosts**, and do not kill their prey immediately. The effects of parasites range from imperceptibly weakening their hosts to totally debilitating or even killing them over time. Parasites are often important in controlling the density of their host species. When host populations are at a high density, parasites can readily spread from one host individual to the next, causing an intense local infestation of the parasite and a subsequent decline in host density.

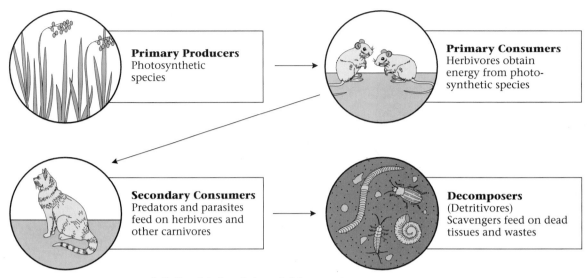

1.5 Trophic levels in a field ecosystem.

Detritivores (also known as **decomposers**) are species that feed on dead plant and animal tissues and wastes, breaking down complex tissues and organic molecules. Detritivores release minerals such as nitrogen and phosphorus back into the environment, where they can be taken up again by plants and algae. The most important detritivores are fungi and bacteria, but a wide range of other species play a role in breaking down organic materials. For example, vultures and other scavengers tear apart and feed on dead animals, dung beetles bury and feed on animal dung, and worms break down fallen leaves and other organic matter. If detritivores were not present to release mineral nutrients by breaking down organic matter, plant growth would decline greatly.

As a general rule, the greatest **biomass** (living weight) in an ecosystem will be that of the primary producers. In any community there are likely to be more individual herbivores than primary carnivores, and more primary carnivores than secondary carnivores. Although species can be organized into these general trophic levels, their actual requirements or feeding habitats within the trophic levels may be quite restricted. For example, a certain aphid species may feed only on one type of plant, and a certain lady beetle species may feed only on one type of aphid. These specific feeding relationships have been termed **food chains.** Such species-specific ecological requirements are an important reason for the inability of many species to increase in abundance within a community. The more common situation in many biological communities, however, is for a species to feed on several items at the trophic level below it, to compete for food with several species at its own trophic level, and in turn to be preyed upon by several species at the trophic level above it. Consequently, a more accurate description of the organization of biological communities is a **food web** in which species are linked together through complex feeding relationships (Figure 1.6). Species at the same trophic level that use approximately the same resources in the environment are considered to be members of a **guild** of competing species.

Keystone species and resources. Within biological communities, certain species may be important in determining the ability of large numbers of other species to persist in the community. These **keystone species** affect the organization of the community to a far greater degree than one would predict based only on their numbers of individuals or biomass (Terborgh 1976; Janzen 1986a). Protecting keystone species is a priority for conservation efforts because if a keystone species is lost from a conservation area, numerous other species might be lost as well. Top predators are among the most obvious keystone species because they are often important in controlling herbivore populations (Redford 1992). The elimination of even a small number of individual predators, constituting a minute portion of the community biomass, potentially can result in dramatic changes in the vegetation and a great loss in biological diversity (Pimm 1991; McLaren and Peterson 1994). For example, in many localities where gray wolves (*Canis lupus*) have been hunted to extinction by humans, populations of deer (*Odocoileus virginianus*) have exploded. The deer severely overgraze

1.6 Diagram of an actual food web studied in Gatun Lake, Panama. Phytoplankton ("floating plants") such as green algae are the primary producers at the base of the web. Zooplankton are tiny, often microscopic, floating animals; they are primary consumers, not photosynthesizers, but they, along with insects and algae, are crucial food sources for fishes in aquatic ecosystems. (After G. H. Orians.)

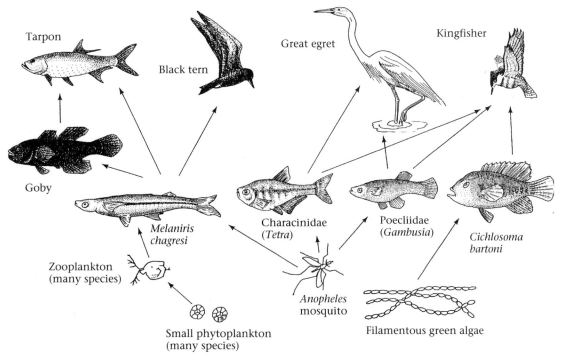

the habitat, eliminating many herbaceous species. The loss of these plants in turn is detrimental to the deer and to other herbivores, including insects. The reduced plant cover may lead to soil erosion, contributing to the loss of species that inhabit the soil.

Bats known as "flying foxes," of the family Pteropodidae, provide other examples of keystone species (Figure 1.7). These bats are the primary pollinators and seed dispersers of numerous economically important tree species in the Old World tropics and Pacific Islands (Cox et al. 1991). When bat colonies are overharvested by hunters and the trees the bats roost in are cut down, the bats' populations decline. As a result, many of the tree species in the remaining forest fail to reproduce. In short, the elimination of a keystone species can create a series of linked extinction events, known as an **extinction cascade**, that results in a degraded ecosystem with much lower biological diversity at all trophic levels. Returning the keystone species to the community may not necessarily restore the community to its original condition if other component species and aspects of the physical environment, such as soil cover, have already been lost.

The identification of keystone species has several important implications for conservation biology. First, as we have seen, the elimination of a keystone species from a community may precipitate the loss of many other species. Second, in order to protect a species of particular interest, it may be necessary to protect the keystone species on which it depends

1.7 Flying foxes—bats of the family Pteropodidae, such as these giant fruit bats—are vital pollinators and seed dispersers in Old World tropical forest communities. Many flying fox species are in danger of extinction. (Photograph © The Wildlife Conservation Society/NYZS.)

either directly or indirectly. Third, if the few keystone species of a community can be identified, these can be carefully protected or even encouraged if the area is being affected by human activity.

Nature reserves are typically compared and valued in terms of their size because, in general, larger reserves contain more species than smaller reserves. However, area alone may not be as significant as the range of habitats and resources that the reserve contains. Particular habitats may contain critical **keystone resources** that occupy only a small area of the habitat yet are crucial to many species in the community. For example, salt licks and mineral pools may provide essential minerals for wildlife, particularly in inland areas with heavy rainfall. The distribution of salt licks can determine the abundance and distribution of vertebrates in an area. The clay licks used by macaws are another example of such a keystone resource. **Deep pools** in streams and springs may be the only refuge for fish and other aquatic species during the dry season when water levels drop. These pools may also be the only sources of drinking water for terrestrial animals for a considerable distance. **Elevational gradients** may be a crucial feature of conservation areas. Many fruit- and nectar-feeding vertebrates and insects require a continuous supply of food, and one way they can supply their needs is by moving among communities searching for new food sources. A steep elevational gradient is typically occupied by a series of different plant communities, so migrating up or down a mountain slope is a common, efficient behavior for an animal in search of new food sources.

Measuring biological diversity

In addition to the definition of biological diversity generally accepted by conservation biologists, there are many other specialized, quantitative definitions of biological diversity that have been developed as a means of comparing the overall diversity of different communities. At its simplest level, diversity has been defined as the number of species found in a community, a measure known as **species richness.** Most definitions also include some measure of how evenly the total number (or abundance) of individuals is divided among species. For example, if there are 10 different bird species in a community of 60 individual birds, an even abundance would be 6 birds per species, while an uneven abundance would be 2 birds per species in 5 species and 50 birds in the sixth species. In the first case, no species would be considered to be dominant, while in the second case, the community would be dominated by the sixth species.

Mathematical indices of biodiversity have been developed to describe species diversity at different geographical scales. The number of species in a single community is usually described as **alpha diversity.** Alpha diversity comes closest to the popular concept of species richness and can be used to compare the number of species in different ecosystem types. The term **beta diversity** refers to the degree to which species composition changes along an environmental gradient. Beta diversity is high, for example, if the species composition of moss communities changes substantially with elevation on a mountain slope, but is low if most of the same species occupy the whole mountainside. **Gamma diversity** applies to larger geographical scales; it is defined as "the rate at which additional species are encountered as geographical replacements within a habitat type in different localities. Thus gamma diversity is a species turnover rate with distance between sites of similar habitat, or with expanding geographic areas" (Cody 1986). In practice, these three indices are often highly correlated. The plant communities of the Amazon, for instance, show high levels of diversity at the alpha, beta, and gamma scales (Gentry 1986). These quantitative definitions of diversity are used primarily in the technical ecological literature and capture only part of the broad definition of biological diversity used by conservation biologists.

The Distribution of Biological Diversity

Where is biological diversity found?

The richest environments in terms of numbers of species appear to be tropical rain forests, coral reefs, large tropical lakes, and the deep sea (Pianka 1966; Groombridge 1992). There is also an abundance of species in tropical dry habitats, such as deciduous forests, shrublands, grasslands, and deserts (Mares 1992), and in temperate shrublands with Mediter-

Table 1.2
Number of mammal species in selected tropical and temperate countries

Tropical country	Number of species	[a]Species per 10,000 km^2	Temperate country	Number of species	[a]Species per 10,000 km^2
Angola	275	76	Argentina	255	57
Brazil	394	66	Australia	299	41
Colombia	358	102	Canada	163	26
Costa Rica	203	131	Egypt	105	31
Kenya	308	105	France	113	39
Mexico	439	108	Japan	186	71
Nigeria	274	82	Morocco	108	39
Peru	359	99	South Africa	279	79
Venezuela	305	92	United Kingdom	77	33
Zaire	409	96	United States	367	60
Average		96	Average		48

Source: After Reid and Miller 1989, using data from WRI/IIED 1988.

[a]To standardize for the size of the country and allow comparisons of species richness, the number of species found in 10,000 square kilometers (the approximate area of the island of Jamaica) is estimated from species–area formulas (see Chapter 2).

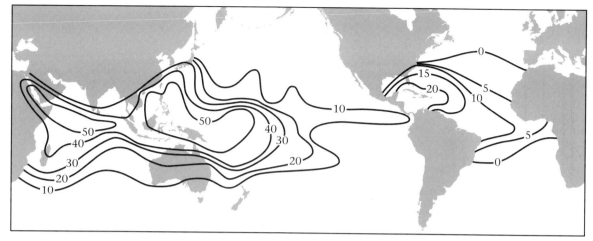

ranean climates, such as those found in South Africa, southern California, and southwestern Australia. In tropical rain forests this diversity is primarily due to the great abundance of animal species in a single class: the insects. In coral reefs and the deep sea the diversity is spread over a much broader range of phyla and classes (Grassle et al. 1991). Diversity in the deep sea may be due to the great age, enormous area, and stability of that environment, as well as specialization on particular sediment types (Etter and Grassle 1992). The great diversity of fishes and other species in large tropical lakes is due to rapid **evolutionary radiation** (Box 1.2) in a series of isolated, productive habitats (Kaufman and Cohen 1993).

For almost all groups of organisms, species diversity increases toward the tropics (Huston 1994). For example, Kenya has 308 species of mammals, while France has only 113 species, despite the fact that the two countries have roughly the same land area (Table 1.2). The contrast is particularly striking in the case of trees and other flowering plants: a hectare of forest in Amazonian Peru or lowland Malaysia might have 200 or more species growing as trees, while an equivalent forest in temperate Europe or the United States would probably contain 30 species per hectare or fewer. Patterns of diversity in terrestrial species are paralleled by patterns in marine species, with a similar increase in species diversity toward the tropics (Figure 1.8). For example, the Great Barrier Reef, off Australia, has 50 genera of reef-building corals at its northern end, where it approaches the tropics, but only 10 genera at its southern end.

The greatest diversity of species is found in tropical forests. Even though tropical forests occupy only 7% of the Earth's land area (see Figure 2.9), they contain over half of the world's species (Whitmore 1990). This estimate is based to some degree on only limited sampling of insects and other arthropods, groups that are thought to contain the majority of the world's species. Estimates of the number of undescribed insect species in

1.8 Global distribution of the genera of reef-forming corals, showing major concentrations in the western Pacific and Indian Oceans and a lesser concentration in the Caribbean. Numbers on the isocline lines indicate the number of genera; the lines connect areas with similar numbers. (After Stehli and Wells 1971.)

Box 1.2   The Origin of New Species

The process whereby one original species evolves into one or more new, distinct species, known as **speciation**, was first described by Charles Darwin and Alfred Russel Wallace more than 100 years ago. The theory of evolution of new species through **natural selection** is both simple and elegant. Individuals within a population show variations in certain characteristics, and some of these characteristics are inherited—they are passed genetically from parents to offspring. These genetic variations are caused by spontaneous changes in the chromosomes and by the rearrangement of chromosomes during sexual reproduction. Differences in genetic characteristics will enable some individuals to grow, survive, and reproduce better than other individuals, an idea often characterized as "survival of the fittest." As a result of the improved survival ability provided by a certain genetic characteristic, the individuals with that characteristic will be more likely to produce offspring than the others; over time, the genetic composition of the population will change.

The gene pool of a population will change over time as the environment of the species changes. These changes may be biological (altered food availability, competitors, prey) as well as physical (changes in climate, water availability, soil characteristics). When a population has undergone so much genetic change that it is no longer able to interbreed with the original species from which it was derived, it can be considered a new species. This process whereby one species is gradually transformed into another species is termed **phyletic evolution.**

For two or more new species to evolve from one original ancestor, there usually must be a geographical barrier that prevents the movement of individuals between the various populations. For terrestrial species, these barriers may be rivers, mountain ranges, or oceans that the species cannot readily cross. Speciation is particularly rapid on islands. Island groups such as the Galápagos and Hawaiian archipelagoes contain many species-rich insect and plant genera that were originally populations of a single invading species. These populations adapted genetically to the local conditions of isolated islands, mountains, or valleys, and have diverged sufficiently from the original species to now be considered separate species. These species will remain re-productively isolated from one another even if their ranges should once again overlap. This process of local adaptation and subsequent speciation is known as **evolutionary radiation** or **adaptive radiation.** Although phyletic evolution has no net effect on biodiversity, adaptive radiation results in much greater diversity.

The origin of new species is normally a slow process, taking place over hundreds, if not thousands, of generations. The evolution of higher taxa, such as new genera and families, is an even slower process, lasting hundreds of thousands or even millions of years. In contrast, human activities are destroying in only a few decades the vast numbers of species built up by these slow natural processes.

One of the most spectacular examples of adaptive radiation is displayed by the honeycreeper family. This family of birds, endemic to the Hawaiian Islands, is thought to have arisen from a single pair of birds that arrived on the islands by chance. The shapes and sizes of the bills are related to the foods eaten by each species: long bills are for feeding on nectar; short, thick bills are for cracking seeds; and short, sharp bills are for eating insects. (After Futuyma 1986.) ▶

tropical forests range from 5 million to 30 million (May 1992); 10 million is considered a reasonable working estimate at present. If the 10 million figure is correct, it would mean that insects found in tropical forests may constitute over 90% of the world's species. About 40% of the world's flow-

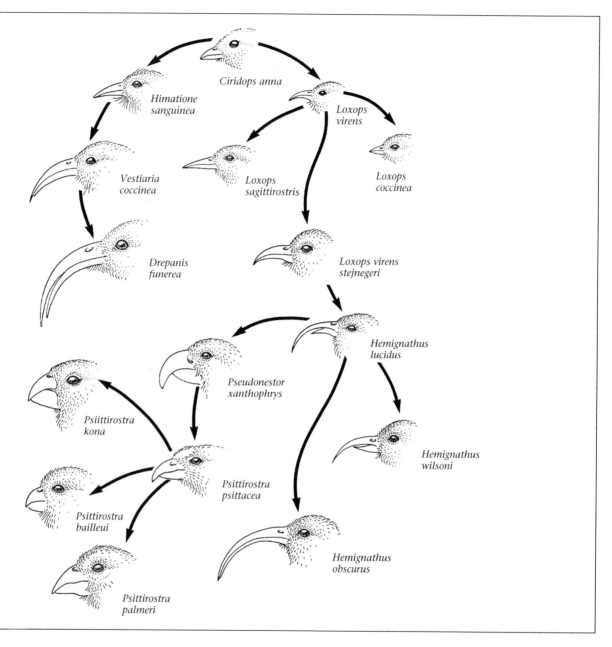

ering plant species are found in tropical forests, while 30% of the world's bird species are dependent on tropical forests (Myers 1980; Diamond 1985).

Coral reefs constitute another concentration of species. Colonies of

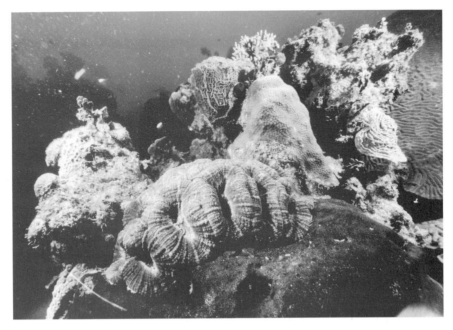

1.9 Coral reefs are built up from the skeletons of billions of tiny individual animals. The intricate coral landscapes create a habitat for many other marine species. (Photograph by Les Kaufman, Boston University.)

tiny coral animals (Figure 1.9) build the large coral reef ecosystems that are the marine equivalent of tropical rain forests in their species richness and complexity. The world's largest coral reef is the Great Barrier Reef off the east coast of Australia, which has an area of 349,000 km². The Great Barrier Reef contains over 300 species of corals, 1500 species of fish, 4000 species of mollusks, and 5 species of turtles, and provides breeding sites for some 252 species of birds (IUCN/UNEP 1988). The Great Barrier Reef contains about 8% of the world's fish species even though it occupies only 0.1% of the ocean surface area (Goldman and Talbot 1976).

Historical factors are also important in defining patterns of species richness, with areas that are geologically older having more species than younger areas. Coral species richness is several times greater in the Indian Ocean and West Pacific than in the Atlantic Ocean, which is geologically younger (see Figure 1.8). Areas that are geologically older have had more time to receive species dispersing from other parts of the world and more time for existing species to undergo adaptive radiation in response to local conditions.

Patterns of species richness are also affected by local variation in topography, climate, and environment (Diamond 1988a; Currie 1991). In terrestrial communities, species richness tends to increase with lower elevation, increasing solar radiation, and increasing precipitation (Figure 1.10). Strong seasonal temperature fluctuations are another factor associated with large numbers of species in the temperate zone (Scheiner and Rey-Benayas 1994). Species richness can also be greater where there is a complex topography that allows genetic isolation, local adaptation, and speciation to occur. For example, a sedentary species occupying a series of isolated mountain peaks may eventually evolve into several different species, each adapted to its local mountain environment. Areas that are geologically complex produce a variety of soil conditions with very sharp boundaries between them, leading to a variety of communities and species adapted to one soil type or another. Among temperate communities, great plant species diversity is found in southwestern Australia, South Africa, and other areas with a Mediterranean climate of mild, moist winters and hot, dry summers. The shrub and herb communities in these areas are apparently rich in species due to their combination of considerable geological age and complexity of site conditions. The greatest species richness in open ocean communities exists where waters from different biological communities overlap, but the locations of these boundary areas are often unstable over time (Angel 1993).

How many species exist worldwide?

Any strategy for conserving biological diversity requires a firm grasp of how many species exist and how those species are distributed. At present,

1.10 The distribution of species richness for tiger beetles (family Cicindelidae) in North America. Isocline lines connect areas with similar numbers of beetles. There is high species diversity in several areas of the southern United States, areas characterized by warm climate, open terrain, and topographic complexity. (From Pearson and Cassola 1992.)

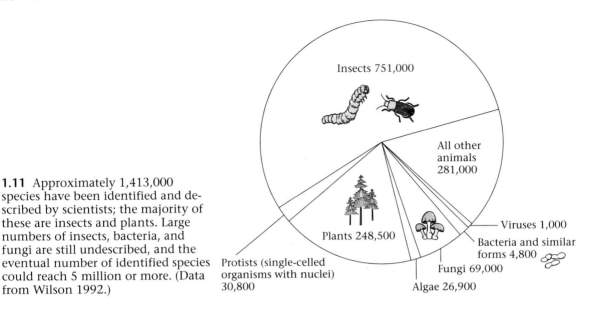

1.11 Approximately 1,413,000 species have been identified and described by scientists; the majority of these are insects and plants. Large numbers of insects, bacteria, and fungi are still undescribed, and the eventual number of identified species could reach 5 million or more. (Data from Wilson 1992.)

about 1.4 million species have been described. At least twice this number of species remain undescribed, primarily insects and other arthropods in the tropics (Figure 1.11; May 1992). Our knowledge of species numbers is imprecise because inconspicuous species have not received their proper share of taxonomic attention. For example, mites, nematodes, and fungi living in the soil and insects living in the tropical forest canopy are small and difficult to study. These poorly known groups could number in the hundreds of thousands or even millions of species. Bacteria are also very poorly known (Hawksworth 1992). Only about 4000 species of bacteria are recognized by microbiologists because of the difficulty of growing and identifying specimens. However, recent work in Norway analyzing bacterial DNA hints that there may be more than 4000 species in a single gram of soil, and an equally large number of species in marine sediments (Giovannoni et al. 1990; Ward et al. 1990). A lack of collecting has particularly hampered our knowledge of the number of species found in the marine environment. The marine environment appears to be a great frontier of biological diversity. An entirely new animal phylum, the Loricifera, was first described in 1983 based on specimens from the deep seas (Kristensen 1983), and there are undoubtedly many more species to be discovered.

Completely new biological communities are still being discovered, often in localities that are extremely remote and inaccessible to humans. Specialized exploration techniques, particularly in the deep sea and the forest canopy, have revealed unusual community structures:

• Diverse communities of animals, particularly insects, are adapted to living in the canopies of tropical trees, rarely if ever descending to the ground (Wilson 1991; Moffat 1994).

- A remote, mountainous rain forest reserve on the border between Vietnam and Laos was only recently surveyed by biologists. To their amazement, they discovered three mammal species new to science, now known as the giant muntjac, the Vu Quang ox, and the slow-running deer (Linden 1994).

- The floor of the deep sea, which remains almost entirely unexplored due to the technical difficulties of transporting equipment and people under high water pressure, has unique communities of bacteria and animals that grow around deep-sea geothermal vents (Lutz 1991; Tunnicliffe 1992). Undescribed, active bacteria have even been found in marine sediments up to 500 meters below the sea floor, where they undoubtedly play a major chemical and energetic role in this vast ecosystem (Parkes et al. 1994).

- A recent drilling project in Sweden turned up evidence of primitive anaerobic bacteria, known as archaebacteria, living within rocky fissures 5 kilometers beneath the Earth's surface (Gold 1992). If this evidence proves valid, it may be that large, undescribed communities of bacteria live inside the Earth, existing on sulfur, methane, and other energy-rich gases.

Extinction and Economics: Losing Something of Value

To discover, catalogue, and preserve the great diversity of species, a new generation of conservation biologists must be trained, and an increased priority must be given to the museums, universities, conservation organizations, and other institutions that support this work. Such a change will require a significant shift in current political and social thinking; governments and communities throughout the world must realize that biological diversity is extremely valuable—indeed, essential—to human existence. Ultimately, change will occur only if people feel that they are truly losing something of value by continuing to damage biological communities. But what is it are we losing? Why should anyone care if a species becomes extinct? What, precisely, is so terrible about extinction?

Patterns of extinction

The diversity of species found on the Earth has been increasing since life first originated. This increase has not been steady, but rather has been characterized by periods of high rates of speciation, followed by periods of minimal change and episodes of **mass extinction** (Sepkoski and Raup 1986; Wilson 1989). The most massive extinction took place at the end of the Permian epoch, 250 million years ago, when 77%–96% of all marine

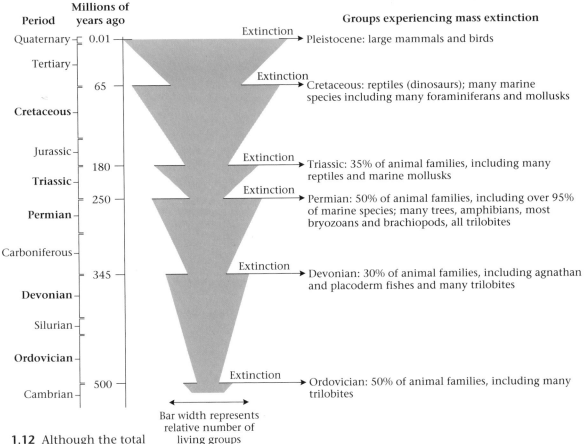

Period	Millions of years ago		Groups experiencing mass extinction

Quaternary — 0.01 — → Extinction → Pleistocene: large mammals and birds

Tertiary —

— 65 — → Extinction → Cretaceous: reptiles (dinosaurs); many marine species including many foraminiferans and mollusks

Cretaceous —

Jurassic —

— 180 — → Extinction → Triassic: 35% of animal families, including many reptiles and marine mollusks

Triassic —

— 250 — → Extinction → Permian: 50% of animal families, including over 95% of marine species; many trees, amphibians, most bryozoans and brachiopods, all trilobites

Permian —

Carboniferous —

— 345 — → Extinction → Devonian: 30% of animal families, including agnathan and placoderm fishes and many trilobites

Devonian —

Silurian —

Ordovician —

— 500 — → Extinction → Ordovician: 50% of animal families, including many trilobites

Cambrian —

Bar width represents relative number of living groups

1.12 Although the total number of families and species has increased over the eons, during each of five episodes of natural mass extinction a large percentage of these groups disappeared. The most dramatic period of loss occurred about 250 million years ago, at the end of the Permian period. We are now at the start of a sixth episode, the Pleistocene extinction, as human populations eliminate species through habitat loss and overharvesting.

animal species are estimated to have become extinct (Figure 1.12; Raup 1979). It is quite likely that some massive perturbation, such as widespread volcanic eruptions or a collision with an asteroid, caused such a dramatic change in the Earth's climate that many species were no longer able to exist. It took the process of evolution about 50 million years to regain the number of families lost during the Permian mass extinction. Species extinctions occur even in the absence of violent disturbance, however. Evolutionary theory states that one species may outcompete another or drive it to extinction through predation. A successful species may evolve into another in response to environmental changes or due to random changes in its gene pool. The factors determining the persistence or failure of a particular species are not entirely clear, but extinction is as much a part of the natural cycle as speciation is.

If extinction is a part of natural processes, why is the loss of species of concern? The answer lies in the relative rates of extinction and speciation.

Speciation is a slow process, occurring through the gradual accumulation of mutations and shifts in allele frequencies over tens of thousands, if not millions, of years. As long as the rate of speciation equals or exceeds the rate of extinction, biodiversity will remain constant or increase. In past geological periods, the loss of existing species was eventually balanced or exceeded by the evolution of new species. However, human activities are causing extinctions at a rate that far exceeds the rate of species replacement. The loss of species occurring at present is unprecedented, unique, and may soon be irreversible.

Environmental economics

Before the trend of species extinctions can be reversed, its fundamental causes must be understood. What factors cause humans to act in a destructive manner? Ultimately, environmental degradation occurs for economic reasons. Forests are logged for revenue from timber sales. Species are hunted for personal consumption, sale, and sport. Marginal land is converted into cropland because people have nowhere else to farm. Species are introduced accidentally or purposefully onto new continents and islands without any consideration for the resulting environmental devastation. Because the underlying cause of environmental damage is so often economic in nature, the solution must incorporate economic principles as well.

An understanding of a few fundamental economic principles will serve to clarify why people treat the environment in what appears to be a short-sighted, wasteful manner. One of the most universally accepted tenets of modern economic thought is that a voluntary transaction takes place only when it is beneficial to both parties involved. A baker who sells his loaves for fifty dollars will find few customers. Likewise, a customer who is willing to pay only five cents for a loaf will soon go hungry. Only when a mutually agreeable price is set that leaves both parties better off will the transaction occur. Adam Smith, an eighteenth-century philosopher whose writings are the foundation of much of modern economic thought, stated, "It is not upon the benevolence of the butcher, the baker, or the brewer that we eat our daily bread, but upon his own self-interest" (*Wealth of Nations*, 1776). All parties involved in an exchange have the expectation of improving their own situation. The sum of each individual acting in his or her own self-interest results in society as a whole becoming wealthier and more prosperous. This concept is referred to as an "invisible hand" guiding the market.

It is beyond the scope of this text to address all the assumptions in and exceptions to this principle of free exchange benefiting society. However, there is one notable exception that directly affects environmental issues. It is generally assumed that the costs and benefits of free exchange are accepted and borne by the participants in the transaction. In some cases, however, certain costs are incurred, or benefits enjoyed, by individuals not directly involved in the exchange. These outside costs or benefits are known as **externalities.** Perhaps the most notable and frequently over-looked externality is the environmental damage that occurs as an indirect consequence of human economic activity. Where externalities exist, the market fails to provide solutions that result in a more prosperous society. This **market failure** results in a misallocation of resources that may allow individuals to benefit at the expense of society.

The fundamental challenge facing the conservation biologist is to ensure that all the costs of a transaction are understood as well as the benefits. Companies or individuals involved in production that results in ecological damage generally do not bear the full cost of their activity. An oil refinery that emits toxic fumes and liquid wastes benefits from the sale of fuel, as does the consumer of the product. Yet the costs of this transaction—increased respiratory disease, decreased visibility, and a polluted environment—are distributed widely through society. Understanding this dichotomy is central to understanding the role of market failure: The wide distribution of the economic *cost* of an activity, combined with a concentrated *benefit* to a small group, creates an economic/ecological conflict.

In response to this challenge, a discipline is being developed that integrates economics, environmental science, and public policy and includes valuations of biological diversity in economic analyses (McNeely 1988; Costanza 1991; Barbier et al. 1994). This discipline is known as **environmental economics.** Conservation biologists are increasingly using the concepts and vocabulary of environmental economics because government officials, bankers, and corporate leaders can be more readily convinced of the need to protect biological diversity if there is an economic justification for doing so.

The environmental costs of large projects are increasingly being calculated in the form of **environmental impact assessments** that consider the present and future effects of the projects on the environment. The environment is often broadly defined to include not just harvestable natural resources, but also air and water quality, the lives of local people, and endangered species. In its most comprehensive form, a **cost–benefit analysis** compares the values gained by a project against the costs of the project and the values lost (Randall 1987). In theory, if the analysis shows that a project is profitable, it should go forward, while if the project is unprofitable, it should be stopped. In practice, cost–benefit analyses are notoriously difficult to carry out because the valuations of the benefits and costs may be difficult to assign and may change over time.

Recent attempts have been made to include the loss of natural resources in calculations of the widely used Gross Domestic Product (GDP) and other indices of national well-being (Daly and Cobb 1989; Repetto 1992). The problem with the GDP as it is usually calculated is that it measures all economic activity in a country, not just beneficial activity. Non-sustainable and unproductive economic activities (including overfishing of coastal waters and poorly managed strip mining) cause the GDP to increase, even though these activities are actually irrelevant or destructive to the long-term well-being of the country. Even environmental disasters such as the Exxon Valdez oil spill and the Gulf War (see Figure 2.15) appear as increases in the GDP because of the temporary increases in jobs and purchases needed for the cleanups. In actuality, the economic costs to a country associated with environmental damage can be considerable and often offset the gains the country apparently attains through agricultural and industrial development (Repetto 1990a,b, 1992). In Costa Rica, for example, the value of the forests destroyed during the 1980s greatly exceeded the income produced from forest products, so that the forestry sector actually represented a drain on the wealth of the country.

Common property resources

Many natural resources, such as clean air, clean water, soil quality, rare species, and even scenic beauty are considered to be **common property resources** that are owned by society at large. These resources are often not assigned a monetary value. People, industries, and governments use and damage these resources without paying more than a minimal cost, and sometimes paying nothing at all, a situation described as **the tragedy of the commons** (Hardin 1968, 1985). In the more complete systems of "green" accounting being developed, such as National Resource Accounting, the use of such common property resources is included as part of the internal cost of doing business instead of being regarded as an externality. When people and organizations have to pay for their actions, they will be likely either to stop damaging the environment or become much more careful (Repetto 1990b, 1992). Some suggestions for bringing this about include higher taxes on fossil fuels, penalties for inefficient energy use and pollution, and mandatory recycling programs. Investment can be redirected to activities that provide the most benefits to the greatest number of people in poverty. Finally, financial penalties for damaging biological diversity could be developed and made so severe that industries would be more careful of the natural world.

Demonstrating the value of biodiversity and natural resources is a complex matter because value is determined by a variety of economic and ethical factors. A major goal of environmental economics is to develop methods for valuing the components of biological diversity. A number of approaches have been developed to assign economic values to genetic variability, species, communities, and ecosystems. One of the most useful is that used by McNeely (1988) and McNeely et al. (1990). In this framework, values are divided between **direct values** (known in economics as *private goods*), which are assigned to those products harvested by people, and **indirect values** (in economics, *public goods*), which are assigned to benefits provided by biological diversity that do not involve harvesting or destroying the resource. Benefits that can be assigned indirect value include water quality, soil protection, recreation, education, scientific research, regulation of climate, and provision of future options for human society. **Existence value** is another kind of indirect value that can be assigned to a benefit—for example, how much people are willing to pay to protect a species from going extinct.

Direct Economic Values

Direct values are assigned to those products that are directly harvested and used by people. These values can often be readily calculated by observing the activities of representative groups of people, by monitoring collection points for natural products, and by examining import and export statistics. Direct values can be further divided into **consumptive use value**, for goods that are consumed locally, and **productive use value**, for products that are sold in markets.

Consumptive use value

Consumptive use value can be assigned to goods such as fuelwood and game that are consumed locally and do not appear in the national and international marketplaces. People living close to the land often derive a considerable proportion of the goods they require for their livelihood from the environment around them. These goods do not typically appear in the GDP of countries because they are neither bought nor sold (Repetto et al. 1989). However, if rural people are unable to obtain these products, as might occur following environmental degradation, overexploitation of natural resources, or even the creation of a protected reserve, then their standard of living will decline, possibly to the point where they are unable to survive and must move to another location.

Studies of traditional societies in the developing world show how extensively these people use their natural environment to supply fuelwood, vegetables, fruit, meat, medicine, cordage, and building materials (Figure 1.13; Prescott-Allen and Prescott-Allen 1982; Myers 1984; Hladick et al. 1993). For example, about 80% of the world's population still relies principally on traditional medicines derived from plants and animals as their primary source of medical treatment (Farnsworth 1988). Over 5000 species are used for medicinal purposes in China, while 2000 species are used in the Amazon basin (Schultes and Raffauf 1990).

One of the crucial requirements of rural people is protein, which they obtain by hunting wild animals for meat. In many areas of Africa, wild game constitutes a significant portion of the protein in the average person's diet: in Botswana about 40%, and in Zaire 75% (Myers 1988b). Throughout the world, 100 million tons of fish, mainly wild species, are harvested each year. Much of this catch is consumed locally.

Consumptive use value can be assigned to a product by considering how much people would have to pay to buy equivalent products in the market if the local sources were no longer available. One example of this

(A)   (B)

1.13 Natural products are critical to the lives of people throughout the world. (A) One of the most important natural products required by local people is fuelwood, particularly in Africa and southern Asia. Here a woman in Burkina Faso gathers kindling. (World Bank Photo by Yosef Hadar, © IBRD.) (B) A wide variety of plants and other natural products are used in Chinese medicine. (Photograph by Catherine Pringle/Biological Photo Service.)

approach was an attempt to estimate the number of wild pigs harvested by native hunters in Sarawak, East Malaysia, in part by counting the number of shotgun shells used in rural areas and interviewing hunters. This pioneering (and somewhat controversial) study estimated that the consumptive use value of the wild pig meat was around $40 million per year (Caldecott 1988). But in many cases, local people do not have the money to buy products in the market. When the local resource is depleted, they are forced into rural poverty, or they migrate to urban centers.

While dependence on local natural products is primarily associated with the developing world, there are rural areas of the United States and Canada where hundreds of thousands of people are dependent on fuelwood for heating and on wild game for meat. Many of these people would be unable to survive in such remote areas if they had to buy fuel and meat.

Productive use value

Productive use value is a direct value assigned to products that are harvested from the wild and sold in commercial markets, at both the national and international levels. These products are typically valued by standard economic methods at the price that is paid at the first point of sale minus the costs incurred up to that point, rather than at the final retail cost of the products; as a result, what may appear to be minor natural products may actually be the starting points of major manufactured products (Godoy et al. 1993). For example, wild cascara (*Rhamnus purshiana*) bark gathered in the western United States is the major ingredient in certain brands of laxatives; the purchase price of the bark is about $1 million, but the final retail price of the medicine is $75 million (Prescott-Allen and Prescott-Allen 1986). The range of products obtained from the natural environment and then sold in the marketplace is enormous, but the major ones are fuelwood, construction timber, fish and shellfish, medicinal plants, wild fruits and vegetables, wild meat and skins, fibers, rattan, honey, beeswax, natural dyes, seaweed, animal fodder, natural perfumes, and plant gums and resins (Myers 1984).

The productive use value of natural resources is significant, even in industrial nations. Prescott-Allen and Prescott-Allen (1986) calculated that 4.5% of the U.S. GDP depends in some way on wild species, an amount averaging about $87 billion per year. The percentage would be far higher for developing countries that have less industry and a higher percentage of the population living in rural areas.

At present, timber is among the most significant products obtained from natural environments, with a value of over $75 billion per year (Reid and Miller 1989). Timber products are being exported at a rapid level from many tropical countries to earn foreign currency, to provide capital for industrialization, and to pay foreign debt. In tropical countries such as Indonesia and Malaysia, timber products are among the top export earners, accounting for billions of dollars per year (Figure 1.14A). Non-wood products from forests, including game, fruits, gums and resins, rattan, and medicinal plants, also have a great productive use value (Figure 1.14B). For example, non-timber products account for 63% of the total foreign exchange earned by India from the export of forest products (Gupta and Guleria 1982). These non-timber products, which are sometimes erroneously called "minor forest products," are in reality very important economically and may be greater in value over time than the one-time timber harvests (Peters et al. 1989). The value of non-timber products, along with the value of forests in other ecosystem functions, provides a strong economic justification for maintaining forests in many areas of the world.

The greatest productive use value for many species lies in their ability

(A)   (B)

1.14 (A) The timber industry is a major source of revenue in many tropical countries. Here "monkey puzzle" trees (*Araucaria araucana*)—a species with a very narrow distribution pattern—are harvested in Chile. (Photograph by Alejandro Frid/Biological Photo Service.) (B) Non-timber forest products are often important in local and national economies. Many rural people supplement their incomes by gathering natural forest products to sell in local markets. Here a Land Dayak family in Sarawak (Malaysia) sells wild honey and edible wild fruits. (Photograph by R. Primack.)

to provide new founder stock for industry and agriculture and for the genetic improvement of agricultural crops (NAS/NRC 1972; Prescott-Allen and Prescott-Allen 1986). Some wild species of plants and animals that are currently harvested on a local scale can be grown on plantations and ranches, and some can be cultured in laboratories. The wild populations provide the initial breeding stock for these colonies and are a source of material for genetic improvement of the domesticated populations. In the case of crop plants, a wild species or variety might provide a particular gene that confers pest resistance or increased yield. This gene needs to be obtained from the wild only once; it then can be incorporated into the breeding stock of the crop species and stored in gene banks. The continued genetic improvement of cultivated plants is necessary not only for increased yield, but also to guard against pesticide-resistant insects and increasingly virulent strains of fungi, viruses, and bacteria (Hoyt 1988). Catastrophic failures of crop plants can often be directly linked to low genetic variability: the 1846 potato blight in Ireland, the 1922 wheat failure in the Soviet Union, and the 1984 outbreak of citrus canker in Florida were all related to low genetic variability among crop plants (Plucknett et al. 1987).

Development of new varieties can also have a noticeable economic effect. Genetic improvements in United States crops were responsible for increasing the value of the harvest by an average of $1 billion per year from 1930 to 1980 (OTA 1987). Genes for high sugar content and large fruit size from wild tomatoes in Peru have been transferred into domestic varieties of tomatoes, resulting in an enhanced value of $80 million to the industry (Iltis 1988). The discovery of a wild perennial relative of corn in the Mexican state of Jalisco (see Chapter 5) is potentially worth billions of dollars to modern agriculture because it could allow the development of a high-yielding perennial corn crop and eliminate the need for annual plowing (Norton 1988).

Wild species can also be used as biological control agents (Julien 1987). Biologists have sometimes controlled exotic, noxious species by searching the pest species' original habitat for a species that limits its population. This control species can then be brought to the new locality, where it can be released to control the pest. One classic example is the case of the prickly pear cactus (*Opuntia* sp.), which was introduced into Australia from South America as a hedgerow plant. The cactus spread out of control and took over millions of hectares of rangeland. In the prickly pear's native habitat, the larvae of a *Cactoblastis* moth feed on this cactus. The moth was successfully introduced into Australia, where it has reduced the cactus to comparative rarity.

The natural world is also an important source of new medicines. Twenty-five percent of prescriptions used in the United States contain active ingredients derived from plants. Two potent drugs derived from the rose periwinkle (*Catharanthus roseus*) of Madagascar, for example, have proved to be effective at treating Hodgkin's disease, leukemia, and other blood cancers. Treatment using these drugs has increased the survival rate of childhood leukemia from 10% to 90%. Many of the most important antibiotics, such as penicillin and tetracycline, are derived from fungi and other microorganisms (Farnsworth 1988; Eisner 1991). Most recently, the fungus-derived drug cyclosporine has proved to be a crucial element in the success of heart and kidney transplants. Many other important new medicines were first identified in animals; poisonous animals such as snakes, arthropods, and marine species have been a rich source of chemicals with valuable medical applications. The 20 pharmaceuticals most used in the United States are all based on chemicals first identified in natural products; these drugs have a combined sales value of $6 billion per year.

The biological communities of the world are being continually searched for new plants, animals, fungi, and microorganisms that can be used to fight human diseases such as cancer and AIDS (Figure 1.15A; Plotkin 1993; Cox and Balick 1994). These searches are generally carried out by government research institutes and pharmaceutical companies. To

(A)   (B)

1.15 (A) Ethnobotanists work with local people —in this case, a native of
Suriname—to collect medicinal plants and gather information on their use.
(Courtesy of Mark Plotkin and Conservation International.) (B) Taxonomists
at INBio are sorting and classifying Costa Rica's rich array of plant and animal species. (Photograph by Steve Winter.)

facilitate the search for new medicines and to profit financially from new
products, the Costa Rican government established the National Biodiversity Institute (INBio), which collects biological products and supplies samples to drug companies (Figure 1.15B). The Merck Company has signed an
agreement to pay INBio $1 million for the right to screen samples and will
pay royalties to INBio on any commercial products that result from the research (Eisner and Beiring 1994). Programs such as these provide financial incentives for countries to protect their natural resources.

Indirect Economic Values

Indirect values can be assigned to aspects of biological diversity, such as
environmental processes and ecosystem services, that provide economic
benefits without being harvested and destroyed during use. Because these
benefits are not goods or services in the usual economic sense, they do not
typically appear in the statistics of national economies, such as the GDP.
However, they may be crucial to the continued availability of the natural
products on which the economies depend. If natural ecosystems are not
available to provide these benefits, substitute sources must be found, often

at great expense. In thinking about how we might value the indirect use values of ecosystems, consider this summary of the consequences of deforestation:

> We must find replacements for wood products, build erosion control works, enlarge reservoirs, upgrade air pollution control technology, install flood control works, improve water purification plants, increase air conditioning, and provide new recreational facilities. These substitutes represent an enormous tax burden, a drain on the world's supply of natural resources, and an increased stress on the natural system that remains. (F. H. Bormann 1976).

Nonconsumptive use value

Biological communities provide a great variety of environmental services that are not consumed through use. This **nonconsumptive use value** is sometimes relatively easy to calculate, as in the case of the value of wild insects that pollinate crop plants. About 100 species of crop plants in the United States require insect pollination of their flowers. The value of these pollinators could be assigned by calculating either how much the crop increases in value through their actions or how much the farmer would have to pay to hire honeybee hives from a commercial beekeeper. Determining the value of other ecosystem services may be more difficult, particularly at the global level. The following is a partial listing of the benefits of conserving biological diversity that typically do not appear on the balance sheets of environmental impact assessments or in GDPs.

Ecosystem productivity. The photosynthetic capacity of plants and algae allows the energy of the sun to be captured in living tissue. The energy stored in plants is sometimes harvested by humans directly as fuelwood, fodder, and wild foods. This plant material is also the starting point for innumerable food chains leading to all of the animal products that are harvested by people. Approximately 40% of the productivity of the terrestrial environment is dominated by human needs for natural resources (Vitousek 1994). Destruction of the vegetation in an area through overgrazing by domestic animals, overharvesting of timber, or frequent fires destroys the system's ability to make use of solar energy, eventually leading to a loss of production of plant biomass and the deterioration of the animal community (including humans) living in the area (Odum 1993). Likewise, coastal estuaries are areas of rapid plant and algal growth that provide the starting point for food chains leading to commercial stocks of fish and shellfish. The U.S. National Marine Fisheries Service has estimated that damage to coastal estuaries has cost the United States over $200 million per year in lost productive use value of commercial fish and shellfish and in lost recreational use value of fish caught for sport (McNeely et al. 1990). Even when degraded or damaged ecosystems are rebuilt or restored—often at great expense—they usually do not perform their ecosystem functions as well as before and almost certainly do not contain their original species diversity. Another critical problem that scientists are investigating at present is how the loss of individual species from biological communities affects ecosystem processes, such as the total growth of plants and the ability of plants to absorb atmospheric carbon dioxide (Schulze and Mooney 1993; Baskin 1994a; Tilman and Downing 1994). How many species must be lost from a community before the ecosystem begins to collapse?

Protection of water and soil resources. Biological communities are of vital importance in protecting watersheds, buffering ecosystems against extremes of flood and drought, and maintaining water quality (Ehrlich and Mooney 1983; Likens 1991). Plant foliage and dead leaves intercept the rain and reduce its impact on the soil, and plant roots and soil organisms aerate the soil, increasing its capacity to absorb water. This increased water-holding capacity reduces the flooding that occurs after heavy rains and allows a slow release of water for days and weeks after the rains have ceased.

When vegetation is disturbed by logging, farming, and other human activities, rates of soil erosion and even landslides increase rapidly, decreasing the value of the land for human activities. Damage to the soil limits the ability of plant life to recover following disturbance and can render the land useless for agriculture. In addition, soil particles suspended in water from runoff can kill freshwater animals, coral reef organisms, and the marine life in coastal estuaries. This silt also makes river water undrinkable for human communities along the rivers, leading to a decline in human health. Increased soil erosion can lead to premature filling of the reservoirs behind dams, leading to a loss of electrical output, and may create sandbars and islands, reducing the navigability of rivers and ports. Unprecedented catastrophic floods in Bangladesh, India, the Philippines, and Thailand have been associated with recent extensive logging in watershed areas; such incidents have led to calls by local people for bans on logging. Flood damage to India's agricultural areas has led to massive government and private tree planting programs in the Himalayas. In the industrial nations of the world wetlands protection is being made a priority to prevent flooding of developed areas. The value of marshland in the region surrounding Boston, Massachusetts, has been estimated at $72,000 per hectare per year solely on the basis of its role in reducing flood damage (Hair 1988).

Regulation of climate. Plant communities are important in moderating local, regional, and probably even global climate conditions (Nobre et al. 1991; Clark 1992). At the local level, trees provide shade and transpire water, which reduces the local temperature in hot weather. This cooling effect reduces the need for fans and air conditioners and increases the comfort and work efficiency of people. Trees are also locally important as windbreaks and in reducing heat loss from buildings in cold weather.

At the regional level, transpiration from plants recycles water back into the atmosphere so that it can return as rain. Loss of vegetation from regions of the world such as the Amazon Basin and West Africa could result in a regional reduction of average annual rainfall (Fearnside 1990). At the global level, plant growth is tied to carbon cycles. A loss of vegetation cover results in reduced uptake of carbon dioxide by plants, contributing to the rising carbon dioxide levels that lead to global warming. Plants are also the source of the oxygen on which all animals, including humans, depend for respiration.

Waste disposal. Biological communities are capable of breaking down and immobilizing pollutants such as heavy metals, pesticides, and sewage that have been released into the environment by human activities (Odum 1993; Greeson et al. 1979). Fungi and bacteria are particularly important in this role. When such ecosystems are damaged and degraded, expensive pollution control systems must be installed and operated to take over these functions.

An excellent example of this ecosystem function is provided by the New York Bight, a 2000-square-mile (5200 km^2) bay at the mouth of the Hudson River. The New York Bight acts as a free sewage disposal system into which is dumped the waste produced by the 20 million people in the New York metropolitan area (Young et al. 1985). If the New York Bight becomes overwhelmed and damaged by a combination of sewage overload and coastal development, an alternative waste disposal system, including massive waste treatment facilities and giant landfills, will have to be developed at a cost of tens of billions of dollars.

Species relationships. Many of the species harvested by people for their productive use value depend on other wild species for their continued existence. Thus, a decline in a wild species of little immediate value to humans may result in a corresponding decline in a harvested species that is economically important. For example, the wild game and fish harvested by people are dependent on wild insects and plants for their food. A decline in insect and plant populations will result in a decline in animal harvests. Crop plants benefit from birds and predatory insects such as praying mantises (family Mantidae), which feed on pest insect species that attack the crops. Many useful wild plant species depend on fruit-eating animals, such as bats and birds, to disperse their seeds (Fujita and Tuttle 1991).

One of the most economically significant relationships in biological communities is that between many forest trees and crop plants and the soil organisms that provide them with essential nutrients. Fungi and bacteria break down dead plant and animal matter, which they use as their energy source; in the process, they release mineral nutrients such as nitrogen into the soil, where they can be used by plants for further growth. The poor growth and massive diebacks of trees that are occurring throughout Europe may be attributable in part to the deleterious effects of acid rain and air pollution on soil fungi (Cherfas 1991).

Recreation and ecotourism. A major focus of recreational activity is the nonconsumptive enjoyment of nature through activities such as hiking, photography, whale-watching, and bird-watching (Duffus and Dearden 1990). The monetary value of these activities, sometimes called the **amenity value**, can be considerable (Figure 1.16). For example, 84% of Canadians participate in nature-related recreational activities that have an estimated value of $800 million per year (Fillon et al. 1985). In the United States, almost 100 million adults and comparable numbers of children are involved each year in some form of nondestructive nature recreation, spending $4 billion in the process on fees, travel, lodging, food, and equipment (Shaw and Mangun 1984). In places of national and international significance for conservation or exceptional scenic beauty, such as Yellowstone National Park, the nonconsumptive recreational use value often dwarfs that of other local industries (Power 1991). Even recreational activities such as sport hunting and fishing, which in theory are consumptive uses, are in practice nonconsumptive because the food value of the animals taken by fishermen and hunters is typically insignificant in comparison with the time and money spent on these activities. Particularly in rural economies, fishing and hunting generate hundreds of millions of dollars. The value of these recreational activities may be even greater than these numbers suggest because many park visitors, sport fishermen, and hunters indicate that they would be willing to pay even higher admission and licensing fees if necessary.

Ecotourism is a growing industry in many developing countries, earn-

1.16 Most people find interacting with other species to be an educational and uplifting experience. Here a group of ecotourists looking at marine wildlife greet a minke whale (*Balaenoptera acutorostrata*) that is being rescued after becoming entangled in a trawler's gill net; the float behind the whale was attached to the net to keep the whale at the surface so it could breathe. Later, rescuers were able to release the whale from the netting. Such meetings—usually taking place at greater distances, as in a more traditional "whale watch" setting or on "photo safaris" in Africa—can enrich human lives. (Photograph by Scott Kraus, New England Aquarium.)

ing approximately $12 billion per year worldwide. Ecotourists visit a country and spend money wholly or in part to experience its biological diversity and to see particular species (Lindberg 1991; Ceballos-Lascuráin 1993). By charging high visitor fees, Rwanda developed a gorilla tourism industry that was the country's third largest foreign currency earner (Vedder 1989) until the recent civil disturbances. Ecotourism has traditionally been a key industry in East African countries such as Kenya and Tanzania and is increasingly part of the tourism picture in many American and Asian countries. In the early 1970s, an estimate was made that each lion at Amboseli National Park in Kenya could be valued at $27,000 per year in tourist revenue, while the elephant herd was worth $610,000 per year (Western and Henry 1979); those values are certainly much higher today. Ecotourism can provide one of the most immediate justifications for protecting biological diversity, particularly when these activities are integrated into overall management plans (Munn 1992). However, there is a danger that tourist facilities will provide a sanitized fantasy experience, rather than allowing visitors to be aware of or even see the serious social and environmental problems that endanger biological diversity (Figure 1.17). Ecotourist activities themselves can also contribute to the degradation of sensitive areas, as when the tourists unwittingly trample wildflowers, break coral, and disrupt nesting bird colonies (Hawkins and Roberts 1994).

Educational and scientific value. Many books, television programs, and movies produced for educational and entertainment purposes are based on nature themes. Increasingly, natural history materials are being incorporated into school curricula (Hair and Pomerantz 1987). These educational programs could probably be valued at billions of dollars per year. A considerable number of professional scientists, as well as highly motivated amateurs, are engaged in ecological observations that have nonconsumptive use value in the form of employment and money spent on goods and services. While these scientific activities provide economic benefits to the areas surrounding field stations, their real value lies in their ability to increase human knowledge, enhance education, and enrich the human experience.

Environmental monitors. Species that are particularly sensitive to chemical toxins can serve as an "early warning system" for monitoring the health of the environment (Hellawell 1986). Some species can even serve as substitutes for expensive detection equipment. Among the best-known indicator species are lichens, which grow on rocks and absorb chemicals in rainwater and airborne pollution (Hawksworth 1990). High levels of toxic materials kill lichens, and each lichen species has distinct levels of tolerance for air pollution. The composition of the lichen community can be used as a biological indicator of the level of air pollution, and the distribution and abundance of lichens can be used to identify areas of contamination around sources of pollution, such as smelters.

1.17 Facilities for ecotourists sometimes create a tropical fantasy that disguises and ignores the realities of Third World problems. (Cartoon from *E. G. Magazin*, Germany.)

Aquatic filter feeders, such as mollusks, are also useful for monitoring pollution because they process large volumes of water and concentrate toxic chemicals, such as poisonous metals, PCBs, and pesticides, in their tissues (Stevens 1988).

Option value

The **option value** of a species is its potential to provide an economic benefit to human society at some point in the future. As the needs of society change, so must the methods of satisfying those needs (Myers 1984). Often the solution to a problem lies in previously untapped animal or plant species. The extent of the search for new natural products is wide-ranging. Entomologists search for insects that can be used as biological control agents, microbiologists search for bacteria that can assist in biochemical manufacturing processes, and zoologists are identifying species that can produce animal protein more efficiently and with less environmental damage than existing domestic species. If biological diversity is reduced in the future, the ability of scientists to locate and utilize new species for such purposes likewise will be decreased.

Health agencies and pharmaceutical companies are making a major effort to collect and screen species for compounds that have the ability to fight human diseases (Plotkin 1988; Eisner and Beiring 1994). The discovery of a potent anticancer chemical in the Pacific yew, a tree native to North American old-growth forests, is only the most recent result of this search. Another such species is the ginkgo tree (*Ginkgo biloba*), which occurs in the wild in a few isolated localities in China. During the last 20 years a $500 million-per-year industry has developed around the cultivation of the ginkgo tree and the manufacture of medicines from its leaves,

1.18 Because valuable medicines can be made from their leaves, ginkgo trees are now being cultivated. Each year the woody stems sprout new shoots and branches, which are harvested. This species is the basis of a pharmaceutical business worth hundreds of millions of dollars each year. (Photograph by Peter Del Tredici, Arnold Arboretum.)

widely used in Europe and Asia to treat problems of blood circulation and stroke (Figure 1.18; Del Tredici 1991).

The growing biotechnology industry is finding new ways to reduce pollution, develop industrial processes, and fight diseases threatening human health (Frederick and Egan 1994). In some cases, newly discovered or well-known species have been found to have exactly those properties needed to deal with a significant human problem. Innovative techniques of molecular biology are allowing unique, valuable genes found in one species to be transferred to another species. Some of the most promising new species being investigated by industrial scientists are the bacteria that live in extreme environments such as deep-sea geothermal vents and hot springs. Bacteria that thrive in unusual chemical and physical environments can often be adapted to special industrial applications of considerable economic value. One of the most important tools of the multibillion-dollar biotechnology industry, the polymerase chain reaction (PCR) technique for multiplying copies of DNA, depends on an enzyme that is stable at high temperatures; this enzyme was originally derived from a bacterium endemic to natural hot springs in Yellowstone National Park.

While most species may have little or no direct economic value, a small proportion may have the potential to supply medical treatments, to support a new industry, or to prevent the collapse of a major agricultural crop. If just one of these species becomes extinct before it is discovered, it will be a tremendous loss to the global economy, even if the majority of the world's species are preserved. Stated another way, the diversity of the world's species can be compared to a manual on how to keep the Earth running effectively. The loss of a species is like tearing a page out of the manual. If we ever need the information from that page to save ourselves and the Earth's other species, we will find that it is irretrievably lost.

A question that is currently being actively debated is: Who owns the commercial development rights to the world's biological diversity? In the past, species were freely collected from wherever they occurred; corporations, often in the developed world, then sold the resulting products at a profit. Increasingly, countries in the developing world are demanding a share in commercial activities resulting from the biological diversity contained within their borders (Vogel 1994). Developing treaties and procedures to carry out this process will be a major challenge in the coming years.

Existence value

Many people throughout the world care about wildlife and plants and are concerned with their protection (Randall 1987). This concern may be associated with a desire to someday visit the habitat of a unique species and see it in the wild, or it may be a fairly abstract identification. Particular species, so-called "charismatic megafauna" such as pandas, lions, elephants, and many birds, elicit strong responses in people. People value these emotions in a direct way by joining and contributing money to conservation organizations that work to protect these species (Figure 1.19). In

1.19 The bald eagle, *Haliaeetus leucocephalus,* national symbol of the United States. People in the United States have indicated a willingness to pay millions of dollars per year to ensure its continued existence. (Photograph by Jessie Cohen, National Zoological Park, Smithsonian Institution.)

the United States, $2.3 billion was contributed in 1990 to environmental wildlife organizations, with the Nature Conservancy, the World Wildlife Fund, Ducks Unlimited, and the Sierra Club topping the list (Groombridge 1992). Citizens also show their concern by directing their governments to spend money on conservation programs. For example, the government of the United States has already spent more than $20 million to protect a single rare species, the California condor (*Gymnogyps californianus*).

Such **existence value** can also be attached to biological communities, such as tropical rain forests and coral reefs, and to areas of scenic beauty. People and organizations contribute large sums of money annually to ensure the continuing existence of these habitats. The money spent to protect biological diversity, particularly in the developed countries of the world, is on the order of hundreds of millions, if not billions, of dollars per year. This sum represents the existence value of species and communities—the amount that people are willing to pay to prevent species from going extinct and habitats from being destroyed.

Ethical Considerations

Even though the methods of environmental economics are a positive development, they can also be viewed as signs of a willingness to accept the present world economic system as it is with only minor changes. Given a world economic system in which millions of children die each year from disease, malnutrition, crime, and war, and in which thousands of unique species become extinct each year due to habitat destruction, we may ask, do we need to make minor adjustments or major structural changes?

A complementary approach to protecting biological diversity and improving the human situation through stringent regulations, incentives, fines, and environmental monitoring is to change the fundamental values of our materialistic society. If the preservation of the natural environment and maintenance of biological diversity became a fundamental value across society, the natural consequences would be a lowered consumption of resources and limited population growth. Many traditional cultures have successfully coexisted with their environment for thousands of years because of societal ethics that encourage personal responsibility and efficient use of resources.

While economic arguments are often advanced to justify the protection of biological diversity, there are also strong ethical arguments for doing so (Rolston 1988, 1989; Naess 1989). These arguments have foundations in the value systems of most religions, philosophies, and cultures and thus can be readily understood by the general public. Ethical arguments for preserving biological diversity appeal to the nobler instincts of people and are based on widely held truths. People will accept these arguments on the basis of their belief systems (Hargrove 1989; Callicott 1994). In contrast, arguments based on economic grounds are still being developed and may eventually prove to be inadequate, highly inaccurate, or unconvincing (Norton 1988). Economic arguments by themselves might provide a basis for valuing species, but they might also be used (and misused) to decide that we ought not to save a species, or that we ought to save one species and not another. In economic terms, a species that has a small physical size, low population numbers, a limited geographical range, an unattractive appearance, no immediate use to people, and no relationship to any species of economic importance will be given a low value; such qualities may characterize a substantial proportion of the world's species, particularly insects, other invertebrates, fungi, nonflowering plants, bacteria, and protists. Costly attempts to preserve these species may not have any short-term economic justification.

Several ethical arguments can be made for preserving all species, regardless of their economic value. The following assertions, based on the intrinsic value of species, are important to conservation biology because they provide the rationale for protecting rare species and species of no obvious economic value.

- *Each species has a right to exist.* All species represent unique biological solutions to the problem of survival. On this basis, the survival of each species must be guaranteed, regardless of its abundance or its importance to humans. This is true whether the species is large or small, simple or complex, ancient or recently evolved, economically important or of little immediate value. All species are part of the community of living beings and have just as much right to exist as humans do. Each species has value for its own sake, an **intrinsic value** unrelated to human needs (Naess 1986). Besides not having the right to destroy species, people have the responsibility of taking action to prevent species from going extinct as the result of human activities. This argument envisions humans as part of a larger biotic community in which we respect and revere all species.

    How can we assign rights of existence and legal protection to nonhuman species when they lack the self-awareness that is usually associated with the morality of rights and duties? Further, how can nonanimal species, such as mosses and fungi, have rights when they lack even a nervous system to sense their environment? Many advocates for environmental ethics believe that species do assert their will to live through their production of offspring and their continuous evolutionary adaptation to a changing environment. The premature extinction of a species due to human activities destroys this natural process, and can be regarded as a "superkilling" (Rolston 1985) because it kills not only living individuals but also future generations of the species and eliminates the processes of evolution and speciation.

- *All species are interdependent.* Species interact in complex ways as parts of natural communities. The loss of one species may have far-reaching consequences for other members of the community.

Other species may become extinct in response, or the entire community may become destabilized as the result of cascades of species extinction. As we learn more about global processes, we are also finding out that many chemical and physical characteristics of the atmosphere, the climate, and the ocean are linked to biological processes in a self-regulating manner. The idea that the Earth is a superecosystem, in which the biotic community has a role in creating and maintaining conditions suitable for life, is set forth in the Gaia hypothesis (Lovelock 1988). If this is the case, our instincts toward self-preservation may impel us to preserve biodiversity. When the natural world prospers, we prosper. We are obligated to conserve the system as a whole because that is the appropriate survival unit.

- *Humans must live within the same ecological limitations as other species do.* All species in the world are constrained by the biological carrying capacity of their environment. Each species utilizes the resources of its environment to survive, and the numbers of a species decline when its resources are damaged. Humans must be careful to minimize the damage they do to their natural environment because such damage harms not only other species but people as well. Much of the pollution and environmental degradation that occurs is unnecessary and could be minimized with better planning.

- *People have a responsibility to act as stewards of the Earth.* If we degrade the natural resources of the Earth and cause species to become extinct, future generations will have to pay the price in terms of a lower standard of living and quality of life. Therefore, people of today should use resources in a sustainable manner so as not to damage species and communities. We might imagine that we are borrowing the Earth from future generations, and when they receive it back from us they will expect to get it in good condition.

- *A respect for human life and human diversity is compatible with a respect for biological diversity.* An appreciation of the complexity of human culture and the natural world leads people to respect all life in its diverse forms. Attempts to bring peace among the nations of the world and to end poverty, crime, and racism will benefit people and biological diversity simultaneously, because violence within and among human societies is one of the principal destroyers of biological diversity. Human maturity leads naturally to an "identification with all life forms" and "the acknowledgment of the intrinsic value of these forms" (Naess 1986). This view sees an expanding circle of moral obligations, moving outward from oneself to include duties to relatives, one's own social group, all humanity, animals, all species, the ecosystem, and ultimately the whole Earth (Figure 1.20; Noss 1992).

- *Nature has spiritual and aesthetic value that transcends its economic*

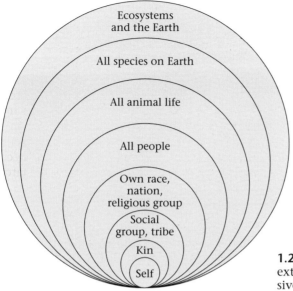

1.20 An ethical sequence in which the individual extends concern outward beyond the self to progressively more inclusive levels. (From Noss 1992.)

value. Throughout history, religious thinkers, poets, writers, artists, and musicians of all varieties have drawn inspiration from nature. For many people, an essential quality of this inspiration requires experiencing nature in an undisturbed setting. Simply reading about species or seeing them in museums, gardens, and zoos will not suffice. Nearly everyone enjoys wildlife and landscapes aesthetically, and many people regard Earth as a divine creation with its own goodness and value that ought to be respected.

- *Biological diversity is needed to determine the origin of life.* Two of the central mysteries in the worlds of philosophy and science are how life originated and how the diversity of life found on Earth today came about. Thousands of biologists are working on these problems and are coming ever closer to the answers. However, when species become extinct, important clues are lost, and the mystery then becomes harder to solve (Stiassny and de Pinna 1994).

Philosophical approaches

Throughout the world, environmental activist organizations such as Greenpeace and EarthFirst! are committed to using their knowledge of environmental issues to protect species and ecosystems. One of the best-developed environmental philosophies that supports this activism is described in *Deep Ecology: Living As If Nature Mattered* (Devall and Sessions 1985; Sessions 1987). **Deep ecology** begins with the premise that all species have value in and of themselves, and that humans have no right to reduce this richness. Because present human activities are destroying the Earth's biological diversity, existing political, economic, technological, and ideological structures must change. These changes entail enhancing the life quality of people, emphasizing improvements in environmental quality, aesthetics, culture, and religion rather than higher levels of material consumption. The philosophy of deep ecology includes an obligation to work to implement the needed changes through political activism and a commitment to personal lifestyle changes (Naess 1989).

Summary

1. Conservation biology is a synthesis of scientific disciplines that deals with today's unprecedented biodiversity crisis. It combines basic and applied research approaches to prevent the loss of biodiversity: specifically, the extinction of species, the loss of genetic variation, and the destruction of biological communities.

2. Conservation biology rests on a number of underlying assumptions that are accepted by most conservation biologists: The diversity of species is good; the extinction of species due to human activities is bad; the complex interaction of species in natural communities is good; the evolution of new species is good; biological diversity has value in and of itself.

3. The Earth's biological diversity includes the entire range of living species, the genetic variation that occurs among individuals within a species, the biological communities in which species live, and the ecosystem-level interactions of the community with the physical and chemical environment.

4. Certain keystone species appear to be important in determining the ability of other species to persist in a community. Keystone resources, such as water holes and salt licks, may occupy only a small fraction of a habitat, but may be crucial to the persistence of many species in the area.

5. The greatest biological diversity is found in the tropical regions of the world, with large concentrations in tropical rain forests, coral reefs, tropical lakes, and the deep sea. The majority of the world's species have still not been described and named.

6. The new field of environmental economics is developing methods for valuing biological diversity and in the process is providing arguments for its protection. Large development projects are increasingly being analyzed by means of environmental impact assessments and cost–benefit analyses before being approved.

7. Components of biological diversity can be given direct economic values, assigned to products harvested by people, or indirect economic values, assigned to benefits provided by biological diversity that do not involve harvesting or destroying the resource. Direct values can be further divided into consumptive use value and productive use value. Consumptive use value is assigned to products that are consumed locally, such as fuelwood, local medicines, and building materials.

8. Productive use value can be assigned to products harvested in the wild and sold in markets, such as commercial timber and fish. Species collected in the wild have great productive use value in their ability to provide new founder stock for domestic species and for the genetic improvement of agricultural crops. Wild species have also been a major source of new medicines.

9. Indirect values can be assigned to aspects of biological diversity that provide economic benefits to people but are not harvested or damaged during these uses. Nonconsumptive use values of ecosystems include ecosystem productivity, protection of soil and water resources, the interactions of wild species with commercial crops, and regulation of climate.

10. Biological diversity is part of the foundation of the outdoor recreation and ecotourism industries. In many countries of the developing world, ecotourism represents one of the major sources of foreign income.

11. Biological diversity also has an option value in terms of its potential to provide future benefits to human society, such as new medicines, biological control agents, and crops. It also has an existence value, based on the amount of money people are willing to pay to protect biological diversity.

12. Protecting biological diversity can be justified on ethical grounds as well as on economic grounds. The value systems of most religions, philosophies, and cultures provide justifications for preserving species that are readily understood by people. These justifications support protecting even species that have no obvious economic value to people.

13. The most central ethical argument is that species have a right to exist based on an intrinsic value unrelated to human needs. People do not have the right to destroy species and must take action to prevent the extinction of species.

Suggested Readings

Barbier, E. B., J. C. Burgess and C. Folke. 1994. *Paradise Lost? The Ecological Economics of Biodiversity*. Earthscan Publications, London. A clear introduction to this new field.

Groombridge, B. (ed.). 1992. *Global Biodiversity: Status of the Earth's Living Resources*. Compiled by the World Conservation Monitoring Centre. Chapman and Hall, London. Huge sourcebook of biodiversity facts and figures. Strong section on environmental economics.

Huston, M. A. 1994. *Biological Diversity: The Coexistence of Species on Changing Landscapes*. Cambridge University Press, Cambridge. Extensive review of the patterns and theories of biological diversity.

Kellert, S. R. and E. O. Wilson (eds.). 1993. *The Biophilia Hypothesis*. Island Press, Washington, D.C. Discussion of humans' inherent biological reasons for valuing and cherishing nature.

McNeely, J. A. et al. 1990. *Conserving the World's Biological Diversity*. IUCN, WRI, CI, WWF-U.S., World Bank, Gland, Switzerland. Outstanding summary of the value of biodiversity and strategies for preservation.

Meffe, G. C., C. R. Carroll and contributors. 1994. *Principles of Conservation Biology*. Sinauer Associates, Sunderland, MA. Excellent advanced textbook.

Plotkin, M. J. 1993. *Tales of a Shaman's Apprentice*. Viking/Penguin, New York. Vivid account of ethnobotanical exploration and efforts to preserve medical knowledge.

Primack, R. 1993. *Essentials of Conservation Biology*. Sinauer Associates, Sunderland, MA. A textbook suitable for undergraduate courses.

Repetto, R. 1992. Accounting for environmental assets. *Scientific American* 266 (June): 94–100. A popular article describing how environmental degradation decreases national wealth.

Wilson, E. O. 1992. *The Diversity of Life*. Belknap Press of Harvard University Press, Cambridge, MA. An outstanding description of biological diversity, written for the general public.

CHAPTER 2

Threats to Biological Diversity

A HEALTHY ENVIRONMENT has great economic, aesthetic, and ethical value. Maintaining a healthy environment means preserving all of its components in good condition: ecosystems, communities, and species. The most serious aspect of environmental damage is the extinction of species. Communities can be degraded and reduced in area, but as long as all of the original species survive, communities still have the potential to recover. Similarly, genetic variation within a species will be reduced as population size is lowered, but species can potentially regain genetic variation through mutation, natural selection, and recombination. However, once a species is eliminated, the unique genetic information contained in its DNA and the special combination of characters that it possesses are forever lost. Once a species goes extinct, its populations cannot be restored, the communities that it inhabited are impoverished, and its potential value to humans can never be realized.

Rates of Extinction

The term "extinct" has many nuances, and its meaning can vary somewhat depending on the context. A species is considered extinct when no member of the species remains alive anywhere in the world: "The Bachman's warbler is extinct" (Figure 2.1). If individuals of a species remain

2.1 One of the first Neotropical migrant songbirds to become extinct as a result of tropical deforestation was the Bachman's warbler (*Vermivora bachmanii*), last seen in the 1960s. The Cuban forests in which this species overwintered were almost entirely cleared for sugarcane fields. The warbler is shown in this Audubon print with the flowering Franklin tree (*Franklinia altamaha*), which is now extinct in the wild, although it can still be found in arboretums and other cultivated gardens.

alive only in captivity or in other human-controlled situations, the species is said to be *extinct in the wild*: "The Franklin tree is extinct in the wild but grows well under cultivation" (Figure 2.1). In both of these situations the species would be considered *globally extinct*. A species is considered *locally extinct* when it is no longer found in an area that it once inhabited but is still found elsewhere in the wild: "The American burying beetle once occurred throughout eastern and central North America; it is now locally extinct in all but three widely separated areas" (Figure 2.2). Some conservation biologists speak of a species being *ecologically extinct* if it persists at such reduced numbers that its effects on the other species in its community are negligible: "The tiger is ecologically extinct; so few tigers remain in the wild that their effect on prey populations is insignificant."

A vital question in conservation biology is, how long will it take for a

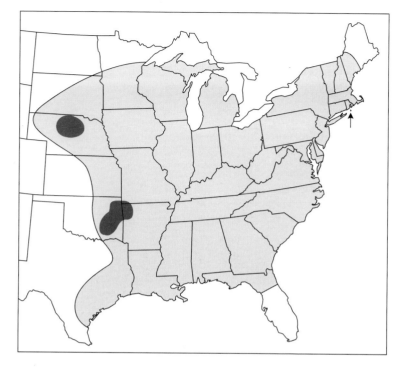

2.2 The American burying beetle (*Nicrophorus americanus*) was once widespread in the eastern and central United States (shaded area) but is now found in only three isolated populations (black areas; Block Island, in Long Island Sound, is highlighted with an arrow). Intensive efforts have been initiated to determine the cause of this decline and develop a recovery plan. (After Kozol et al. 1994.)

given species to become extinct following a severe reduction in its range or the degradation or fragmentation of its habitat? When populations fall below a certain critical number of individuals, they are very likely to become extinct. In some populations, a few individuals might persist for years or decades, and even reproduce, but their ultimate fate would be extinction. In woody plants in particular, isolated, nonreproductive individuals can persist for hundreds of years. These species have been called "the living dead": even though technically the species is not extinct while a few individuals live, the population is no longer reproductively viable, so the species' future is limited to the life spans of the remaining individuals (Gentry 1986; Janzen 1986b).

In order to successfully preserve species, conservation biologists must identify the human activities that affect the stability of populations and drive species to extinction. They must also determine the factors that make a population vulnerable to extinction.

Human-caused extinctions

The global diversity of species reached an all-time high in the present geological period. The most advanced groups of organisms—insects, vertebrates, and flowering plants—reached their greatest diversity about 30,000 years ago. However, since that time species richness has decreased as human populations have grown. At the present time a phenomenal 40% of

Table 2.1
Three ways in which humans dominate the global ecosystem

1. LAND SURFACE
Human land use and need for resources have transformed as much as half of the Earth's ice-free land surface.

2. NITROGEN CYCLE
Each year human activities, such as cultivating nitrogen-fixing crops, using nitrogen fertilizers, and burning fossil fuels, release more nitrogen into terrestrial systems than is added by natural biological and physical processes.

3. ATMOSPHERIC CARBON CYCLE
By the middle of the twenty-first century, human use of fossil fuels will have resulted in a doubling of the level of carbon dioxide in the Earth's atmosphere.

Source: Data from Vitousek 1994.

the total net primary productivity of the terrestrial environment is used or wasted in some way by people; this represents about 25% of the total primary productivity of the Earth (Table 2.1).

    The first noticeable effects of human activity on extinction rates can be seen in the elimination of large mammals from Australia and North and South America at the time humans first colonized these continents many thousands of years ago. Shortly after humans arrived, 74% to 86%

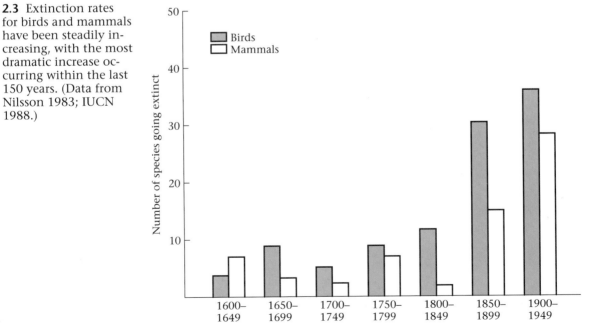

2.3 Extinction rates for birds and mammals have been steadily increasing, with the most dramatic increase occurring within the last 150 years. (Data from Nilsson 1983; IUCN 1988.)

Table 2.2

Recorded extinctions, 1600 to the present

Taxon	Recorded extinctions[a]				Approximate number of species	Percentage of taxon extinct
	Mainland[b]	Island[b]	Ocean	Total		
Mammals	30	51	4	85	4,000	2.1
Birds	21	92	0	113	9,000	1.3
Reptiles	1	20	0	21	6,300	0.3
Amphibians[c]	2	0	0	2	4,200	0.05
Fishes[d]	22	1	0	23	19,100	0.1
Invertebrates[d]	49	48	1	98	1,000,000+	0.01
Flowering plants[e]	245	139	0	384	250,000	0.2

Source: After Reid and Miller 1989; data from various sources.

[a] Numerous additional species have presumably gone extinct without ever being recorded by scientists.

[b] Mainland areas are those with landmasses of 1 million km² or greater (the size of Greenland or larger); smaller landmasses are considered islands.

[c] There has been an alarming decrease in amphibian populations in the last 20 years; some scientists believe that many amphibian species are on the verge of becoming extinct.

[d] The figures given are primarily representative of North America and Hawaii.

[e] The numbers for flowering plants include extinctions of subspecies and varieties as well as species.

of the megafauna—mammals weighing more than 44 kg (100 lbs.)—in these areas became extinct. These extinctions were probably caused directly by hunting (Martin and Klein 1984) and indirectly by burning and clearing of forests. On all continents, there is an extensive record of prehistoric human alteration and destruction of habitat coinciding with a high rate of species extinctions.

How has human activity affected extinction rates in more recent times? Extinction rates are best known for birds and mammals because these species are relatively large, well studied, and conspicuous. Extinction rates for the other 99.9% of the world's species are just rough guesses at the present time. However, extinction rates are uncertain even for birds and mammals, because some species that were considered extinct have been rediscovered, and other species that are presumed to be **extant** (still living) may actually be extinct (Diamond 1988b). Based on the available evidence, the best estimate is that about 85 species of mammals and 113 species of birds have become extinct since the year 1600 (Table 2.2), representing 2.1% of mammal species and 1.3% of birds (Reid and Miller 1989; Smith et al. 1993). While these numbers initially may not seem alarming, the trend of these extinction rates is upward, with the majority of extinctions occurring in the last 150 years (Figure 2.3). The extinction rate for birds and mammals was about one species every decade during the period 1600–1700, but it rose to one species every year during the period 1850–1950. This increase in the rate of species extinction is an indication of the seriousness of the threat to biological diversity. Many species

Table 2.3
Numbers of species threatened with extinction in major groups of animals and plants, and some key families and orders

Group	Approximate number of species	Number of species threatened with extinction	Percentage of species threatened with extinction
VERTEBRATE ANIMALS			
Fishes	24,000	452	2
Amphibians	3,000	59	2
Reptiles	6,000	167	3
Boidae (constrictor snakes)	17[a]	9	53
Varanidae (monitor lizards)	29[a]	11	38
Iguanidae (iguanas)	25[a]	17	68
Birds	9,500	1,029	11
Anseriformes (waterfowl)	109[a]	36	33
Psittaciformes (parrots)	302[a]	118	39
Mammals	4,500	505	11
Marsupialia (marsupials)	179[a]	86	48
Canidae (wolves)	34[a]	13	38
Cervidae (deer)	14[a]	11	79
PLANTS			
Gymnosperms	758	242	32
Angiosperms (flowering plants)	240,000	21,895	9
Palmae (palms)	2,820	925	33

Source: Data from Smith et al. 1993 and Mace 1994.
[a] Number of species for which information is available.

not yet technically extinct have been decimated by human activities and persist only in very low numbers. These species may be considered ecologically extinct in that they no longer play a role in community organization. The future of many such species is doubtful (Table 2.3). About 11% of the world's remaining bird species are threatened with extinction; the same percentage holds for mammal species. Table 2.3 also shows certain animal groups for which the danger is even more severe, such as the family of lizards known as iguanas (Mace 1994). The threat to some freshwater fishes and mollusks may be equally severe (Williams and Nowak 1993). Plant species are also threatened, with gymnosperms (conifers, ginkgos, and cycads) and palms among the especially vulnerable groups. While extinction does occur as a natural process, more than 99% of modern species extinctions can be attributed to human activity (Raup and Stanley 1978).

Extinction rates on islands

The highest species extinction rates during historic times have occurred on islands (see Table 2.2). Most of the known extinctions of birds, mammals, and reptiles during the last 350 years have occurred on islands (King 1985; Groombridge 1992), and more than 80% of the endemic plants of some oceanic islands are extinct or in danger of extinction. A species is **endemic** to the location where it occurs naturally. Island species are particularly vulnerable to extinction because many of them are endemic to only one or a few islands and have only one or a few local populations. Recorded extinction rates may also be higher on islands simply because these areas are better studied than continental areas.

Species may be endemic to a wide geographical area, like the black cherry tree (*Prunus serotina*), which is found across North America, Central America, and South America; or they may be endemic to a small geographical area, like the giant Komodo dragon, which is known only from several small islands in the Indonesian archipelago. A more extreme example is the Haleakala silversword plant, which is found only in one volcanic crater on the island of Maui. Isolated geographical units, such as remote islands, old lakes, and solitary mountain peaks, often have high percentages of endemic species. In contrast, geographical units of equivalent area that are not isolated typically have much lower percentages of endemic species. One of the most notable examples of an isolated area with a high rate of endemism is the island of Madagascar (Myers 1986). Here, the tropical moist forests are spectacularly rich in endemic species: 93% of the 28 primate species, 99% of the 144 species of frogs, and over 80% of the plant species on the island are endemic to Madagascar. By comparison, only 33% of the plant species that occur in Europe are found nowhere else. If the communities on Madagascar or other isolated islands are destroyed or damaged, or populations are intensively harvested, then these endemic species will become extinct. In contrast, mainland species often have many populations over a wide area, so that the loss of one population is not catastrophic for the species. Even in mainland areas, however, certain local regions are noted for their concentrations of endemic species, resulting from such factors as geological age and a wide variety of habitats (Figure 2.4).

One intensively studied island group is the Hawaiian archipelago (Olson 1989). There were 98 species of endemic birds in the Hawaiian islands before the arrival of the Polynesians in 400 A.D. The Polynesians introduced the Polynesian rat, the domestic dog, and the domestic pig; they also began clearing the forest for agriculture. As a result of increased predation and disturbance, about 50 of the bird species became extinct prior to the arrival of Europeans in 1778. The Europeans brought cats, new species of rats, the Indian mongoose, goats, cattle, and the barn owl. They also unwittingly brought bird diseases, and they cleared even more land for agriculture and human settlements. Since then, an additional 17 bird species have become extinct. Many of the remaining endemic species have declining populations and are near extinction. Plant species on many islands are also threatened with extinction, mainly through habitat de-

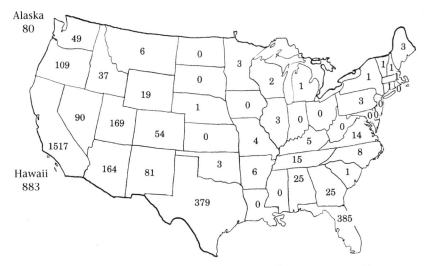

2.4 The number of plant species endemic to the different states in the United States varies greatly. For example, 379 plant species are found only in Texas and nowhere else in the United States. New York, in contrast, has only one endemic species. California, with its large area and vast array of habitats, including deserts, mountains, seacoasts, old-growth forests, and myriad others, is home to more endemic species than any other state. The island archipelago of Hawaii, far from the mainland, hosts many endemic species despite its small area. (From Gentry 1986.)

struction (Table 2.4). In Hawaii, fully 91% of the naturally occurring plant species are endemic to the islands. About 10% of these endemic species have become extinct, and 40% of the remaining endemics are threatened with extinction (Davis et al. 1986).

Extinction rates at sea and on the mainland

Of all the animal and plant species known to have gone extinct in the period from 1600 to the present, almost half were island species (see Table 2.2), even though islands represent only a small fraction of the Earth's surface. In contrast, it has been estimated that only five species—four species of marine mammals and a limpet—have become extinct in the world's vast oceans during modern times. This calculation is almost certainly an underestimate, because marine species are not as well known as terrestrial species, but it may also reflect the greater geographical range of individual marine species. However, the significance of these marine losses may be greater than the numbers suggest because many of the marine mammals are top predators that have a major effect on marine communities. Also, marine species have greater diversity at the phylum level than do terrestrial species, so the extinction of even a few marine species can represent a serious loss to global biological diversity.

Table 2.4
Number of plant species and their status for various islands and island groups

Island(s)	Native species	Endemic species	Percentage endemic	Number of endemics threatened	Percentage of endemics threatened
Ascensión	25	11	44	9	82
Azores	600	5	9	23	42
Galápagos	543	229	42	135	59
Hawaiian	970	883	91	±353	40
Juan Fernandez	147	118	80	93	79
Madeira	760	131	17	86	66
New Caledonia	3250	2474	76	146	6
New Zealand	2000	±1620	81	±132	8
Norfolk	174	48	28	45	94
Rodrigues	145	40	28	36	90

Source: After Reid and Miller 1989; data from Davis et al. 1986 and Gentry 1986.

The majority of freshwater fish and flowering plant extinctions have occurred in mainland areas simply because of the vastly greater numbers of species in these regions. In a recent survey of the rich freshwater fish fauna of the Malay Peninsula, only 122 of the 266 species of fish known to exist on the basis of earlier collections could still be found (Mohsin and Ambak 1983). In North America, over one-third of the freshwater fish species are in danger of extinction (Moyle and Leidy 1992).

Island biogeography and modern extinction rates

Studies of island communities have led to the development of general rules on the distribution of biological diversity, synthesized as the **island biogeography model** of MacArthur and Wilson (1967). The central observation that this model was built to explain is the **species–area relationship**: islands with large areas have more species than islands with small areas (Figure 2.5). This rule makes intuitive sense, because large islands will tend to have a greater variety of local environments and community types than small islands. Also, larger islands allow greater geographical isolation and a larger number of populations per species, increasing the likelihood of speciation and decreasing the probability of extinction of newly evolved as well as recently arrived species.

The island biogeography model has been used to predict the number and percentage of species that would become extinct if habitats were destroyed (Simberloff 1986). It is assumed that if an island has a certain number of species, reducing the area of natural habitat on the island would result in the island being able to support only a number of species corresponding to that on a smaller island (Figure 2.6). This model has been extended from islands to national parks and nature reserves that are sur-

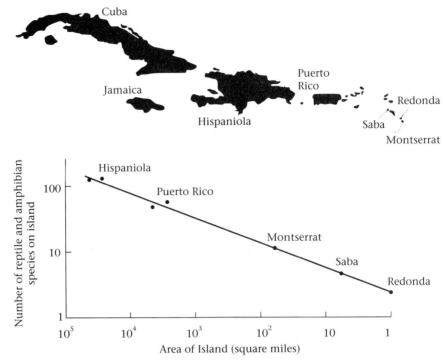

2.5 The number of species on an island can be predicted from the area of the island. In this figure, the number of species of reptiles and amphibians is shown for seven islands in the West Indies. The number of species on large islands such as Cuba and Hispaniola far exceeds that on the tiny islands of Saba and Redonda. (From Wilson 1989.)

rounded by damaged habitat. These reserves can be viewed as **habitat islands** in an inhospitable "sea" of unsuitable habitat. The model predicts that when 50% of an island (or a habitat island) is destroyed, approximately 10% of the species occurring on the island will be eliminated. If these species are endemic to the area, they will become extinct. When 90% of the habitat is destroyed, 50% of the species will be lost; and when 99% of the habitat is gone, about 75% of the original species will be lost.

Predictions of extinction rates based on habitat loss vary considerably because each group of species and each geographical area has particular species–area relationships. Because tropical forests account for the great majority of the world's species, estimating present and future rates of species extinction in rain forests gives an approximation of global rates of extinction. If deforestation continues until all of the tropical forests except those in national parks and other protected areas are cut down, about two-thirds of all plant and bird species will be driven to extinction (Simberloff 1986).

Using a conservative value of 1% of the world's rain forests being destroyed per year, Wilson (1989) estimated that 0.2%–0.3% of all species—20,000 to 30,000 species if based on a total of 10 million species—would be lost per year. In more immediate units, 68 species would be lost each day, or 3 species each hour. Over the 10-year period from 1993 to 2003,

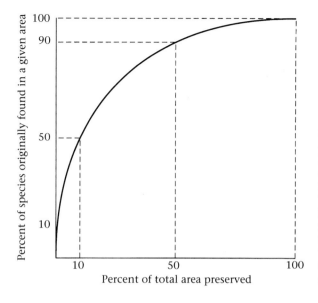

2.6 According to the island biogeography model, the number of species present increases asymptotically with area to a maximum value. In practical terms, this means that if the area approach of habitat is reduced by 50%, the number of species lost may be 10%; if the habitat is reduced by 90%, the number species lost may be 50%. The shape of the curve is different for each region of the world and each group of species, but this model gives a general indication of the effect of habitat destruction on species extinctions and the persistence of species in the remaining habitat.

approximately 250,000 species would become extinct. Other methods using the rates of extinction in tropical rain forests estimate a loss of between 2% and 11% of the world's species per decade (Reid and Miller 1989; Koopowitz et al. 1994). The variation in rates is caused by different estimates of the rate of deforestation, different values for the species-area curves, and different mathematical approaches (Heywood et al. 1994). Extinction rates might be somewhat lower if species-rich areas could be targeted for conservation efforts. Extinction rates might also be higher because the highest rates of deforestation are occurring in countries with large concentrations of rare species (Balmford and Long 1994). Regardless of which figure is the most accurate, all of these estimates indicate that hundreds of thousands of species are headed for extinction within the next 50 years.

In addition to the global extinctions that are the primary focus of conservation biology, many species are experiencing a series of local extinctions across their range. Formerly widespread species are now often restricted to a few small pockets of their former habitat. For example, the American burying beetle, which was once found all across central and eastern North America, is now found only in three isolated populations (see Figure 2.2). Biological communities are impoverished by such local extinctions. For example, the Middlesex Fells, a local conservation area in metropolitan Boston, contained 338 native plant species in 1894; only 227 native species remained when the area was surveyed 98 years later (Drayton and Primack 1995). Fourteen of the plant species that were lost had been listed as "common" in 1894. These large numbers of local extinctions serve as important biological warning signs that something is wrong with the environment. Action is needed to prevent further local extinctions as well as the global extinctions of species that are known to be experiencing local extinction on a massive and widespread scale.

Causes of Extinction

If species and communities are adapted to local environmental conditions, why are they facing extinction? Shouldn't species and communities tend to persist in the same place over time? The answers to these questions are obvious: massive disturbances caused by people have altered, degraded, and destroyed the landscape on a vast scale, driving species and even whole communities to the point of extinction. The major threats to biological diversity that result from human activity are habitat destruction, habitat fragmentation, habitat degradation (including pollution), the overexploitation of species for human use, the introduction of exotic species, and the increased spread of disease. Most threatened species face at least two or more of these problems, which are speeding their way to extinction and hindering efforts to protect them (Groombridge 1992).

These six threats to biological diversity are all caused by an ever-increasing use of the world's natural resources by the exponentially expanding human population. Until the last few hundred years, the rate of human population growth was relatively slow, with the birth rate only slightly exceeding the mortality rate. The greatest destruction of biological communities has occurred during the last 150 years, during which the human population grew from 1 billion in 1850, to 2 billion in 1930, to 5.9 billion in 1995, and will reach an estimated 6.5 billion by the year 2000 (Figure 2.7). Human numbers have increased because birth rates have remained high while mortality rates have declined as a result of both modern medical discoveries (specifically, the control of disease) and the presence of more reliable food supplies (Keyfitz 1989). Population growth has slowed in the industrialized countries of the world but is still high in many areas of tropical Africa, Latin America, and Asia—areas where the greatest biological diversity is also found (WRI/UNEP/UNDP 1994).

People use natural resources such as fuelwood, wild meat, and wild plants, and people convert vast amounts of natural habitat to agricultural and residential purposes, so human population growth by itself is partially responsible for the loss of biological diversity. Some scientists have argued that controlling the size of the human population is the key to protecting biological diversity (Hardin 1993; Meffe et al. 1993). However, human population growth is not the only cause of species extinction and habitat destruction. If one examines the situation throughout the world in both developing and industrial nations, it is clear that species extinctions and the destruction of ecosystems are not always caused by individual citizens obtaining their basic needs. The rise of industrial capitalism and materialistic modern societies has produced an accelerated demand for natural resources, particularly in the developed countries. Inefficient and unequal usage of natural resources is also a major cause of the decline in biological diversity. In many countries there is extreme inequality in the distribution of wealth, with the majority of the wealth (money, good farmland, timber resources, etc.) owned by a small percentage of the population. As a result, rural people are forced to destroy biological communities and hunt endangered species to extinction because they are poor and have no land or resources of their own (Dasmann et al. 1973; Kummer and Turner 1994; Skole et al. 1994).

In many cases, the causes of habitat destruction are the large-scale industrial and commercial activities associated with a global economy, such as mining, cattle ranching, commercial fishing, forestry, plantation agriculture, manufacturing, and dam construction, initiated with the goal of making a profit (Meyer and Turner 1994). Many of these projects are sanctioned by national governments and international development banks and are touted as providing jobs, commodities, and tax revenues. However, their use of natural resources is often neither efficient nor cost-effective because the emphasis in these industries is on short-term gains, often made at the expense of the long-term viability of the natural resources, the environment, and, ultimately, the people and businesses that depend on the resources.

The responsibility for the destruction of biological diversity in species-rich tropical areas also lies in the unequal use of natural resources worldwide. People in industrialized countries (and the wealthy minority in the developing countries) consume a disproportionate share of the world's energy, minerals, wood products, and food (Parikh and Parikh 1991; WRI/IUCN/UNEP 1992). Each year, the average citizen of the United States uses 43 times more petroleum products, 34 times more aluminum, and 58 times more phosphate fertilizer than the average citizen of India (WRI/UNEP/UNDP 1994). This excessive consumption of resources is not sustainable in the long run, and if this pattern is adopted by the expanding middle class in the developing world, it will cause massive environmental disruption. The affluent citizens of developed countries need to confront their excessive consumption of resources and reevaluate their lifestyles as they offer aid to curb population growth and protect biological diversity in the developing world (Figure 2.8).

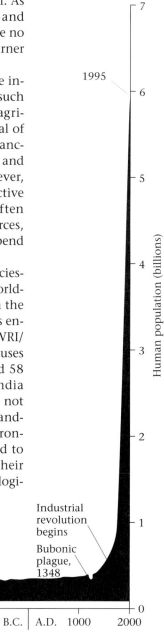

2.7 The human population has increased spectacularly since the seventeenth century. At current growth rates, the population will double in less than 40 years.

2.8 The wealthy developed countries often criticize the poorer, developing nations for a lack of sound environmental policies, but seem unwilling to acknowledge that their own excessive consumption of resources is a major part of the problem. (Cartoon by Scott Willis, © *San Jose Mercury News*.)

Habitat Destruction

The major threat to biological diversity is loss of habitat, and the most important means of protecting biological diversity is habitat preservation. Habitat loss is known to be the primary threat to the majority of verte-

Table 2.5

Factors responsible for some extinctions and threatened extinctions

Group	Percentage due to each cause[a]					
	Habitat loss	Over-exploitation[b]	Species introductions	Predators	Other	Unknown
EXTINCTIONS						
Mammals	19	23	20	1	1	36
Birds	20	11	22	0	2	37
Reptiles	5	32	42	0	0	21
Fishes	35	4	30	0	4	48
THREATENED EXTINCTIONS[c]						
Mammals	68	54	6	8	12	—
Birds	58	30	28	1	1	—
Reptiles	53	63	17	3	6	—
Amphibians	77	29	14	—	3	—
Fishes	78	12	28	—	2	—

Source: From Reid and Miller 1989, based on data from various sources.

[a] These values represent the percentage of species that are influenced by the given factor. Some species may be influenced by more than one factor; thus some rows may exceed 100%.

[b] Overexploitation includes commercial, sport, and subsistence hunting as well as live animal capture for any purpose.

[c] Threatened species and subspecies include those in the IUCN categories endangered, vulnerable, and rare, as defined in Chapter 3.

Table 2.6
Loss of primary forest habitat in some countries of the Old World tropics

Country	Primary forest remaining (× 1000 ha)	Percentage of habitat lost
AFRICA		
Gambia	122	89
Ghana	4,254	82
Kenya	2,274	71
Madagascar	13,049	75
Rwanda	184	80
Zaire	83,255	57
Zimbabwe	17,169	56
ASIA		
Bangladesh	482	96
India	49,929	78
Indonesia	60,403	51
Malaysia	18,008	42
Myanmar (Burma)	24,131	64
Philippines	<1,000	97
Sri Lanka	610	86
Thailand	13,107	73
Vietnam	6,758	76

Source: WRI/UNEP/UNDP 1994.

brate species currently facing extinction (Table 2.5; Groombridge 1992), and this is undoubtedly true for invertebrates, plants, and fungi as well. In many parts of the world, particularly on islands and where human population density is high, most of the original habitat has been destroyed. More than 50% of the primary forest wildlife habitat has been destroyed in 47 out of 57 Old World tropical countries (Table 2.6). In tropical Asia, fully 65% of the forest wildlife habitat has been lost, with particularly high rates of destruction reported for the Philippines, Bangladesh, Sri Lanka, Vietnam, and India. Sub-Saharan Africa has lost most of its wildlife habitat, with habitat loss being most severe in Gambia, Ghana, and Rwanda. The biologically rich countries of Zaire and Zimbabwe are relatively better off, still having about half of their wildlife habitat. Present rates of deforestation vary considerably among countries, with particularly high annual rates of 1.5%–2% reported in such tropical countries as Vietnam, Paraguay, Mexico, Côte d'Ivoire, and Costa Rica. In the Mediterranean region, which has been densely populated by humans for thousands of years, only 10% of the original forest cover remains.

Table 2.7
Range loss for some Southeast Asian primates and the percentage of their original habitat now protected

Species	Original range (× 1000 ha)	Remaining range (× 1000 ha)	Percentage of range lost	Percentage now protected
Orangutan	55,300	20,700	63	2.1
Siamang	46,511	16,980	63	6.8
Bornean gibbon	39,500	25,300	36	5.1
Mentawai gibbon	650	450	31	22.9
Indochinese gibbon	34,933	8,753	75	3.1
Long-tailed macaque	38,318	12,332	68	3.4
Proboscis monkey	2,969	1,775	40	4.1
Douc langur	29,600	7,227	76	3.1
Javan lutong	4,327	161	96	1.6
Francois' leaf monkey	9,740	1,411	86	1.2

Source: IUCN/UNEP 1986.

For many important wildlife species, the majority of the habitat in their original range has been destroyed, and very little of the remaining habitat is protected. Table 2.7 gives such statistics for some Asian primates. More than 95% of the original habitats of both the Javan gibbon and the Javan lutong have been destroyed, and they are protected on less than 2% of their original range. The orangutan, a great ape that lives in Sumatra and Borneo, has lost 63% of its habitat and is also protected in only 2% of its range.

Threatened rain forests

The destruction of tropical rain forests has come to be synonymous with the loss of species. Tropical moist forests occupy 7% of the Earth's land surface, but are estimated to contain over 50% of its species. The original extent of tropical rain forests and related moist forests has been estimated at 16 million km^2, based on current patterns of rainfall and temperature (Figure 2.9; Myers 1984, 1986, 1991b; Sayer and Whitmore 1991). A combination of ground surveys, aerial photos, and remote sensing data from satellites showed that in 1982 only 9.5 million km^2 remained, an area about equal in size to the continental United States. A recensus in 1985 showed a loss of almost another million km^2 during this three-year period. At the present time, as much as 180,000 km^2 of rain forest is being lost per year—an area larger than the state of Florida—with 80,000 km^2 completely destroyed and 100,000 km^2 degraded to the point at which species composition and ecosystem processes are greatly altered. Tropical forest ecosystems are easily degraded because their soils are often thin and nutrient-poor and are readily eroded by heavy rainfall. At present, there is considerable discussion in the scientific literature about the original extent and current area

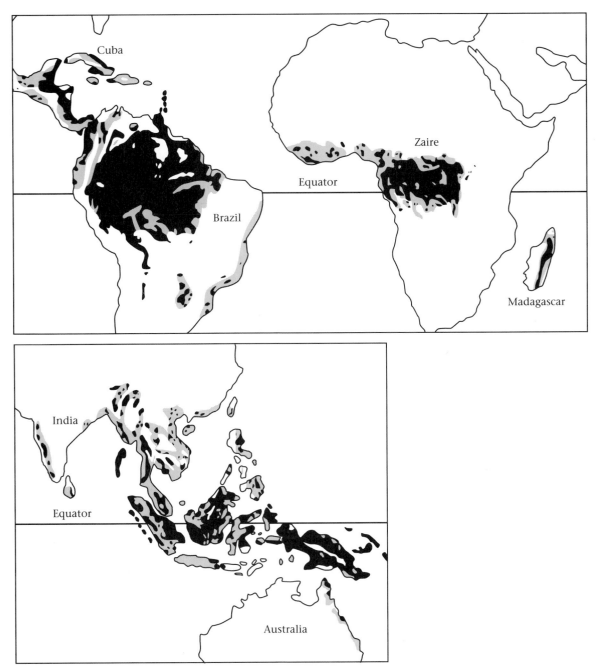

2.9 Tropical rain forests are found predominantly in wet, equatorial areas of the Americas, Africa, and Asia. Tropical forests once covered the entire shaded area, but in recent years human activities have resulted in the loss of a great deal of rain forest, reducing the limits to the areas shown in black. (After Repetto 1990a; maps based on data from the Smithsonian Institution.)

2.10 Tropical forests in the Brazilian Amazon are being cut down to make way for cattle ranches. Similar scenes are common in Southeast Asia, where logging by timber companies is followed by shifting cultivation. (Photograph from The Woods Hole Research Center.)

of tropical forests as well as the rates of deforestation (Groombridge 1992; WRI/UNEP/UNDP 1994). Despite the difficulty of obtaining accurate numbers, there is a general consensus that tropical deforestation rates are alarmingly high. Extending the projections forward reveals that at the current rate of loss, there will be very little intact tropical forest left after the year 2040 except in the relatively small areas under protection. The situation is actually even more grim than these projections indicate because the human population is still increasing and poverty is on the rise, putting ever greater demands on the dwindling supply of rain forest.

On a global scale, about half of rain forest destruction results from small-scale cultivation of crops by farmers. Some of this land is converted into permanent farmland and pastures, but much of it is used for **shifting cultivation**, in which patches of forest are cleared, burned, and cultivated for a few seasons, until the soil fertility declines to the point at which the land must be abandoned. The land then returns to secondary forest. A further 25,000 km^2 is degraded each year for fuelwood production, mostly to supply local villagers with wood for cooking fires. Another 45,000 km^2 per year is destroyed through commercial clear-cutting and selective logging operations. The remaining 20,000 km^2 per year is cleared for cattle ranches (Figure 2.10). Logging, farming, and cattle ranching on rain forest lands are often related to demand in industrialized countries for cheap agricultural products, such as rubber, palm oil, cocoa, timber, plywood, and beef. The relative importance of these activities varies by geographical region, with logging being a more significant activity in tropical Asia, cattle ranching being more prominent in tropical America, and farming and fuelwood gathering more important in tropical Africa (Kummer and Turner 1994).

A number of places can be singled out as examples of how rapid and serious rain forest destruction can be.

- *Madagascar.* The moist forests of Madagascar, with their rich array of endemic species, originally covered 112,000 km^2. By 1985, they had been reduced to 38,000 km^2 by a combination of shifting cultivation, cattle grazing, and fire. The present rate of deforestation on Madagascar is about 1,100 km^2 per year, which means that by the year 2020 there may be no moist forests left except in the 1.5% of the island under protection (Myers 1986; Green and Sussman 1990). Because Madagascar is the only place where lemurs occur in the wild, the loss of Madagascar's forests will result in the extinction of many lemur species (Figure 2.11).

- *The Atlantic Coast of Brazil.* Another area of high endemism is the Atlantic Coast forest of northern Brazil. Fully half of its tree species are endemic to the area, and the region supports a number of rare and endangered animals, including the golden lion tamarin. In recent decades, the Atlantic Coast forest has been almost entirely cleared for sugar cane, coffee, and cocoa production; less than 5% of the original forest remains (Myers 1986). The remaining forest is not in one large block, but is divided into isolated fragments that may be unable to support viable populations of many wide-ranging species. The single largest patch of forest remaining is only 7000 km^2, and this patch is highly disturbed in places.

- *Coastal Ecuador.* The coastal region of Ecuador originally was covered by a rich forest filled with endemic species. It was minimally disturbed by human activity until 1960. At that time, roads were developed and forests cleared to establish human settlements and

2.11 The aye-aye (*Daubentonia madagascariensis*) is one of the endangered endemic lemur species of Madagascar. The aye-aye is the subject of conservation efforts in the field as well as captive breeding programs. All 28 lemur species—an entire order of primates found nowhere else in the world—are in danger of becoming extinct on Madagascar. (Photograph © David Haring, Duke University Primate Research Center.)

oil palm plantations. One of the only surviving fragments is the 1.7 km^2 Rio Palenque Science Reserve. This tiny conservation area has 1025 recorded plant species, of which 25% are not known to occur anywhere else (Gentry 1986). Over 100 undescribed plant species have been recorded at this site. Many of these species are known only from a single individual plant and are doomed to certain extinction.

Other threatened habitats

Other habitat types besides the rain forest are equally threatened with destruction.

- *Tropical dry forests.* The land occupied by tropical dry forests is more suitable for agriculture and cattle ranching than is the land occupied by tropical rain forests. Consequently, human population density is five times greater in dry forest areas of Central America than in adjacent rain forest areas (Murphy and Lugo 1986). Today, the Pacific Coast of Central America has less than 2% of its original extent of deciduous dry forest remaining (Janzen 1988a).

- *Wetlands and aquatic habitats.* Wetlands are of critical importance as habitats for fish, aquatic invertebrates, and birds, and are a resource for flood control, drinking water, and power production (Mitchell 1992; Moyle and Leidy 1992; Dugan 1993). Wetlands are often filled in or drained for development or altered by channelization of watercourses, dams, and chemical pollution. All of these factors are affecting the Florida Everglades, one of the prime wildlife refuges in the United States, now on the verge of ecological collapse (Holloway 1994). During the last 200 years, over half of the wetlands in the United States have been destroyed, resulting in 40%–50% of the freshwater snail species in the southeastern United States becoming either extinct or endangered (Maltby 1988). Destruction of wetlands has been equally severe in other areas of the industrialized world, such as Europe and Japan. In the last few decades, one of the major threats to wetlands in developing countries has been massive development projects involving drainage, irrigation, and dams, organized by governments and often financed by international aid agencies.

  Although many wetland species are widespread, some aquatic systems are known for their high levels of endemism. For example, Lake Victoria in East Africa has one of the richest endemic fish faunas in the world, but 250 of its species are in danger of extinction due to water pollution and introductions of exotic fishes that prey on the endemic fishes (Kaufman 1992).

- *Mangroves.* One of the most important wetland communities in tropical areas is the mangrove forest. Mangrove species are among the few woody plants that can tolerate salt water. Mangrove forests occupy coastal areas with saline or brackish water, typically where there are muddy bottoms. Such habitats are similar to those occupied by salt marshes in the temperate zone. Mangrove forests are extremely important as breeding grounds and feeding areas for shrimp and fish, and as a source of wood for poles, charcoal, and industrial production. In Australia, two-thirds of the species caught by commercial fishermen are dependent to some degree on the mangrove ecosystem (WRI/IIED 1986). Despite their great economic value, mangrove forests are often cleared for rice cultivation and commercial shrimp and prawn hatcheries, particularly in Southeast Asia, where as much as 15% of the mangrove forest has been removed for aquaculture (ESCAP 1985). The Philippines has lost more than half of its mangrove forest over the last 100 years.

- *Grasslands.* Temperate grassland is another habitat type that has been almost completely destroyed by human activity. It is relatively easy to convert large areas of grassland into farmland and cattle ranches. Illinois and Indiana originally contained 15 million ha of tall-grass prairie, but now only 1400 ha of this habitat—one ten-thousandth of the original area—remains undisturbed; the rest has been converted into farmland (Chadwick 1993). This remaining area of prairie is divided up into many small fragments, widely scattered across the landscape.

- *Coral reefs.* Tropical coral reefs contain an estimated one-third of the ocean's fish species, although they occupy only 0.2% of its surface area. Already, 5%–10% of all coral reefs have been destroyed, and as many as 50% could be destroyed in the next few decades. In the Caribbean, a combination of overfishing, hurricane damage, and disease is responsible for the dramatic decline of a large proportion of the coral reefs and their replacement by fleshy macroalgae (Hughes 1994). Elkhorn and staghorn corals, which were formerly common and gave structure to the community, have become rare in many locations.

Desertification

Many biological communities in seasonally dry climates have been degraded into artificial deserts by human activities, a process known as **desertification** (Breman 1992; Allan and Warren 1993). Such communities include tropical grasslands, scrub, and deciduous forest, as well as temperate shrublands and grasslands such as those found in the Mediterranean region, southwestern Australia, South Africa, Chile, and southern California. While these areas initially may be suitable for agriculture, repeated cultivation leads to soil erosion and a loss of the water-holding capacity of the soil. Land may also be chronically overgrazed by domestic livestock such as cattle, sheep, and goats (Figure 2.12), and woody plants may be cut down for fuel (Fleischner 1994; Milton et al. 1994). The result

2.12 Overgrazed grassland takes on the appearance of a desert, leading to the elimination of native species. (Photograph courtesy of the U.S. Fish and Wildlife Service and U.S. Forest Service.)

is a progressive and largely irreversible degradation of the biological community and a loss of soil cover, to the point at which the area takes on the appearance of a desert. Worldwide, 9 million km² of arid lands have been converted into deserts by this process (Dregné 1983). The process of desertification is most severe in the Sahel region of Africa, where most of the native large mammal species are threatened with extinction. The human dimensions of the problem are illustrated by the fact that the Sahel region is estimated to have 2.5 times more people than the land can sustainably support. Further desertification appears to be almost inevitable, except in the limited areas where intensification of agriculture is possible (Breman 1992).

Habitat Fragmentation

In addition to being destroyed outright, habitats that formerly occupied large areas are often divided into small pieces by roads, fields, towns, and a wide range of other human activities. **Habitat fragmentation** is the process whereby a large, continuous area of habitat is both reduced in area and divided into two or more fragments (Wilcove et al. 1986; Shafer 1990). When habitat is destroyed, a patchwork of habitat fragments may be left behind. These fragments are often isolated from one another by a highly modified or degraded landscape (Figure 2.13). This situation can be described by the island model of biogeography, with the fragments functioning as habitat islands in an inhospitable human-dominated "sea." Fragmentation occurs during almost any severe reduction in habitat area, but it can also occur even when habitat area is reduced to only a minor degree, as when the original habitat is divided by roads, railroads, canals, power lines, fences, oil pipelines, fire lanes, or other barriers to the free movement of species (Schonewald-Cox and Buechner 1992).

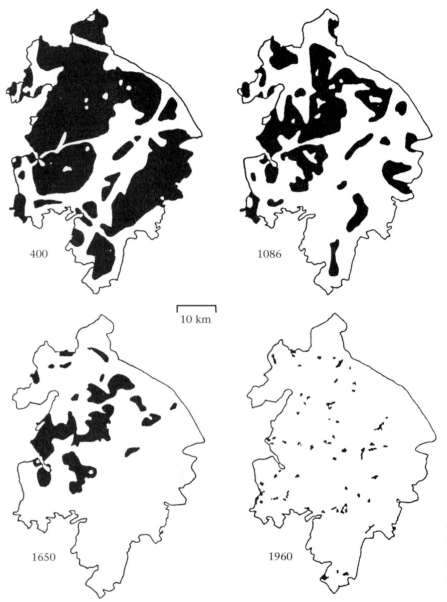

400

1086

10 km

1650

1960

2.13 The forested areas of Warwickshire, England (shown in black) have been fragmented and reduced in area over the centuries from 400 to 1960 A.D. (From Wilcove et al. 1986.)

Habitat fragments differ from the original habitat in two important ways: (1) fragments have a greater amount of edge per area of habitat, and (2) the center of each habitat fragment is closer to an edge. A simple example will illustrate these characteristics and the problems that can occur because of them.

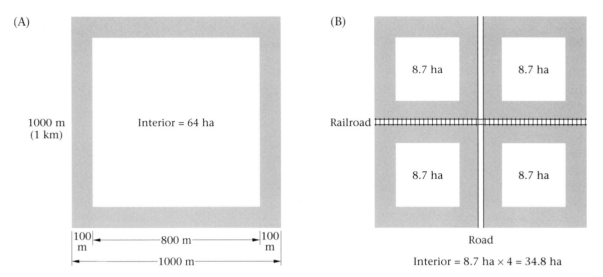

(A)

1000 m
(1 km)

Interior = 64 ha

|100 m| ← 800 m → |100 m|

← 1000 m →

(B)

8.7 ha   8.7 ha

Railroad

8.7 ha   8.7 ha

Road

Interior = 8.7 ha × 4 = 34.8 ha

2.14 A hypothetical example shows how habitat area is reduced by fragmentation and edge effects. (A) A 1–km² protected area. Assuming that edge effects (shaded area) penetrate 100 m into the reserve, approximately 64 ha are available as usable interior habitat for nesting birds. (B) The fragmentation of the reserve by a road and a railway, although they take up little actual area, extends the edge effects so that almost half the nesting habitat is destroyed.

Consider a square conservation reserve 1000 m (1 km) on each side (Figure 2.14). The total area of the reserve is 1 km² (100 ha). The perimeter (or edge) of the reserve totals 4000 m. A point in the middle of the reserve is 500 m from the nearest point on the perimeter. If domestic cats forage 100 m into the forest from the perimeter of the reserve and prevent forest birds from successfully raising their young, then only the 64 ha in the reserve's interior is available to the birds for breeding. Edge habitat, unsuitable for breeding, occupies 36 ha.

Now imagine the reserve being divided into four equal quadrants by a north–south road 10 m wide and by an east–west railroad track that is also 10 m wide. The rights-of-way remove a total of 2 × 1000 m × 10 m of area (2 ha) from the reserve. Because only 2% of the reserve is being removed by the road and railroad, government planners argue that the effects on the reserve are negligible. However, the reserve has now been divided into four fragments, each of which is 495 m × 495 m in area. The distance from the center of each fragment to the nearest point on the perimeter has been reduced to 247 m, which is less than half of the former distance. Because cats can now forage into the forest from the road and railroad as well as the perimeter, birds can successfully raise young only in the most interior areas of each of the four fragments. Each of these interior areas is 8.7 ha, for a total of 34.8 ha. Even though the road and railroad removed only 2% of the reserve area, they reduced the habitat available to the birds by about half.

Habitat fragmentation also threatens the persistence of species in more subtle ways. First, fragmentation may limit a species' potential for dispersal and colonization. Many bird, mammal, and insect species of the forest interior will not cross even very short stretches of open area because of the danger of predation. As a result, many species do not recolonize fragments after the original population has disappeared (Lovejoy et al. 1986; Bierregaard et al. 1992). Furthermore, when animal dispersal is reduced by habitat fragmentation, plants with fleshy fruits or sticky seeds that depend on the animals to disperse their seeds will be affected as well. Thus, isolated habitat fragments will not be colonized by many native species that could potentially live in them. As species become extinct within individual fragments through natural successional and population processes, new species will fail to arrive due to these dispersal barriers, and the number of species in the habitat fragment will decline over time.

A second harmful aspect of habitat fragmentation is that it may reduce the foraging ability of native animals. Many animal species, either as individuals or as social groups, need to be able to move freely across the landscape among widely scattered or seasonally available resources such as fruits, seeds, grasses, or pools of water. A given resource may be needed for only a few weeks of the year, or even only once in a few years, but when a habitat is fragmented, species confined to a single habitat fragment may be unable to migrate over their normal home range in search of that scarce resource. For example, fences may prevent the natural migration of large grazing animals such as wildebeest or bison, forcing them to overgraze an unsuitable habitat and eventually leading to starvation of the animals and degradation of the habitat.

Habitat fragmentation may also precipitate population decline and extinction by dividing an existing widespread population into two or more subpopulations, each in a restricted area. These smaller populations are more vulnerable to inbreeding depression, genetic drift, and other problems associated with small population size (see Chapter 3). While a large area of habitat may have supported a single large population, it is possible that none of its fragments can support a subpopulation large enough to persist for a long period.

Edge effects

Habitat fragmentation dramatically increases the amount of edge relative to the amount of interior habitat, as demonstrated above (see Figure 2.14). The microenvironment at a fragment edge is different from that of the forest interior. Some of the more important **edge effects** are greater fluctuations in levels of light, temperature, humidity, and wind (Kapos 1989; Bierregaard et al. 1992). These edge effects are often evident up to 500 meters into the forest (Laurance 1991). Because plant and animal species are often precisely adapted to certain temperature, humidity, and light levels, these changes will eliminate many species from forest fragments. Shade-tolerant wildflower species of the temperate forest, late-successional tree species of the tropical forest, and humidity-sensitive animals such as amphibians are often rapidly eliminated by habitat fragmentation, leading to a shift in the species composition of the community.

A dense tangle of vines and other fast-growing pioneer species often grows up at the forest edge in response to the higher light levels. These tangles of vegetation may create a barrier that reduces the effects of environmental disturbance on the interior of the fragment. In this sense, the forest edge plays an important role in preserving the composition of the forest fragment, but in the process, the species composition of the forest edge is dramatically altered and the area occupied by forest interior species is further reduced.

When a forest is fragmented, the increased wind, lower humidity, and higher temperatures at the forest edge make fires more likely. Fires may spread into habitat fragments from nearby agricultural fields that are burnt regularly, as in sugarcane harvesting, or from the activities of farmers practicing shifting cultivation (Gomez-Pompa and Kaus 1992). In Indonesian Borneo, several million hectares of tropical moist forest burned during an unusual dry period in 1982 and 1983; a combination of forest fragmentation due to farming and selective logging, accumulation of brush after selective logging, and human-caused fires contributed to this environmental disaster (Leighton and Wirawan 1986).

Habitat fragmentation increases the vulnerability of the fragments to invasion by exotic species and native pest species. The forest edge is a disturbed environment in which pest species can easily become established, increase in numbers, and then disperse into the interior of the fragment (Paton 1994). Omnivorous animals such as raccoons, skunks, and blue jays may increase in numbers along forest edges, where they can obtain foods from both undisturbed and disturbed habitats. These aggressive feeders eat the eggs and nestlings of forest birds, often preventing successful reproduction for many bird species hundreds of meters from the nearest forest edge. Nest-parasitizing cowbirds, which live in fields and edge habitats, use habitat edges as an invasion point into forest interiors, where their nestlings destroy the eggs and nestlings of forest songbirds. The combination of habitat fragmentation, increased nest predation, and destruction of tropical forests is probably responsible for the dramatic decline of many migratory songbird species of North America, such as the red-eyed vireo, the Eastern wood pewee, and the hooded warbler (Terborgh 1989, 1992b), though there is still no consensus on its causes and geographical extent (James et al., in press).

Habitat fragmentation also brings wild populations into contact with domestic plants and animals. Diseases of domestic species can then spread more readily to wild species, which often have low immunity to them. There is also a potential for diseases to spread from wild species to domestic plants, animals, and even people, once the level of contact increases.

Habitat Degradation and Pollution

Even when a habitat is unaffected by overt destruction or fragmentation, the communities and species in that habitat can be profoundly affected

2.15 Although it causes extensive damage to ecological communities over widespread areas, air pollution is often subtle and easy for humans to ignore. The massive air pollution generated by oil well fires set during the 1991 Persian Gulf War was a more conspicuous example of this constant threat. (Photograph © Reuters/Bettmann.)

by human activities. Biological communities can be damaged and species driven to extinction by external factors that do not change the dominant plant structure of the community, so that the damage is not immediately apparent. For example, in a temperate deciduous forest, physical degradation of a habitat might be caused by frequent uncontrolled ground fires; these fires might not kill the mature trees, but the rich perennial wildflower community and insect fauna on the forest floor would be gradually eliminated. Frequent boating and diving in coral reef areas typically degrade the community as fragile species are crushed by divers' flippers, boat hulls, and anchors. The most subtle form of environmental degradation is environmental pollution, the most common causes of which are pesticides, chemicals and sewage released by industries and human settlements, emissions from factories and automobiles, and sediment deposits from eroded hillsides. The general effects of pollution on water quality, air quality, and even the global climate are cause for great concern, not only as threats to biological diversity but also because of their effects on human health. Sometimes, as in the case of the massive oil spills and 500 oil well fires that resulted from the Persian Gulf War, environmental pollution is highly visible and dramatic (Figure 2.15).

Pesticide pollution

The dangers of pesticides were brought to the world's attention in 1962 by Rachel Carson's influential book *Silent Spring.* Carson described the process known as **biomagnification**, through which DDT (dichlorodiphenyltrichloroethene) and other organochlorine pesticides become more concentrated as they ascend the food chain. These pesticides, used on crop plants to kill insects and sprayed on water bodies to kill mosquito larvae, were harming wildlife populations, particularly birds that ate large amounts of insects, fish, or other animals exposed to DDT and its by-products. Birds with high levels of pesticides concentrated in their tissues, particularly raptors such as hawks and eagles, were weakened and tended to lay eggs with abnormally thin shells, which cracked during incubation. As a result of their failure to raise young, populations of these birds showed dramatic declines throughout the world. In lakes and estuaries, DDT and other pesticides became concentrated in predatory fishes and marine mammals such as dolphins. In agricultural areas, beneficial and endangered insect species were killed along with harmful species. At the same time, mosquitoes and other targeted insects evolved resistance to the chemicals, so that ever-larger doses of DDT were required to suppress the insect populations. Recognition of this situation led to a ban on the use of organochloride pesticides in many industrialized countries. The ban eventually allowed the partial recovery of many bird species, most notably peregrine falcons, ospreys, and bald eagles (Cade et al. 1988; Porteous 1992). Nevertheless, the continuing use of these pesticides in other countries is cause for concern, not only for the sake of endangered animal species, but also because of their potential long-term effects on people, particularly workers who handle the chemicals in the field and people who eat agricultural products treated with them.

Water pollution

Water pollution has negative consequences for human populations: it destroys food sources such as fish and shellfish and contaminates drinking water. Important as well is the damage water pollution does to aquatic communities (Figure 2.16; Moyle and Leidy 1992). Rivers, lakes, and oceans are often used as open sewers for industrial wastes and residential sewage. Pesticides, herbicides, petroleum wastes and spills, heavy metals (such as mercury, lead, and zinc), detergents, and industrial wastes can injure and kill organisms living in aquatic environments. In contrast to wastes dumped in the terrestrial environment, which have primarily local effects, toxic wastes in aquatic environments can be carried by currents and diffused over a wide area. Toxic chemicals, even at very low levels, may be concentrated to lethal levels by aquatic organisms that filter large volumes of water while feeding. Bird and mammal species that prey on the filter feeders are exposed in turn to these concentrated levels of toxic chemicals.

Even essential minerals that are beneficial to plant and animal life can become harmful pollutants at high levels. At present, human activities release more nitrogen into biological communities each year than is taken up by natural biological processes (see Table 2.1). Human sewage, agricultural and lawn fertilizers, detergents, and industrial processes often release large amounts of nitrates and phosphates into aquatic systems, starting a process known as **cultural eutrophication.** Although small amounts of

2.16 Aquatic habitats such as rivers, lakes, estuaries, and the open ocean are often used as dumping grounds for sewage, rubbish, and industrial wastes, to the detriment of biological communities. (After Eales 1992.)

these nutrients can stimulate plant and animal growth, high concentrations often result in thick "blooms" of algae at the water's surface. These algal blooms may be so dense that they outcompete other plankton species and shade out bottom-dwelling plant species. As the algal mat becomes thicker, its lower layers sink to the bottom and die. The bacteria and fungi that decompose the dying algae multiply in response to this added sustenance and consequently absorb all of the oxygen in the water. Without oxygen, much of the remaining animal life dies off. The result is a greatly impoverished and simplified community, consisting only of species that can tolerate polluted water and low oxygen levels.

Eroding sediments from logged or farmed hillsides can also harm aquatic ecosystems. The sediments cover submerged plant leaves and other green surfaces with a muddy film that reduces light availability and diminishes the rate of photosynthesis. Increasing water turbidity may prevent animal species from seeing, feeding, and living in the water and reduce the depth at which light penetrates and photosynthesis can occur. Increased sediment loads are particularly harmful to many coral species, which require crystal-clear water to survive.

Air pollution

Human activity has altered and contaminated the Earth's atmosphere. In the past, people assumed that the atmosphere was so vast that materials released into the air would be widely dispersed and their effects would be minimal. But today several types of air pollution are damaging ecosystems.

- *Acid rain.* Industries such as smelting operations and coal- and oil-fired power plants release huge quantities of nitrates and sulfates into the air, which combine with moisture in the atmosphere to produce nitric acid and sulfuric acid. In the United States alone, 21 million metric tons of nitrates and 19 million metric tons of sulfates are released into the atmosphere each year (WRI/UNEP/UNDP 1994). The acids are incorporated into cloud systems and dramatically lower the pH (the standard measure of acidity) of rainwater. Acid rain in turn lowers the pH of soil moisture and water bodies such as ponds and lakes. By itself, the acidity is damaging to many plant and animal species. As the acidity of water bodies is increased by acid rain, many fish either fail to spawn or die outright (Figure 2.17). Increased acidity and water pollution are two likely factors behind the recent dramatic decline in amphibian populations throughout the world. Most amphibian species depend on bodies of water for at least part of their life cycle, and a decline in water pH causes a corresponding increase in the mortality of eggs and larvae (Beebee et al. 1990; Blaustein and Wake 1995). Acidity also inhibits the microbial process of decomposition, lowering the rate of mineral recycling and ecosystem productivity. Many ponds and lakes in industrialized areas of the world have lost large portions of their animal communities as a result of acid rain (France and Collins 1993). Many of these damaged water bodies are in supposedly pristine ar-

2.17 The pH scale, indicating ranges at which acidity becomes lethal to fish. Studies indicate that fish are indeed disappearing from heavily acidified lakes. (After Cox 1993, based on data from the U.S. Fish and Wildlife Service.)

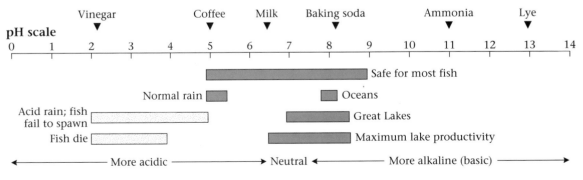

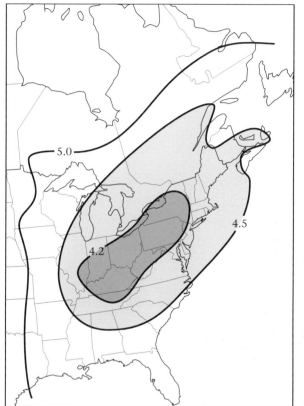

2.18 In North America, acid rain has its strongest effects in the eastern United States and Canada because prevailing winds carry air pollution east from the industrial heartland. Lower pH values indicate greater acidity; normal rainfall has a pH of 5.0 or greater.

eas hundreds of kilometers from major sources of urban and industrial pollution (Figure 2.18); already acidification is evident in 39% of lakes in Sweden and 34% of lakes in Norway (Moiseenko 1994).

- *Ozone production and nitrogen deposition.* Automobiles, power plants, and other industrial activities release hydrocarbons and nitrogen oxides as waste products. In the presence of sunlight, these chemicals react with the atmosphere to produce ozone and other secondary chemicals, collectively called **photochemical smog.** Although ozone in the upper atmosphere is important in filtering out harmful ultraviolet radiation, high concentrations of ozone at ground level damage plant tissues and make them brittle, harming biological communities and reducing agricultural productivity. Biological communities throughout the world can also be damaged and altered when these airborne nitrogen compounds are deposited by rain and dust, leading to potentially toxic levels of this nutrient.

- *Toxic metals.* Leaded gasoline, mining and smelting operations, and other industrial activities release large quantities of lead, zinc, and other toxic metals into the atmosphere. These compounds are di-

2.19 Forests throughout the world are experiencing diebacks, thought to be caused in part by the effects of acid rain combined with nitrogen deposition, ozone damage, insect attack, and disease. These dead trees were photographed on Mt. Mitchell, North Carolina, in 1988. (Photograph by Jim MacKenzie, WRI.)

rectly poisonous to plant and animal life. The effects of these toxic metals are particularly evident in areas surrounding large smelting operations, where life can be destroyed for miles around.

The effects of air pollution on forest communities have been intensively studied because forests have such great economic value in terms of wood production, watershed management, and recreation. It is widely accepted that acid rain damages and weakens many tree species and makes them more susceptible to attacks by insects, fungi, and disease (Figure 2.19). Widespread deaths of forest trees over large areas of Europe and eastern North America have been linked to acid rain and other components of air pollution such as nitrogen deposition and ozone (Hinrichsen 1987; MacKenzie and El-Ashry 1988). When the trees die, other species in the forest also become extinct on a local scale. Even when communities are not destroyed by air pollution, species composition may be altered as more susceptible species are eliminated. Lichens—symbiotic organisms composed of fungi and algae that can survive in some of the harshest natural environments—are particularly susceptible to air pollution.

Levels of air pollution continue to rise throughout the world. Increases in air pollution will be particularly severe in the many Asian countries with dense (and growing) human populations and increasing industrialization. The heavy reliance of China on high-sulfur coal and the rapid increase in automobile ownership in Southeast Asia are examples of potential threats to biological diversity in those regions. Hope for controlling air pollution in the future depends on motor vehicles with dramatically lower emissions of pollutants, increased development of mass transit systems, more efficient scrubbing processes for industrial smokestacks, and the reduction of overall energy use through conservation and efficiency measures.

Global climate change

Carbon dioxide, methane, and other trace gases in the atmosphere are transparent to sunshine, allowing light energy to pass through the atmosphere and warm the surface of the Earth. However, these gases and water vapor (in the form of clouds) trap the energy radiating from the Earth's surface as heat, slowing the rate at which heat leaves the Earth and radiates back into space. These gases have been called **greenhouse gases** because they function much like greenhouse glass, which is transparent to sunlight but traps energy inside the greenhouse once it is transformed into heat (Figure 2.20). The denser the concentration of gases, the more heat is trapped near the Earth, and the higher the planet's surface temperature.

The greenhouse effect has been important in allowing life to flourish on Earth—without it, the temperature at the Earth's surface would fall dramatically. The problem that exists today, however, is that concentrations of greenhouse gases are increasing so much as a result of human activity that they could affect the Earth's climate, creating an episode of global warming. During the past 100 years, global atmospheric levels of carbon dioxide (CO_2), methane, and other trace gases have been steadily increasing, primarily as a result of the burning of fossil fuels such as coal, oil, and natural gas (Graedel and Crutzen 1989). The cutting down and burning of forests to create farmland and the burning of fuelwood for heating and cooking also contribute to rising concentrations of CO_2. The CO_2 concentration in the atmosphere has increased from 290 parts per million (ppm) to 350 ppm over the last 100 years, and it is projected to reach 400–550 ppm by the year 2030. Even if immediate, massive efforts are made to reduce CO_2 production, there will be little immediate reduction in present atmospheric CO_2 levels because each CO_2 molecule resides in the atmosphere for an average of 100 years before being removed by plants and natural geochemical processes. Because of this time lag, levels of CO_2 in the atmosphere will continue to rise.

Many scientists believe that increased levels of greenhouse gases have affected the world's climate already, and that these effects will increase

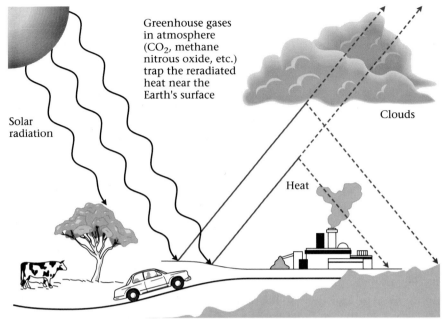

Greenhouse gases
in atmosphere
(CO_2, methane
nitrous oxide, etc.)
trap the reradiated
heat near the
Earth's surface

Clouds

Solar
radiation

Heat

2.20 In the greenhouse effect, gases and water vapor form a blanket around the Earth that acts like the glass roof of a greenhouse, trapping heat near the Earth's surface. (From Gates 1993.)

Light waves are transformed into
infrared radiation (heat) and reradiated

in the future (Gates 1993). The best evidence seems to show that world climate has warmed by 0.5°C during the twentieth century (Jones and Wigley 1990). There is a growing consensus among meteorologists that the world climate will probably warm by an additional 2°–6°C over the twenty-first century as a result of increased atmospheric levels of carbon dioxide and other gases. It seems likely that many species will be unable to adjust quickly enough to survive this human-engendered global warming, which will occur far more rapidly than previous natural climate shifts. While the details of global climate change are still being debated by scientists, there is no doubt that the effects of such a rapid rise in temperature on biological communities will be profound. For example, climatic regions in the northern and southern temperate zones will be shifted toward the poles. Species adapted to the eastern deciduous forests of North America will have to migrate 500–1000 km northward over the twenty-first century to keep up with this climate shift (Davis and Zabinski 1992). Although widely distributed, easily dispersed species will be able to adjust to these changes, many species with limited distributions or poor dispersal ability will undoubtedly become extinct. These extinctions will be accelerated by habitat fragmentation, which may create barriers to dispersal.

Warming temperatures will also cause melting of mountain glaciers and shrinkage of the Greenland ice sheet. As a result of this release of water over the next 50–100 years, sea levels could rise by 0.2–1.5 meters. This rise in sea level will flood low-lying coastal wetland communities and many major urban areas. Particularly where human settlements, roads, and flood control barriers have been built adjacent to wetlands, the migration of wetland species will be blocked. It is possible that rising sea levels could destroy 25%–80% of the coastal wetlands of the United States (Smith and Tirpak 1988). In low-lying countries such as Bangladesh, much of the land area could be under water within 100 years.

Rising sea levels will be potentially detrimental to many coral species, which grow at a precise depth in the water that has the right combination of light and current. Certain coral reefs may be unable to grow quickly enough to keep pace with the rise in sea level and will gradually be "drowned" (Grigg and Epp 1989). Damage could be compounded if ocean temperatures also rise (Brown and Ogden 1993). Abnormally high water temperatures in the Pacific Ocean in 1982 and 1983 led to the death of the symbiotic algae that live inside corals; the "bleached" corals then suffered a massive dieback, with an estimated loss of coral over 70%–95% of the area.

Global climate change and increasing concentrations of atmospheric CO_2 have the potential to radically restructure biological communities, favoring those species that are able to adapt to the new conditions (Bazzaz and Fajer 1992). There is some evidence that this process of change has already begun (Grabherr et al. 1994; Phillips and Gentry 1994). Because the implications of global climate change are so far-reaching, biological communities, ecosystem functions, and climate need to be carefully monitored in the future. Concern over global climate change, however, should not divert attention from the massive habitat destruction that is still the principal cause of species extinction: saving intact communities from destruction and restoring degraded communities are still the most important and immediate priorities for conservation.

Overexploitation

People have always hunted and harvested the food and other resources they needed to survive. As long as human populations were small and their methods of collection unsophisticated, people could sustainably harvest and hunt the plants and animals of their environment without driving species to extinction. However, as human populations have increased, their use of the environment has escalated. Methods of harvesting have also become dramatically more efficient (Redford 1992; Wilkie et al. 1992). Guns are used instead of blowpipes, spears, or arrows for hunting in the tropical rain forests and savannahs. Powerful motorized fishing boats and efficient "factory ships" harvest fish from all the world's oceans. Small-scale local fishermen have outboard motors on their canoes and boats, allowing them to harvest more rapidly and over a wider area than previously possible. Even in preindustrial societies, intense exploitation has led to the decline and extinction of local species. As an example, ceremonial cloaks worn by the Hawaiian kings were made from the feathers of the mamo bird; a single cloak used the feathers of 70,000 birds of this now-extinct species. Predator species may also decline when their prey are overharvested by people. Overexploitation by humans is estimated to threaten about a third of the currently endangered, vulnerable, and rare species of vertebrates (Groombridge 1992), which places it second only to habitat loss and degradation in importance.

In traditional societies, restrictions often existed to prevent the overexploitation of natural resources: for example, the rights to specific harvesting territories were rigidly controlled; hunting in certain areas was banned; there were prohibitions against taking females, juveniles, and undersized individuals; certain seasons of the year and times of the day were closed for harvesting; or certain efficient types of harvesting were not allowed. These kinds of restrictions, which allowed traditional societies to harvest communal resources on a long-term, sustainable basis, are very similar to the rigid fishing restrictions developed and proposed for many fisheries in industrialized nations.

In much of the world today, however, resources are exploited as rapidly as possible. If a market exists for a product, local people will search their environment to find and sell it. Whether people are poor and hungry or rich and greedy, they will use whatever methods are available to secure the product. Sometimes traditional societies even decide to sell their rights to a resource, such as a forest or mining area, in order to use the money to buy desired goods. In rural areas the traditional controls that regulated the extraction of natural products have generally weakened, and in many areas into which there has been substantial human migration, or where civil unrest and war have occurred, such controls may no longer exist at all. In countries beset with civil conflict, such as Somalia, the former Yugoslavia, and Rwanda, there has been a proliferation of firearms among rural people and a breakdown of food distribution networks. In such situations the resources of the natural environment will be taken by whoever can exploit them.

Overexploitation of resources often occurs rapidly when a commercial market develops for a previously unexploited or locally used species. One of the most pervasive examples is the international trade in furs, which has reduced species such as the chinchilla (*Chinchilla* spp.), vicuña (*Vicugna vicugna*), giant otter (*Pteronura brasiliensis*), and numerous cat species to very low numbers. The legal and illegal trade in wildlife is responsible for the decline of many species (Figure 2.21; Poten 1991; Hemley 1994). Overharvesting of butterflies by insect collectors, of orchids, cacti, and other plants by horticulturists, of marine mollusks by shell collectors, and of tropical fishes for aquarium hobbyists are further examples in which whole biological communities have been targeted to supply an enormous international demand.

2.21 Industrialized countries can develop large markets for products gathered from the wild, often leading to the overexploitation of resources. Here a buyer of raccoon skins lies on top of his stock. Although the raccoon is not currently threatened, such overharvesting by trappers imperils many other fur-bearing species. (Photograph courtesy of In Defense of Animals.)

The pattern in many cases of overexploitation is distressingly familiar. A resource is identified, a commercial market is developed for that resource, and the local human populace mobilizes to extract and sell the resource. The resource is extracted so thoroughly that it becomes rare or even extinct, and the market identifies another species or another region to exploit in place of the first. Commercial fishing fits this pattern well, with the industry working one species after another to the point of diminishing return. Commercial forestry companies often behave similarly, with loggers extracting less desirable tree species or trees of smaller size in successive cutting cycles until there is little timber left in the forest.

An extensive body of literature has developed in the fields of wildlife management, fisheries, and forestry to describe the **maximum sustainable yield** that can be obtained each year from a resource (Getz and Haight 1989). The maximum sustainable yield is the greatest amount of the resource that can be harvested each year and replaced by natural population growth. Calculations using the population growth rate and the carrying capacity (the largest population that the environment can support) are used to estimate the maximum sustainable yield. In highly controlled situations in which a resource can be easily quantified, it may be possible to achieve sustainable use. However, in many real-world situations, harvesting a species at the theoretical maximum sustainable yield is not possible, and attempts to do so often lead to an abrupt species decline (Ludwig et al. 1993). For example, fishing industry representatives use such calculations to support their position that harvesting levels of Atlantic bluefin tuna can be maintained at the present rate, even though the population of this species has declined by 90% in recent years (Safina 1993). In order to satisfy local business interests and protect jobs, governments often set harvesting levels too high, which results in damage to the resource base. Illegal harvesting may result in additional resource removal not accounted for in official records, and a considerable proportion of the stock not harvested may be damaged during harvesting operations. An additional difficulty presents itself if harvest levels are kept fairly constant even though the resource base fluctuates; a normal harvest of a fish species during a year when fish stocks are low due to unusual weather conditions may severely reduce or destroy the species. Species that migrate across national boundaries and through international waters are particularly difficult to harvest sustainably due to the problems of coordinating international agreements and monitoring compliance. In order to protect species from total destruction, governments are increasingly closing fishing grounds to allow populations to recover. Such a policy, while admirable and necessary, clearly demonstrates that models of maximum sustainable yield are often inappropriate and invalid for the real world.

The hope for many overexploited species is that as they become rare, it will no longer be commercially viable to harvest them and their numbers will have a chance to recover. Unfortunately, populations of many species, such as the rhinoceros and certain wild cats, may already have been reduced so severely that they will be unable to recover. In some cases, rarity can even increase demand: as the rhinoceros becomes more rare, the price of its horn rises, making it even more valuable as a commodity on the black market. In rural areas of the developing world, desperate people may search even more intensively for the few remaining individuals of rare plant and animal species to collect and sell so that they can buy food for their families.

One of the most heated debates over the harvesting of wild species has involved the hunting of whales, species to which the general public of certain Western countries has a very strong emotional attachment. After the recognition that many whale species had been hunted to dangerously low levels, the International Whaling Commission finally banned all commercial whaling in 1986. Despite that ban, certain species, such as the blue whale and the right whale, remain at densities far below their original numbers (Best 1988), although other species, such as the humpback and gray whale, appear to be recovering (Table 2.8). The reason for the slow recovery of some species may be that hunting is not the only unnatural cause of whale mortality. Right whales frequently are killed when they collide with ships, a problem that may be occurring in other, less familiar species as well (Kraus 1990). Furthermore, each year thousands of dolphins and an unknown number of whales suffocate when they become entangled in drift nets, gill nets, and other deep-sea fishing equipment intended for tuna, cod, and other commercial fish. Efforts to limit or ban drift-net

Table 2.8
Worldwide populations of whale species harvested by humans

Species	Numbers prior to whaling[a]	Present numbers	Main diet items
BALEEN WHALES			
Blue	228,000	14,000	Plankton
Bowhead	30,000	7,800	Plankton
Fin	548,000	120,000	Plankton, fish
Gray	20,000	21,000	Crustaceans
Humpback	115,000	10,000	Plankton, fish
Minke	140,000	725,000	Plankton, fish
Northern right	Unknown	1,000	Plankton
Sei	256,000	54,000	Plankton, fish, squid
Southern right	100,000	3,000	Plankton
TOOTHED WHALES			
Beluga	Unknown	50,000	Fish, crustaceans
Narwhal	Unknown	35,000	Fish, squid, crustaceans
Sperm	2,400,000	1,950,000	Fish, squid

Source: After Myers 1993.
[a] Pre-exploitation population numbers are highly speculative.

fishing have been only partly effective and have caused acrimony in trade relations between countries. These problems are exacerbated by a growing trend toward the hunting of smaller, more common whale species despite the ban; countries with a long tradition of whaling, such as Norway and Japan, continue to take limited harvests of common whale species, and local fisheries in developing countries often hunt small cetaceans when there is nothing else to catch.

Introductions of Exotic Species

The geographical ranges of many species are restricted by major environmental and climatic barriers to dispersal. Mammals of North America are unable to cross the Pacific to reach Hawaii, marine fishes in the Caribbean are unable to cross Central America to reach the Pacific, and freshwater fishes in one African lake have no way of crossing the land to reach nearby, isolated lakes. Oceans, deserts, mountains, and rivers all restrict the movement of species. As a result of geographical isolation, patterns of evolution have proceeded in different ways in each major area of the world; for example, the biota of the Australia–New Guinea region is strikingly different from that of the adjacent region of Southeast Asia. Islands, the most isolated of habitats, tended to evolve unique endemic biotas.

Humans have radically altered this pattern by transporting species throughout the world. In preindustrial times, people carried cultivated plants and domestic animals from place to place as they set up new farming areas and colonies. Animals such as goats and pigs were set free on uninhabited islands by European seafarers to provide food on return visits. In modern times a vast array of species have been introduced, deliberately and accidentally, into areas where they are not native (Grove and Burdon 1986; Drake et al. 1989; Hedgpeth 1993). Many species introductions have occurred by the following means.

- *European colonization.* European settlers arriving at new colonies released hundreds of European bird and mammal species in places like New Zealand, Australia, and South Africa to make the countryside seem familiar and to provide game for hunting.

- *Horticulture and agriculture.* Large numbers of plant species have been introduced and grown in new regions as ornamentals, agricultural crops, or pasture grasses. Many of these species have escaped from cultivation and have become established in the local community.

- *Accidental transport.* Species are often transported by people unintentionally; common examples include weed seeds that are accidentally harvested with commercial seeds and sown in new localities, rats and insects that stow away aboard ships and airplanes, and disease and parasitic organisms transported along with their host species. Ships frequently carry exotic species in their ballast. Soil ballast dumped in port areas brings in weed seeds and soil arthropods, and water ballast introduces algae, invertebrates, and small fishes. Ballast water being released by ships into Coos Bay, Oregon, was found to contain 367 marine species originating in Japanese waters (Carlton and Geller 1993).

The great majority of exotic species do not become established in the places to which they are introduced because the new environment is not suitable to their needs. However, a certain percentage of species do establish themselves in their new homes, and many of these increase in abundance at the expense of native species. These exotic species may displace native species through competition for limiting resources. Introduced animal species may prey upon native species to the point of extinction, or they may so alter the habitat that many natives are no longer able to persist.

Many areas of the world are strongly affected by exotic species. Consider that approximately 4600 exotic plant species have been recorded in the Hawaiian Islands, about three times the total number of native species there (St. John 1973). Many North American wetlands are completely dominated by exotic perennials: purple loosestrife from Europe dominates marshes in eastern North America, while Japanese honeysuckle forms dense tangles in bottomlands of the southeastern United States. More than half of the freshwater fish species in Massachusetts were introduced from elsewhere, and these exotic species constitute the majority of the fish biomass (Hartell 1992). Insects introduced deliberately, such as most honeybees and bumblebees, and accidentally, such as fire ants and African honeybees, can build up huge populations. The effects of these exotic insects on the native insect fauna can be devastating, eliminating numerous species from the area (Porter and Savignano 1990). At some localities in the southern United States, the diversity of insect species declines by 40% following the invasion of exotic fire ants.

Exotic species on islands

The effects of exotic species are generally greatest on islands and in continental areas that have experienced human disturbance. The isolation of island habitats encourages the development of a unique assemblage of endemic species, but it also leaves those species particularly vulnerable to depredations by invading species (Gagné 1988; Loope et al. 1988). Animals introduced onto islands have efficiently preyed upon endemic animal species and have grazed down native plant species to the point of extinction. Introduced plant species with tough, unpalatable foliage are better able to coexist with the introduced grazers than are the more palatable native plants, so the exotics begin to dominate the landscape as the native vegetation dwindles. Island animal species adapted to a community with few predators may have few defenses against introduced predators. Moreover, island species often have no natural immunities to mainland diseases; when exotic species are introduced to the island, they frequently carry pathogens or parasites that, though relatively harmless to the carrier, can devastate the native populations.

Two examples illustrate the effects of introduced species on the biota of islands:

- *Plants of Santa Catalina Island.* Forty-eight native plant species have been eliminated from Santa Catalina Island off the coast of California, primarily due to grazing by introduced goats and other exotic mammals (Thorne 1967).

- *Birds of the Pacific Islands.* The brown tree snake (*Boiga irregularis;* Figure 2.22) has been introduced onto a number of islands in the Pacific Ocean. The snake eats eggs, nestlings, and adult birds; on Guam alone, it has reduced 10 endemic bird species to the point of extinction (Savidge 1987).

Exotic species in aquatic habitats

Exotic species can have severe effects on lakes, streams, and even entire marine ecosystems (Mills et al. 1994). Freshwater communities in particular are similar to oceanic islands in that they are isolated habitats surrounded by vast stretches of uninhabitable terrain, and are likewise vulnerable to the introduction of exotic species. Commercial and sport fish species are

2.22 The brown tree snake (*Boiga irregularis*) has been introduced onto many Pacific islands, where it has devastated populations of endemic birds. This adult snake has just swallowed a bird. (Photograph by Julie Savidge.)

often introduced into aquatic environments where they do not naturally occur. Over 120 fish species have been introduced into marine and estuarine systems and inland seas; although some of these introductions have been deliberate attempts to increase fisheries, most of them were the unintentional result of canal building and the transport of ballast water in ships (Baltz 1991). Often these exotic species are larger and more aggressive than the native fish fauna, and through a combination of competition and direct predation, they eventually drive the local fishes to extinction.

Aggressive aquatic exotics include plants and invertebrate animals as well as fishes. One of the most alarming recent invasions in North America was the arrival in 1988 of the zebra mussel (*Dreissena polymorpha*) in the Great Lakes. This small, striped native of the Caspian Sea apparently was a stowaway in the ballast tanks of a European tanker. Within two years zebra mussels had reached densities of 700,000 individuals per square meter in parts of Lake Erie, choking out native mussel species in the process (Figure 2.23; Stolzenburg 1992). Zebra mussels have been found in the Detroit, Cumberland, and Tennessee Rivers; as it spreads southward, this exotic species is causing enormous economic damage to fisheries, dams, power plants, and boats as well as devastating the aquatic communities it encounters.

The ability of exotic species to invade

Why are some exotic species so easily able to invade and dominate new habitats and displace native species? One reason is the absence of their natural predators, pests, and parasites in the new habitat. Rabbits introduced into Australia, for example, spread uncontrollably, grazing native

2.23 The zebra mussel (*Dreissena polymorpha*), a native of the Caspian Sea, was accidentally introduced into the Great Lakes and associated rivers in 1988. Since then the species has formed dense populations over a wide and ever-increasing area, outcompeting and choking out native species. In this case, thumbnail-size zebra mussels have almost totally encrusted a crayfish shell. (Photograph courtesy of Ontario Ministry of Natural Resources and GLSGN Graphics Library.)

plants to the point of extinction, because there were no effective checks on their numbers. Control efforts have focused in part on introducing into Australia diseases that help control rabbit populations elsewhere.

Human activity may create unusual environmental conditions, such as nutrient pulses, an increased incidence of fire, or enhanced light availability, to which exotic species can adapt more readily than native species. The highest concentrations of exotics are often found in habitats that have been most altered by human activity. In Southeast Asia, for example, progressive degradation of forests results in a progressively smaller proportion of native species living in the habitat (Figure 2.24). Explosive increases in some exotic plant species, such as the European biennial garlic mustard (*Alliaria officinalis*) in the eastern United States, may be due to increased atmospheric nitrogen deposition and other altered soil conditions.

Exotic species are considered to be the most serious threat facing the biota of the United States National Park system. While the effects of habitat degradation, fragmentation, and pollution can potentially be corrected and reversed in a matter of years or decades as long as the original species are present, exotic species that are well established may be impossible to remove from communities (Coblentz 1990). Exotic species may have built up such large numbers and become so widely dispersed and so thoroughly integrated into the community that eliminating them may be extraordinarily difficult and expensive.

An additional class of exotics are species that have increased their ranges within continental areas because they are suited to the ways in which humans have altered the environment (Soulé 1990). Within North America, fragmentation of forests, suburban development, and easy access to garbage have allowed the numbers and ranges of coyotes, red foxes, and herring gulls to increase. As these aggressive species increase, they do so at the expense of native species that are less competitive and less able to resist predation. Native species that build up to unusually high numbers be-

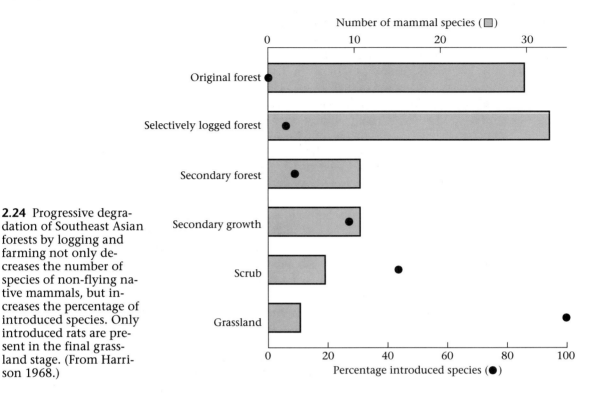

2.24 Progressive degradation of Southeast Asian forests by logging and farming not only decreases the number of species of non-flying native mammals, but increases the percentage of introduced species. Only introduced rats are present in the final grassland stage. (From Harrison 1968.)

cause they can adapt well to human activities represent a further challenge to the management of vulnerable species and protected areas.

Another special class of exotics is those that have close relatives in the native biota. When exotics hybridize with native species and varieties, unique genotypes may be eliminated from local populations, and taxonomic boundaries may become obscured. Such appears to be the fate of native trout species when confronted by commercial species. In the American Southwest, the Apache trout (*Oncorhynchus apache*) has had its range reduced by habitat destruction and competition fish species that have been introduced. The species has also hybridized extensively with the rainbow trout (*O. mykiss*), an introduced sport fish (Dowling and Childs 1992).

Increased Spread of Disease

Infections by disease organisms are common in both wild and captive populations (May 1988; Scott 1988; Aguirre and Starkey 1994). Infections may come from **microparasites,** such as viruses, bacteria, fungi, and protozoa, or **macroparasites,** such as helminth worms and parasitic arthropods. Such diseases may be the single greatest threat to some rare species. The last population of black-footed ferrets (*Mustela nigrepes*) known to exist in the wild was destroyed by the canine distemper virus in 1987

- *Species that are characteristically found in stable environments.* Many species are adapted to environments where disturbance is minimal, such as old stands of tropical rain forest or the interiors of temperate deciduous forests. When these forests are logged, grazed, burned, or otherwise altered by human activity, many native species are unable to tolerate the changed microclimatic conditions (more light, less moisture, greater temperature variation) and the resulting influx of exotic species. Also, species in stable environments typically delay reproduction to an advanced age and produce only a few young. Such species are often unable to rebuild their populations fast enough to avoid extinction following one or more episodes of habitat disturbance.

- *Species that form permanent or temporary aggregations.* Species that group together in specific places are highly vulnerable to local extinction. For example, bats forage widely at night but typically roost together in particular caves during the day. Hunters entering those caves during the day can rapidly harvest every individual in the population. Herds of bison, flocks of passenger pigeons, and schools of fish all represent aggregations that have been exploited and completely harvested by people. Some species of social animals may be unable to persist when their population size falls below a certain number because they can no longer forage, mate, or defend themselves.

- *Species that are hunted or harvested by people.* Overharvesting can rapidly reduce the population size of a species that is economically valuable to humans. If hunting and harvesting are not regulated, either by law or by local custom, the species can be driven to extinction.

These characteristics of extinction-prone species are not independent, but tend to group together into categories of characteristics. For example, species with large body size tend to have low population densities and large home ranges—all characteristics of extinction-prone species. By identifying characteristics of extinction-prone species, conservation biologists can anticipate the need for managing populations of vulnerable species.

Summary

1. Human activity has already driven many species to extinction. Since 1600, about 2.1% of the world's mammal species and 1.3% of its bird species have gone extinct. The rate of extinction is accelerating, and many extant species are teetering on the brink of extinction. More than 99% of modern species extinctions are attributable to human activity.

2. Many species that occupy islands are especially vulnerable to extinction because they are endemic to only one or a few islands. An island

biogeography model has been used to predict that current rates of habitat destruction will result in the loss of about 25,000 species per year over the next 10 years. Many biological communities are being gradually impoverished by local extinctions of species.

3. Slowing human population growth is part of the solution to the biological diversity crisis. In addition, large-scale industrial activities, logging, and agriculture are often unnecessarily destructive of the natural environment in their pursuit of short-term profit. Efforts to reduce the high consumption of natural resources in wealthy industrialized countries and to eliminate poverty in developing countries are also important parts of the overall strategy to protect biological diversity.

4. The major threat to biological diversity is loss of habitat, and the most important means of protecting biological diversity is preserving habitat. Habitats particularly threatened with destruction are rain forests, tropical dry forests, wetlands in all climates, temperate grasslands, mangrove forests, and coral reefs.

5. Habitat fragmentation is the process whereby a large, continuous area of habitat is both reduced in area and divided into two or more fragments. Habitat fragmentation can lead to the rapid loss of the species remaining because it creates barriers to the normal processes of dispersal, colonization, and foraging. Environmental conditions in the fragments may change, and pests may become more common.

6. Environmental pollution eliminates many species from biological communities even where the structure of the community is not obviously disturbed. The range of environmental pollution includes excessive use of pesticides; contamination of water sources with industrial wastes, sewage, and fertilizers; and air pollution resulting in acid rain, excess nitrogen deposition, photochemical smog, and ozone.

7. Global climate patterns may change within the twenty-first century because of the large amounts of carbon dioxide entering the atmosphere, produced by the burning of fossil fuels. Predicted temperature increases could be so rapid that many species will be unable to adjust their ranges and will probably become extinct.

8. Growing rural poverty, increasingly efficient methods of hunting and harvesting, and the globalization of the economy combine to encourage the overexploitation of many species to the point of extinction. Traditional societies had customs to prevent overharvesting of resources, but these customs are breaking down.

9. Humans have deliberately and accidentally moved thousands of species to new regions of the world. Some of these exotic species have negative effects on native species.

10. Levels of disease and parasites often increase when animals are confined to a nature reserve and cannot disperse over a wide area. Animals

held in captivity are particularly prone to high levels of disease. Diseases sometimes spread between related species of animals.

11. Species most vulnerable to extinction have particular characteristics, such as very narrow geographic ranges, only one or a few populations, small population size, declining population size, and economic value to humans that leads to overexploitation.

Suggested Readings

Adams, D. and M. Carwardine. 1990. *Last Chance to See*. Harmony Books, New York. A light but poignant account of the imminent threat of extinction facing many well-known species.

Bierregaard, R. O., T. E. Lovejoy, V. Kapos, A. A. Dos Santos and R. W. Hutchings. 1992. The biological dynamics of tropical rainforest fragments. *BioScience* 42: 859–866. A summary of an extensive long-term study of rain forest fragmentation in Brazil; other articles in the same issue focus on tropical community ecology and conservation.

BioScience. May 1994. A special issue of this journal that focuses on global patterns of land use change, with articles on Amazonia, Southeast Asia, and Africa.

Carson, R. 1962. *Silent Spring*. Reprinted in 1982 by Penguin, Harmondsworth, England. This book's descriptions of the harmful effects of pesticides on birds created heightened public awareness of environmental problems when it was first published.

Drake, J. A. et al. (eds.). 1989. *Biological Invasions: A Global Perspective*. John Wiley & Sons, Chichester. The effects of invasions on a wide range of ecosystems.

Gates, D. M. 1993. *Climate Change and Its Biological Consequences*. Sinauer Associates, Sunderland, MA. A clear and thorough description of both past and predicted climate changes and their effects.

Hardin, G. 1993. *Living within Limits: Ecology, Economics, and Population Taboos*. Oxford University Press, New York. Blunt advice on controlling human numbers.

Jones, R. F. 1990. Farewell to Africa. *Audubon* 92: 50–104. An excellent extended essay on the problems faced by wildlife in Africa.

Ludwig, D., R. Hilborn and C. Walters. 1993. Uncertainty, resource exploitation, and conservation: Lessons from history. *Science* 260: 17, 36. An excellent short statement about why commercial exploitation so often destroys its resource base. See the 1993 volume of *Ecological Applications* for more articles on this topic.

MacArthur, R. H. and E. O. Wilson. 1967. *The Theory of Island Biogeography*. Princeton University Press, Princeton, NJ. This classic text outlining the island biogeography model has been highly influential in shaping modern conservation biology.

Terborgh, J. 1992. Why American songbirds are vanishing. *Scientific American* 264 (May): 98–104. A variety of theories are examined in light of recent evidence.

Wilson, E. O. 1989. Threats to biodiversity. *Scientific American* 261 (September): 108–116. How extinction rates are increasing due to human activities.

CHAPTER 3

Conservation at the Population and Species Levels

CONSERVATION EFFORTS are often directed toward protecting species that are declining in numbers and in danger of becoming extinct. In order to successfully maintain species under the restricted conditions imposed by human activities, conservation biologists must determine the stability of populations under certain circumstances. Will a population of an endangered species persist or even increase in a nature reserve? Alternatively, is the species declining, and does it require special attention to prevent it from going extinct?

Many national parks and wildlife sanctuaries have been created to protect "charismatic megafauna," such as lions and tigers, that are important as national symbols and as tourist attractions. However, merely designating the communities in which these species live as protected areas may not stop their decline and extinction, even when they are legally protected. Sanctuaries generally are created only after most populations of a threatened species have already been severely reduced by habitat loss, habitat degradation, habitat fragmentation, or overharvesting. Under these circumstances, a species tends to dwindle rapidly toward extinction. Also, individuals outside the reserve boundaries remain unprotected and at risk.

The Problems of Small Populations

As a general rule, an adequate conservation plan for an endangered species requires that as many individuals as possible be preserved within the greatest possible area of protected habitat. However, this general statement does not provide specific guidelines to assist planners, land managers, politicians, and wildlife biologists who are trying to protect species from extinction. The problem is exacerbated by the fact that planners often must proceed without a firm understanding of the range and habitat requirements of the species. For example, to preserve the red-cockaded woodpecker, does longleaf pine habitat in the southeastern United States need to be preserved for 50, 500, 5000, 50,000, or even more individuals? Furthermore, planners must reconcile conflicting demands on finite resources—a problem vividly demonstrated in the "owls versus jobs" debate over the conservation of the northern spotted owl, an endangered species that occupies valuable old-growth timber stands in the Pacific Northwest.

In a groundbreaking paper, Shaffer (1981) defined the number of individuals necessary to ensure the survival of a species as its **minimum viable population (MVP):** "A minimum viable population for any given species in any given habitat is the smallest isolated population having a 99% chance of remaining extant for 1000 years despite the foreseeable effects of demographic, environmental, and genetic stochasticity, and natural catastrophes." In other words, an MVP is the smallest population that can be predicted to have a very high chance of persisting for the foreseeable future. Shaffer emphasized the tentative nature of this definition, saying that the survival probabilities could be set at 95%, 99%, or any other percentage, and that the time frame might similarly be adjusted, for example, to 100 years or 500 years. The key point of the MVP is that it allows a quantitative estimate to be made of how many individuals are needed to preserve a species (Menges 1991).

Shaffer (1981) compares MVP protection efforts to flood control efforts. In planning flood control systems and regulating building on wetlands, it is not sufficient to use average annual rainfall as a guideline. We recognize the need to plan for severe flooding, which may occur only once every 50 years. Likewise, in protecting natural systems, we understand that certain catastrophic events, such as massive hurricanes, earthquakes, forest fires, volcanic eruptions, epidemics, and die-offs of food items, may occur at even longer intervals. To plan for the long-term protection of an endangered species, we not only have to provide for the requirements of the species in average years, but also for its needs in exceptional years. In drought years, for instance, animals may migrate well beyond their normal ranges to obtain the water they need to survive.

Obtaining an accurate estimate of the MVP for a particular species may require a detailed demographic study of the population and an environmental analysis of the site, which may be expensive and require months or even years of research (Thomas 1990). Some biologists have suggested a general rule of attempting to protect 500–1000 individuals for vertebrate species, as this number seems adequate to preserve genetic variability (Lande 1988). Protecting this number of individuals may be adequate to allow a minimum number of individuals to survive in catastrophic years and return the population to former levels. For species with extremely variable population sizes, such as certain invertebrates and annual plants, it has been suggested that protecting a population of about 10,000 individuals would be an effective strategy.

Once a minimum viable population size has been established for a species, the **minimum dynamic area (MDA),** the amount of suitable habitat necessary for maintaining the MVP, can be estimated. The MDA can be estimated by studying the home range sizes of individuals and groups (Thiollay 1989). Estimates have been made that reserves of 10,000 to 100,000 ha are needed to maintain many small mammal populations (Schonewald-Cox 1983). To preserve populations of wide-ranging grizzly bears in Canada, the areas needed are enormous: 49,000 km^2 for 50 individuals, and 2,420,000 km^2 for 1000 individuals (Noss and Cooperrider 1994).

One of the best-documented examples of determining minimum viable population size comes from a study of the persistence of 120 bighorn sheep (*Ovis canadensis*) populations in the deserts of the southwestern United States (Berger 1990). Some of these populations have been followed for up to 70 years. The striking observation was made that 100% of the populations with fewer than 50 individuals went extinct within 50 years, while virtually all of the populations with more than 100 individuals persisted over this time period (Figure 3.1). Field evidence from long-term studies of birds on the Channel Islands supports the need for large populations to ensure population persistence; only populations of more than 100 pairs had a greater than 90% chance of surviving for 80 years (Jones and Diamond 1976). On the other hand, there is no need to give up entirely on small populations: many populations of birds have apparently survived for 80 years with 10 or fewer breeding pairs.

Exceptions notwithstanding, large populations are needed to protect most species, and species with small populations are in real danger of going extinct. Small populations are subject to rapid decline in numbers and local extinction for three main reasons: genetic problems resulting from loss of genetic variability, inbreeding, and genetic drift; demographic fluctuations due to random variations in birth and death rates; and environmental fluctuations due to variations in predation, competition, incidence of disease, and food supply, as well as natural catastrophes resulting from single events that occur at irregular intervals, such as fires, floods, or droughts.

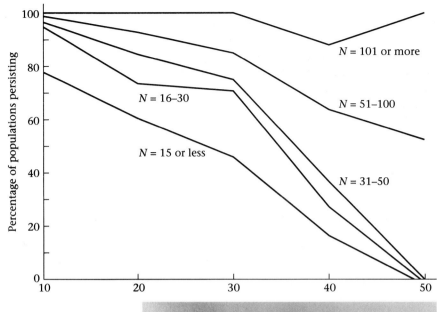

3.1 The relationship between the size of populations of bighorn sheep and the percentage of populations that persist over time. The numbers on the graph indicate population size (*N*). Populations with more than 100 sheep almost all persisted beyond 50 years, while populations with fewer than 50 sheep died out within 50 years. (After Berger 1990; photograph by Mark Primack.)

Loss of genetic variability

Genetic variability is important in allowing populations to adapt to a changing environment (see Chapter 1). Individuals with certain alleles or combinations of alleles may have just the characteristics needed to survive and reproduce under the new conditions. Within a population, particular alleles may vary in frequency from common to very rare. In small populations, allele frequencies may change from one generation to the next simply due to chance, depending on which individuals mate and leave offspring, a process known as **genetic drift**. When an allele is at a low frequency in a small population, it has a significant probability of being lost in each generation due to chance. Considering the theoretical case of an isolated population in which there are two alleles per gene, Wright (1931) proposed a formula to express the expected drop in heterozygosity (individuals possessing two different allele forms of the same gene) per generation (ΔF) for a population of breeding adults (N_e):

$$\Delta F = \frac{1}{2N_e}$$

According to this equation, a population of 50 individuals would show a decline in heterozygosity of 1% (1/100) per generation due to the loss of rare alleles; a population of 10 individuals would show a decline of 5% (1/20, or 5/100) per generation (Figure 3.2).

   This formula demonstrates that significant losses of genetic variability can occur in isolated small populations. However, migration of individuals among populations and the regular mutation of genes tend to increase the amount of genetic variability within a population and balance the effects of genetic drift. Even a low frequency of movement of individuals between populations minimizes the loss of genetic variability associated with small population size (Lacey 1987). If only one new immigrant arrives every generation in an isolated population of about 100 individuals, the effect of genetic drift will be negligible. Such **gene flow** appears to be the major factor preventing the loss of genetic variability in Galápagos finches (Grant and Grant 1992). Although the mutation rates found in nature—about 1 in 1000 to 1 in 10,000 per gene per generation—may

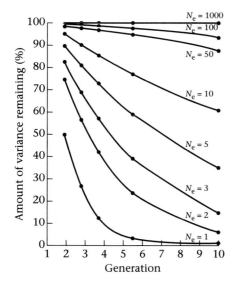

3.2 Genetic variability is lost randomly over time through genetic drift. This graph shows the average percentage of genetic variability remaining over 10 generations in theoretical populations of various population sizes (N_e). After 10 generations, there is a loss of genetic variability of approximately 40% with a population size of 10, 65% with a population size of 5, and 95% with a population size of 2.

make up for random losses of alleles in large populations, they are ineffective at countering genetic drift in small populations of about 100 individuals or fewer.

In addition to theories and simulations, field data also show that small population size leads to a more rapid loss of alleles from the population. In a New Zealand conifer species, small populations suffered much higher losses of genetic variability than large populations (Billington 1991). When 11 pairs of plant species were compared, rare species were consistently found to have lower genetic variability than common species in the same genus (Karron 1987). An extensive review of studies of genetic variability in plants showed that only 8 of 113 species had no measurable genetic variability and that most of those 8 species had very limited ranges (Hamrick and Godt 1989).

Small populations subjected to genetic drift have greater susceptibility to a number of deleterious genetic effects, such as inbreeding depression, loss of evolutionary flexibility, and outbreeding depression. These factors may contribute to a decline in population size and a greater probability of extinction (Ellstrand and Elam 1993; Thornhill 1993; Loeschcke et al. 1994).

Inbreeding depression. A variety of mechanisms prevent inbreeding in most natural populations. In large populations of most animal species, individuals do not normally mate with close relatives. Individuals often disperse away from their place of birth, or are inhibited from mating with relatives through unique individual odors or other sensory cues. In many plants, a variety of morphological and physiological mechanisms encourage cross-pollination and prevent self-pollination. In some cases, however, particularly when population size is small and no other mates are available, these mechanisms fail to prevent inbreeding. Mating among close relatives, such as parents and their offspring, siblings, and cousins, and self-fertilization in hermaphroditic species may result in **inbreeding depression**, characterized by fewer offspring or offspring that are weak or sterile (Ralls et al. 1988). For example, plants of the scarlet gilia (*Ipomopis aggregata*) that come from populations with fewer than 100 individuals produce smaller seeds with a lower rate of seed germination and exhibit a greater susceptibility to environmental stress than do plants from larger populations (Heschel and Paige 1995). Such symptoms, associated with inbreeding depression and loss of genetic variation, are lessened when plants from small populations are cross-pollinated using pollen from plants of large populations.

The most plausible explanation for inbreeding depression is that it allows the expression of harmful alleles inherited from both parents (Charlesworth and Charlesworth 1987; Barrett and Kohn 1991;). Inbreeding depression can be a severe problem in small captive populations in zoos and domestic breeding programs, and also appears to be significant in some wild populations (Jiménez et al. 1994; Keller et al. 1994).

Outbreeding depression. Individuals of different species rarely mate in the wild, due to a number of behavioral, physiological, and morphological mechanisms that ensure that mating happens only within a species. However, when a species is rare or its habitat is damaged, outbreeding—mating between different species—may occur. Individuals unable to find mates within their own species may mate with a related species. The resulting offspring are often weak or sterile due to the lack of compatibility of the chromosomes and enzyme systems inherited from their different parents, a condition known as **outbreeding depression** (Templeton 1986; Thornhill 1993). These hybrid offspring may also no longer have the precise combination of genes that allowed individuals to survive in a particular set of local conditions. Outbreeding depression can also result from matings between different subspecies, or even matings between divergent genotypes or populations of the same species. Captive breeding programs must guard against outbreeding depression by avoiding the pairing of individuals from the extremes of the species' geographical range.

Outbreeding depression may be particularly important in plants, in which mate selection is to some degree a matter of the chance movement of pollen (Waser and Price 1989). A rare plant species growing near a closely related common species may become overwhelmed by the pollen of the common species, leading to sterile offspring or a blurring of species boundaries (Ellstrand 1992).

Loss of evolutionary flexibility. Rare alleles and unusual combinations of alleles that confer no immediate advantages may be uniquely suited for some future set of environmental conditions. Loss of genetic variability in a small population may limit the ability of the population to respond to long-term changes in the environment, such as pollution, new diseases, or global climate change (Allendorf and Leary 1986). Without sufficient genetic variability, a species may become extinct.

Effective population size. How many individuals are needed to maintain genetic variability in a population? Franklin (1980) suggested that 50 individuals might be the minimum number necessary to maintain genetic variability. This figure was based on the practical experience of animal breeders, which indicates that animal stocks can be maintained with a loss of 2%–3% of the variability per generation. Wright's formula shows that a population of 50 individuals will lose only 1% of its variability per generation, so using this figure would be erring on the safe side. However, because this figure is based on work with domestic animals, its applicability to the wide range of wild species is uncertain. Using data on mutation rates in *Drosophila* fruit flies, Franklin (1980) suggested that in populations of 500 individuals, the rate of new genetic variability arising through mutation might balance the variability being lost due to small population size. This range of values has been referred to as the 50/500 rule: isolated populations need to have at least 50 individuals and preferably 500 individuals to maintain genetic variability.

The 50/500 rule is difficult to apply in practice because it assumes that a population is composed of N individuals that all have an equal probability of mating and having offspring. However, many individuals in a population do not produce offspring due to factors such as age, poor health, sterility, malnutrition, small body size, or social structures that prevent some animals from finding mates. As a result of these factors, the **effective population size** (N_e) of breeding individuals is often substantially smaller than the actual population size. Because the rate of loss of genetic variability is based on the effective population size, loss of genetic variability can be quite severe even when the actual population size is much larger (Kimura and Crow 1963; Lande and Barrowclough 1987; Nunney and Elam 1994). An effective population size that is smaller than expected can exist under any of the following circumstances.

Unequal sex ratio. By random chance, the population may consist of unequal numbers of males and females. If, for example, a population of a monogamous goose species (in which one male and one female form a long-lasting pair bond) consists of 20 males and 6 females, only 12 individuals will be involved in mating activity. In this case, the effective population size is 12, not 26. In other animal species, social systems may prevent many individuals from mating even though they are physiologically capable of doing so: in elephant seals, for example, a dominant male may control a large group of females and prevent other males from mating with them.

The effect of unequal numbers of breeding males and females on N_e can be described by the general formula:

$$N_e = \frac{4N_m N_f}{N_m + N_f}$$

where N_m and N_f are the numbers of breeding males and breeding females, respectively, in the population. In general, as the sex ratio of breeding individuals becomes increasingly unequal, the ratio of the effective population size to the number of breeding individuals (N_e/N) also goes down.

Variation in reproductive output. In many species the number of offspring varies substantially among individuals. This is particularly true in plants, in which some individuals may produce a few seeds while others produce thousands of seeds. Unequal production of offspring leads to a substantial reduction in N_e because a few individuals in the present generation will be disproportionately represented in the gene pool of the next generation (Crow and Morton 1955).

Population fluctuations and bottlenecks. In some species, population size varies dramatically from generation to generation. Particularly good examples of populations with such variation are checkerspot butterflies in California (Murphy et al. 1990), annual plants, and amphibians (Pechmann et al. 1991). In populations that show such extreme fluctuations, the effective population size is somewhere between the lowest and the highest number of individuals. However, the effective population size tends to be determined by the years with the smallest numbers; a single year of drastically reduced population numbers will substantially lower the value of N_e.

This principle is involved in a phenomenon known as a **population bottleneck.** When a population is greatly reduced in size, rare alleles in the population will be lost if no individuals possessing those alleles survive and reproduce (Carson 1983). With fewer alleles present and a decline in heterozygosity, the average fitness of the individuals in the population may decline. A special category of bottleneck, known as the **founder effect,** occurs when a few individuals leave a large population to establish a new population. The new population often has less genetic variability than the larger original population.

The lions of Ngorongoro Crater in Tanzania provide a well-studied example of a genetic bottleneck (Packer et al. 1991; Packer 1992). The lion population consisted of 60–75 individuals until an outbreak of biting flies in 1962 reduced the population to 9 females and 1 male. Two years later, 7 additional males immigrated into the crater; there has been no further immigration since that time. The small number of founders, the isolation of the population, and variation in reproductive success among individuals apparently created a genetic bottleneck even though the population has subsequently increased to 75–125 animals. In comparison with the large Serengeti lion population nearby, the Crater lions show reduced genetic variability, high levels of sperm abnormalities (Figure 3.3), and reduced reproductive rates.

Nevertheless, population bottlenecks need not always lead to reduced heterozygosity. If a population expands rapidly in size after a temporary bottleneck, the former level of heterozygosity may be restored even though the number of alleles present is severely reduced (Nei et al. 1975; Allendorf and Leary 1986). An example of this phenomenon is the high level of heterozygosity found in the greater one-horned rhinoceros in Nepal (Figure 3.4). In the mid 1960s, this population consisted of fewer than 30 breeding individuals, but by 1988 it had recovered to almost 400 individuals (Dinerstein and McCracken 1990).

These examples demonstrate that effective population size is often substantially less than the total number of individuals in a population. Particularly where there is a combination of factors, such as fluctuating population size, numerous nonreproductive individuals, and an unequal sex ratio, the effective population size may be far lower than the number of individuals alive in a good year. For example, using special genetic techniques, the effective population size of a population of Chinook salmon was measured as 85, despite an apparent breeding population of 2000 adults. This disparity was attributed to the unequal breeding success of the adults (Bartley et al. 1992).

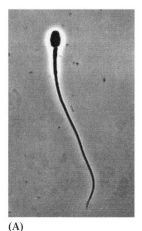

(A)

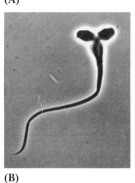

(B)

(C)

3.3 Males of the isolated and inbred population of lions at Ngorongoro Crater in Tanzania exhibit a high level of sperm abnormalities. (A) Normal lion sperm. (B) Bicephalic ("two-headed") sperm. (C) Nonfunctional sperm with a coiled flagellum. (Photographs by D. Wildt.)

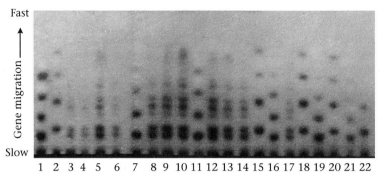

3.4 Starch gel electrophoresis reveals that the population of greater one-horned rhinoceros (*Rhinoceros unicornis*) at Chitwan National Park in Nepal shows high levels of genetic variation. This technique is based on the fact that the proteins (in this case, an enzyme called LDH) produced by different alleles of a gene migrate at different rates across an electrically charged starch gel plate, appearing as bands at different distances from the starting point at the bottom of the gel. Each column represents one individual animal. Note that animals 10 and 11, for example, have bands at different positions, indicating that these two individuals are genetically different from each other for the enzyme LDH. (From Dinerstein and McCracken 1990.)

Demographic variation

In an idealized stable environment, a population will increase until it reaches the carrying capacity of the environment. At that point the average birth rate per individual equals the average death rate, and there is no net change in population size. In a real population, however, individuals do not usually produce the average number of offspring, but rather, may have no offspring, fewer than the average, or more than the average. As long as population size is large, the average provides an accurate description of what is occurring in the population. Similarly, the average death rate in a population can be determined by studying large numbers of individuals.

Once population size drops below about 50 individuals, individual variation in birth and death rates begins to cause the population size to fluctuate randomly up or down (Gilpin and Soulé 1986; Menges 1992). If population size fluctuates downward in any one year due to a higher than average number of deaths and a lower than average number of births, the resulting smaller population will be even more susceptible to demographic fluctuations in subsequent years. Random fluctuations upward in population size are eventually bounded by the carrying capacity of the environment, and the population may again fluctuate downward. Consequently, once a population becomes small due to habitat destruction and fragmentation, this demographic variation, also known as **demographic stochasticity**, becomes an important factor, and the population has a higher probability of going extinct due to chance alone (Mac-Arthur and Wilson 1967; Richter-Dyn and Goel 1972). The chance of extinction is also greater in species that have low birth rates, such as elephants, because these species take longer to recover from a chance reduction in population size.

When populations drop below a critical number, there is also the possibility of a decline in birth rate due to deviation from an equal sex ratio. For example, the last five surviving individuals of the extinct dusky sparrow were all males, so there was no opportunity to establish a captive breeding program. Likewise, the last three individuals left in Illinois of the rare lakeside daisy (*Hymenoxys acaulis* var. *glabra)* are unable to produce viable seeds when cross-pollinating among themselves because they belong to the same self-infertile mating type (De Mauro 1993).

In many animal species, small populations may be unstable due to the collapse of the social structure once the population falls below a certain number. Herds of grazing mammals and flocks of birds may be unable to find food and defend themselves against attack when their numbers fall below a certain level. Animals that hunt in packs, such as wild dogs and lions, may need a certain number of individuals to hunt effectively. Many animal species that live in widely dispersed populations, as do bears or whales, may be unable to find mates once the population density drops below a certain point. This phenomenon is known as the **Allee effect.** In plant species, as population size decreases, the distance between plants increases; pollinating animals may not visit more than one of the isolated, scattered plants, resulting in a loss of seed production (Bawa 1990). This combination of random fluctuations in demographic characteristics, unequal sex ratios, decreased population density, and disruption of social behavior contributes to instabilities in population size, often leading to local extinction.

Environmental variation and catastrophes

Random variation in the biological and physical environment, known as **environmental stochasticity**, can also cause variation in the population size of a species. For example, the population of an endangered rabbit species might be affected by fluctuations in the population of a deer species that eats the same types of plants as the rabbits, in the population of a fox species that preys on the rabbits, and in the presence of parasites and diseases affecting the rabbits. Fluctuations in the physical environment might also strongly influence the rabbit population; rainfall during an average year might encourage plant growth and allow the population to increase, while dry years might limit plant growth and cause rabbits to starve.

Natural catastrophes at unpredictable intervals, such as droughts, storms, floods, earthquakes, volcanic eruptions, fires, and cyclical die-offs in the surrounding biological community, can also cause dramatic fluctuations in population levels. Natural catastrophes can kill part of a population or even eliminate the entire population from an area. Numerous examples exist of die-offs in populations of large mammals, including many cases in which 70%–90% of the population dies (Young 1994). Even though the probability of a natural catastrophe in any one year is low, over the course of decades and centuries, natural catastrophes have a high likelihood of occurring.

Modeling efforts by Menges (1992) and others have shown that random environmental variation is generally more important than random demographic variation in increasing the probability of extinction in populations of small to moderate size. In these models, environmental variation substantially increases the risk of extinction even in populations showing positive population growth under the assumption of a stable environment (Mangel and Tier 1994). In general, introducing environmental variation into population models, in effect making them more realistic, results in populations with lower growth rates, lower population sizes, and higher probabilities of extinction. Menges (1992) introduced environmental variation into models of plant populations that had been developed by field ecologists working with palms. When only demographic variation was considered, these plant models suggested that the minimum viable population size, in this case the number of individuals needed to give the population a 95% probability of persisting for 100 years, was about 140 mature individuals. When moderate environmental variation was included, however, the minimum viable population size increased to 380 individuals.

Extinction vortices

The smaller a population becomes, the more vulnerable it is to further demographic variation, environmental variation, and genetic factors, which tend to reduce its size even more. This tendency of small populations to decline toward extinction has been likened to an **extinction vortex** (Gilpin and Soulé 1986). For example, a natural catastrophe, a new disease, or human disturbance could reduce a large population to a small size. This small population could then suffer from inbreeding depression, resulting in a lowered juvenile survival rate. This increased death rate could result in an even lower population size and even more inbreeding. Similarly, random demographic variation often reduces population size, resulting in even greater demographic fluctuations and a greater probability of extinction. These three factors—environmental variation, demographic variation, and loss of genetic variability—act together so that a decline in population size caused by one factor will increase the vulnerability of the population to the other factors (Figure 3.5). Once a population has declined, it will often become extinct unless highly favorable conditions allow it to increase to a larger size. Such populations require a careful program of population and habitat management to reduce demographic and

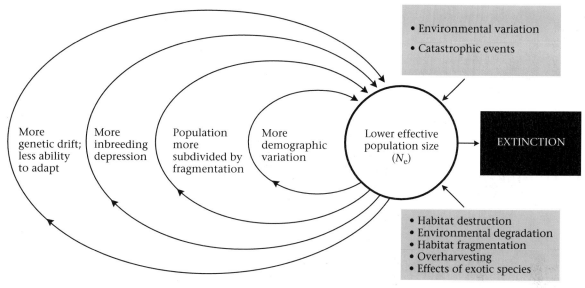

3.5 Extinction vortices progressively lower population size, leading to local extinctions of species. Once a population drops below a certain size, it enters a vortex, in which the factors that affect small populations tend to drive its size progressively lower. (After Gilpin and Soulé 1986, and Guerrant 1992.)

environmental variation and thus minimize the effects of small population size (Schonewald-Cox et al. 1983).

Natural History and Autecology

The key to protecting and managing a rare or endangered species is an understanding of its biological relationship to its environment and the status of its populations. This information is generally called the **natural history,** or sometimes simply the **ecology,** of the species, while as a scientific discipline, learning about individual species is known as **autecology.** With information concerning a rare species' natural history, managers are able to make more effective efforts to maintain the species and identify the factors that place it at risk of extinction (Gilpin and Soulé 1986).

The following are categories of autecological questions that need to be answered in order to design and implement effective population-level conservation efforts. For most species, only a few of these questions can be answered without further investigation. Decisions on management, however, often have to be made before this information is available or while it is being gathered. The exact types of information gathered will obviously depend on the characteristics of the species.

- *Environment.* What are the habitat types in which the species is found, and how much area is there of each? How variable is the environment in time and space? How frequently is the environment affected by catastrophic disturbance?

- *Distribution*. Where is the species found in its habitat? Does the species move and migrate among habitats, or to different geographical areas, over the course of a day or over a year? How efficient is the species at colonizing new habitats?

- *Biotic interactions*. What types of food and other resources does the species need? What other species compete with it for those resources? What predators, pests, and parasites affect its population size?

- *Morphology*. How do the shape, size, color, and surface texture of individuals allow the species to exist in its environment?

- *Physiology*. What quantities of food, water, minerals, and other necessities does an individual need to survive, grow, and reproduce? How efficient is an individual at using its resources? How vulnerable is the species to extremes of climate, such as heat, cold, wind, and rain?

- *Demography*. What is the current population size, and what was it in the past? Are the numbers of individuals stable, increasing, or decreasing?

- *Behavior*. How do the actions of an individual allow it to survive in its environment? How do individuals in a population mate and produce offspring? In what ways do individuals of the species interact among themselves, either cooperatively or competitively?

- *Genetics*. How much of the variation among individuals in morphological and physiological characteristics is genetically controlled?

Gathering natural history information

The basic information needed for an effort to conserve a species or determine its status can be obtained from three major sources.

- *Published literature*. Library indexes such as *Biological Abstracts* or *Zoological Record,* often accessible by computer, provide easy access to a variety of books, articles, and reports. The Internet provides ever-increasing access to databases, electronic bulletin boards, and specialized discussion groups. Sometimes sections of the library will have related material shelved together, so that finding one book leads to other books. Also, once one key reference is obtained, its bibliography can often be used to discover earlier useful references. The *Science Citation Index,* available in many libraries, is another valuable tool for tracing the literature forward in time; for example, by looking in the current *Science Citation Index* for the name of W. K. Kenyon, who wrote several important scientific papers on the Hawaiian monk seal between 1959 and 1981, recent papers on the Hawaiian monk seal that cited his works can be located.

- *Unpublished literature*. A considerable amount of information in conservation biology is contained in unpublished reports by individuals, government agencies, and conservation organizations. This so-called "gray literature" is sometimes cited in published literature or mentioned by leading authorities in conversations and lectures. Often, a report known through word of mouth can be obtained through direct contact with the author or with conservation organizations. (A list of such sources of information is given in the Appendix.)

- *Fieldwork.* The natural history of a species usually must be learned through careful observations in the field. Fieldwork is usually necessary because only a tiny percentage of the world's species have been studied, and because the ecology of many species changes from one place to another. Only in the field can the conservation status of a species, and its relationships to the biological and physical environment, be determined. While much natural history information can be obtained through careful observation, many of the other techniques used are technical and are best learned by study under the supervision of an expert or by reading manuals (for example, Rabinowitz 1993; Heyer et al. 1994).

Monitoring populations

The way to learn the status of a rare species of special concern is to census the species in the field and monitor its populations over time. By repeatedly censusing a population on a regular basis, changes in the population over time can be determined (Simberloff 1988; Schemske et al. 1994). Long-term census records can help to distinguish long-term population trends of increase or decrease, possibly caused by human disturbance, from short-term fluctuations caused by variations in weather or unpredictable natural events (Pechmann et al. 1991; Cohn 1994). Monitoring is effective at showing the response of a population to a change in its environment; for example, a decline in an orchid species was shown in this way to be connected with heavy cattle grazing in its habitat (see below). Monitoring efforts can also be targeted at particularly sensitive species, such as butterflies, using them as indicators of the long-term stability of ecological communities (Sparrow et al. 1994).

Monitoring studies are increasing dramatically as government agencies and conservation organizations become more concerned with protecting rare and endangered species (Goldsmith 1991). A review of projects monitoring rare and endangered plants in the United States showed a phenomenal increase in the number of research projects initiated from 1974 to 1984: only one project was initiated in the three years from 1974 to 1976, while more than 120 projects were initiated from 1982 to 1984 (Palmer 1987). The most common types of monitoring projects were inventories (40%) and population demographic studies (40%); survey studies were somewhat less frequently used (20%).

An **inventory** is simply a count of the number of individuals present in a population. By repeating an inventory over successive time intervals, it can be determined whether the population is stable, increasing, or decreasing in numbers. The inventory is an inexpensive and straightforward method. It might answer such questions as: How many individuals exist in the population at present? Has the population been stable in numbers during the period for which inventory records exist? Inventories conducted over a wider area can help to determine the range of a species and its areas of local abundance.

A population **survey** involves the use of a repeatable sampling method to estimate the density of a species in a community. An area can be divided into sampling segments and the number of individuals in each segment counted. These counts can then be averaged and used to estimate the actual population size. Survey methods are used when a population is very large or its range extensive. Survey methods are particularly valuable when stages in a species' life cycle are inconspicuous, tiny, or hidden, such as the seed and seedling stages of many plants or the larval stages of aquatic invertebrates.

Demographic studies follow known individuals in a population to determine their rates of growth, reproduction, and survival. Individuals of all ages and sizes must be included in such a study. Either the whole population or a subsample can be followed. In a complete population study, all individuals are counted, aged if possible, measured for size, sexed, and tagged or marked for future identification; their positions on the site are mapped, and tissue samples are sometimes collected for genetic analysis. The techniques used to conduct a population study vary depending on the characteristics of the species and the purpose of the study. Each discipline has its own technique for following individuals over time: ornithologists band birds' legs, mammalogists often attach tags to animals' ears, and botanists attach aluminum tags to trees (Figure 3.6; see Goldsmith 1991). Information from demographic studies can be used in life history formulas to calculate the rate of population change and to identify vulnerable stages in the life cycle (Menges 1986; Caswell 1989).

Demographic studies can provide information on the age structure of a population. A stable population typically has an age distribution with a characteristic ratio of juveniles, young adults, and older adults. An absence or low number of any age class, particularly of juveniles, may indicate that the population is in danger of declining. Similarly, a large number of juveniles and young adults may indicate that the population is stable or even expanding. Careful analysis of long-term data, or of changes in the population over time, is often needed to distinguish short-term fluctuations from long-term trends.

Demographic studies can also reveal the spatial characteristics of a species, which can be very important in maintaining the viability of separate populations. The number of populations of the species, movement among the populations, and the stability of the populations in space and

(A)

(B)

time are all important considerations, particularly for species that occur in an aggregate of temporary or fluctuating populations linked by migration, known as a **metapopulation** (see below). Some examples of monitoring studies follow.

- *Hawaiian monk seals.* Population inventories of the Hawaiian monk seal (*Monachus schauinslandi*) documented a decline from almost 100 adults in the 1950s to fewer than 14 in the late 1960s (Figure 3.7; Gerrodette and Gilmartin 1990). The number of pups similarly declined during this period. On the basis of these trends, the Hawaiian monk seal was declared an endangered species under the U.S. Endangered Species Act in 1976, and conservation efforts were implemented that reversed the trend (Ackerman 1992).

- *Marine mollusks.* In Transkeii, South Africa, people living on the coast collect and eat marine mollusks, such as the brown mussel, the abalone, and the turban shell (Lasiak 1991). A survey method was used to determine whether traditional collecting methods are likely to deplete shellfish populations: the frequency and size distributions of mollusks were compared in protected and exploited rocky areas. Even though collection depleted the adult populations in exploited areas, they were quickly replaced by larvae, probably due to immigration from nearby protected areas and adjacent, inaccessible subtidal areas.

3.6 Monitoring populations requires specialized techniques suited to each species. (A) An ornithologist checks the health and weight of a piping plover on Cape Cod. Note the identification band on the bird's leg. (Photograph by Laurie McIvor.) (B) At Bako National Park, Sarawak, on the island of Borneo, marked trees in permanent research plots are measured and monitored for growth and survival. Here Forest Department staff measure a tree for its girth at breast height. (Photograph by R. Primack.)

3.7 Inventories of Hawaiian monk seal populations on Green Island, Kure Atoll (black trace) and on Tern Island, French Frigate Shoals (shaded trace) revealed that this species was in danger of extinction. Population counts were plotted from either a single count, the mean of several counts, or the maximum of several counts. Note the effect on seal populations of the Coast Guard stations on the islands. (After Gerrodette and Gilmartin 1990.)

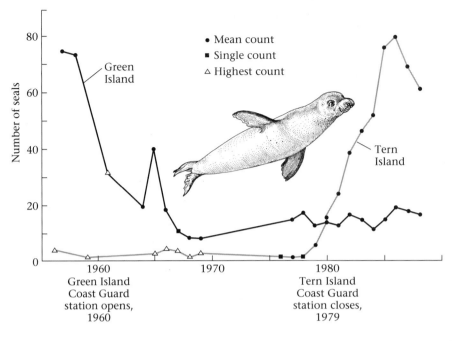

- *Early spider orchid.* The early spider orchid (*Ophrys sphegodes*) has shown a substantial decline in range during the last half of the twentieth century in Britain. A nine-year demographic study of this species showed that the plants were unusually short-lived for perennial orchids, with only half of the individuals surviving beyond two years (Hutchings 1987). This short half-life makes the species unusually vulnerable to unfavorable conditions. In one population in which the species was declining in numbers, demographic analysis highlighted soil damage caused by cattle grazing as the key element in the population decline. A change in land use to sheep grazing only during times when the plants are not flowering and fruiting has allowed the population to make a substantial recovery.

Monitoring studies are playing an increasingly important role in conservation biology. Monitoring has a long history in temperate countries, particularly Britain (Goldsmith 1991). In North America, the Breeding Bird Survey has been censusing bird abundance at about 1000 locations for the past 30 years, and this information is now being used to determine the stability of migrant songbird populations over time (James et al., in press). Some of the most elaborate monitoring projects have established permanent research plots in tropical forests, such as the 50 ha site at Barro Colorado Island in Panama, to monitor changes in species and communities over time (Condit et al. 1992; Dallmeier 1992). These studies have shown that many tropical tree and bird species are more dynamic in numbers than had previously been suspected (Bierregaard et al. 1992; Primack 1992; Primack and Hall 1992), suggesting that MVP estimates may need to be revised upward.

Population viability analysis

Population viability analysis (PVA) is an extension of demographic analysis that focuses on determining whether a species has the ability to persist in an environment (Shaffer 1991; Boyce 1992; Ruggiero et al. 1994). PVA is a method of looking at the range of requirements that a species has and the resources available in its environment in order to identify vulnerable stages in its natural history (Gilpin and Soulé 1986). PVA can be useful in understanding the effects of habitat loss, habitat fragmentation, and habitat degradation on a rare species. Although PVA is still being developed as an approach for predicting species persistence, and does not yet have a standard methodology or statistical framework (Shaffer 1990; Thomas 1990; Burgman et al. 1993), its methods of systematically and comprehensively examining species data are natural extensions of autecology, natural history research, and demographic studies. Such attempts to use statistics to predict future trends in population sizes must be used with caution and a large dose of common sense, however, in regard to the changing levels of human impact on species (Harcourt 1995).

Attempts to utilize population viability analysis have already begun. One of the most thorough examples of PVA, combining genetic and demographic analyses, is a study of the Tana River crested mangabey (*Cercocebus galeritus galeritus*), an endangered primate confined to the floodplain forests in a nature reserve along the Tana River in eastern Kenya (Figure 3.8; Kinnaird and O'Brien 1991). As its habitat has been reduced in area and fragmented by agricultural activities in the last 15–20 years, the species has experienced a decline in overall population size of about 50%, as well as a decline in the number of groups. While the number of mangabeys in 1989 was about 700 individuals, the effective population size was only about 100 due to a large proportion of nonreproductive individuals and variation in the number of offspring produced by different individuals. With such a low effective population size, the mangabey is in danger of losing significant amounts of its genetic variability. To maintain an effective population size of 500 individuals, the number considered sufficient to maintain genetic variability, a population of about 5000 mangabeys would have to be maintained. In addition, a demographic analysis of the population suggests that in the current situation, the probability of the population going extinct over the next 100 years is 40%. To assure that the population has a 95% probability of persisting for 100 years, based on demographic factors alone, the population size would have to be almost 8000 individuals.

Both the genetic and the demographic analyses suggest that the long-term future of the present mangabey population is bleak. Given the restricted range and habitat of the species and the growing human population in the area, a goal of increasing the population size to 5000–8000 individuals is probably unrealistic. A management plan that combines increases in the area of protected forests, enrichment plantings of existing forests to increase the numbers of mangabey food plants, and establishment of corridors to facilitate movement between forest fragments might increase the survival probability of the Tana River crested mangabey.

Conservation efforts on behalf of the African elephant have taken on international importance because of the species' precipitous decline in numbers and its symbolic importance as a representative of wildlife throughout the world. A population viability analysis of elephant populations on semiarid land at Tsavo National Park in Kenya indicated that a minimum reserve size of about 2500 km^2 is needed to attain a 99% prob-

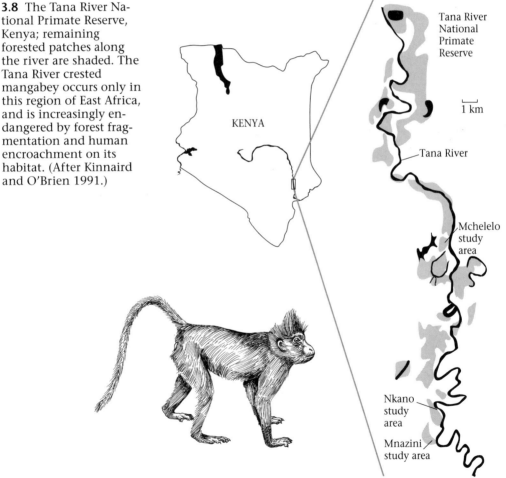

3.8 The Tana River National Primate Reserve, Kenya; remaining forested patches along the river are shaded. The Tana River crested mangabey occurs only in this region of East Africa, and is increasingly endangered by forest fragmentation and human encroachment on its habitat. (After Kinnaird and O'Brien 1991.)

KENYA

Tana River National Primate Reserve

1 km

Tana River

Mchelelo study area

Nkano study area

Mnazini study area

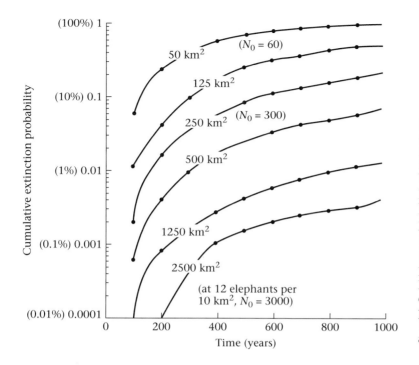

3.9 Cumulative probability of extinction (log scale) over time for elephant populations in different-sized protected areas. With a density of 12 elephants per 10 km^2, a 2500 km^2 protected area has an initial population (N_0) of 3000 elephants; the probability of extinction in 100 years is close to 0%, and in 1000 years is just 0.4%. A population in a protected area of 250 km^2 with an initial population of 300 elephants has a 20% probability of extinction in 1000 years. (After Armbruster and Lande 1993.)

ability of population persistence for 1000 years (Figure 3.9; Armbruster and Lande 1993). At densities of about 12 animals per 10 km^2, this translates into an initial population size of about 3000 animals. At this reserve size, the population could tolerate a modest degree of harvesting without substantially increasing its probability of extinction.

The metapopulation

Over the course of time, populations of a species may become extinct on a local scale, and new populations may form on other nearby, suitable sites. These species may be characterized by one or more **core** populations, with fairly stable numbers, and several **satellite areas** with fluctuating populations (Bleich et al. 1990). Populations in the satellite areas may become extinct in unfavorable years, but the areas are recolonized by migrants from the core population when conditions become more favorable. This system of temporary or fluctuating populations linked by migration is known as a **metapopulation** (Figure 3.10). In some species, every population is short-lived, and the distribution of the species changes dramatically with each generation. Many species that live in ephemeral habitats, such as herbs found on frequently flooded stream banks or in recently burned forests, are characterized by metapopulations made up of a shifting mosaic of temporary populations linked by some degree of migration (Menges 1990; Murphy et al. 1990).

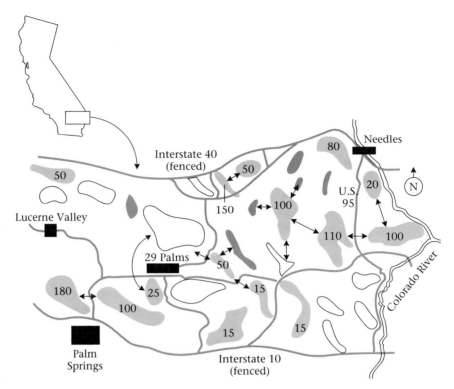

3.10 Mountain sheep (*Ovis canadensis*) in the southeastern California desert have a shifting mosaic of populations best described as a metapopulation. Mountain ranges shown with light shading had populations of the sizes indicated in 1990; unshaded mountain ranges were unpopulated in 1990 but had resident populations in the past. Mountains shown with dark shading have never had resident populations. Arrows indicate observed migrations of sheep. (After Bleich et al. 1990.)

The target of a population study is typically one or several populations, but an entire metapopulation may need to be studied if this would result in a more accurate portrayal of the species than a single-population study. Metapopulation models have the advantage of recognizing that local populations are dynamic and that there is movement of organisms from one local population to another (Hanski 1989; Olivieri et al. 1990; Stacey and Taper 1992). The recognition that infrequent colonization events and migrations are occurring also allows biologists to consider the impact of founder effects and genetic drift on the species. The following are two examples in which the metapopulation approach has proved to be more useful than a single-population description in understanding and managing species.

The endemic Furbish's lousewort, *Pedicularis furbishiae,* occurs along a river in Maine that is subject to periodic flooding (Menges 1990). Flooding often destroys some existing populations, but it also creates exposed riverbank habitat suitable for the establishment of new populations. Studies of any single population would give an incomplete picture of the species because the current populations are short-lived. The metapopulation is really the appropriate unit of study, and the watershed is the appropriate unit of management.

The checkerspot butterfly (*Euphydryas* spp.) has been extensively stud-

3.11 Studies of the bay check-erspot butterfly (*Euphydryas editha bayensis*) have been used to demonstrate the metapopulation approach. Core populations of this species colonize unoccupied satellite areas during favorable years. (Photograph courtesy of Dennis Murphy, Stanford University.)

ied in California (Figure 3.11; Ehrlich and Murphy 1987; Murphy et al. 1990). Individual butterfly populations often become extinct, but dispersal and colonization of unoccupied habitat allow the species to survive. Environmental stochasticity and lack of habitat variation at a particular site often cause extinctions of local populations. The largest and most persistent populations are found in large areas that have both moist, north-facing slopes and warmer, south-facing slopes. Butterflies migrating out from these core populations often colonize the unoccupied satellite areas.

In metapopulation situations, destruction of the habitat of one central, core population could result in the extinction of numerous satellite populations that depend on the core population for periodic colonization. Also, human disturbances that inhibit migration, such as fences, roads, and dams, can reduce the rate of migration among habitat patches and so reduce or even eliminate the probability of recolonization after local extinction (Lamberson et al. 1992; Harrison 1994). In such situations, a metapopulation model may not be appropriate. Metapopulation models highlight the dynamic nature of population processes and show how the elimination of a few core populations could lead to the extinction of a species over a much wider area. Effective management of a species often requires an understanding of these metapopulation dynamics.

Long-term monitoring of species and ecosystems

Long-term monitoring of ecosystem processes (temperature, rainfall, humidity, soil acidity, water quality, discharge rates of streams, soil erosion, etc.), communities (species present, amount of vegetative cover, amount of biomass present at each trophic level, etc.), and population numbers (number of individuals present of particular species) is necessary because it is otherwise difficult to distinguish normal year-to-year fluctuations from long-term trends (Magnuson 1990; Primack 1992). For example, many

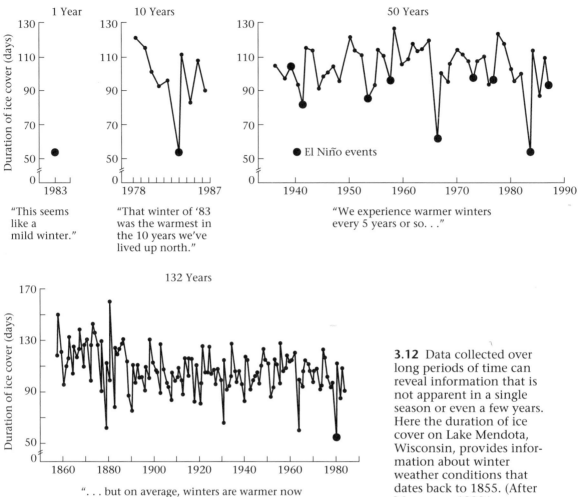

3.12 Data collected over long periods of time can reveal information that is not apparent in a single season or even a few years. Here the duration of ice cover on Lake Mendota, Wisconsin, provides information about winter weather conditions that dates back to 1855. (After Magnuson 1990.)

amphibian, insect, and annual plant populations are highly variable from year to year, so many years of data are required to determine whether a particular species is actually declining in abundance or merely experiencing a number of low-population years in accord with its regular pattern of variation. Monitoring is particularly important in integrated conservation and development projects in which the long-term protection of biological diversity is an important goal (Kremen et al. 1994).

A challenge in understanding change in ecosystems is created by the fact that effects may lag for many years behind their initial causes. For example, acid rain and other components of air pollution may weaken and kill trees over a period of decades, increasing the amount of soil erosion

into adjacent streams and ultimately making the aquatic environment unsuitable for the larvae of certain rare insect species. In such a case, the
cause (air pollution) may have occurred decades before the effect (insect
decline) is detectable.

Acid rain, global climate change, vegetation succession, nitrogen deposition, and invasions of exotic species are all examples of processes that
cause long-term changes in biological communities but are often hidden
from our short-term perspective (Figure 3.12). Some long-term information is available from weather stations, annual census counts of birds,
forestry plots, water authorities, and old photographs of vegetation, but
the number of long-term monitoring efforts for biological communities is
inadequate for most conservation purposes. To remedy this situation,
many scientific research stations have begun to implement programs for
monitoring ecological change over the course of decades and centuries.
One such program is the system of 172 Long-Term Ecological Research
(LTER) sites established by the U.S. National Science Foundation (Swanson and Sparks 1990). These sites will provide an early warning system for
disruption or decline of ecosystem functions.

Establishment of New Populations

Instead of only passively observing endangered species as they decline toward extinction, many conservation biologists have begun to develop approaches to save these species. Some exciting new methods are being developed to establish new wild and semi-wild populations of rare and
endangered species and to increase the size of existing populations (Gipps
1991; Bowles and Whelan 1994). These experiments offer the hope that
species now living only in captivity can regain their ecological and evolutionary roles within the biological community. Populations in the wild
may have less chance of being destroyed by catastrophes (such as epidemics or wars) than confined captive populations. Further, simply increasing the number and size of populations of a species generally lowers
its probability of extinction.

Such establishment programs are unlikely to work effectively, however,
unless the factors leading to the decline of the original wild populations
are clearly understood and then eliminated, or at least controlled (Campbell 1980). For example, if an endemic bird species has been hunted nearly
to extinction in the wild by local villagers, its nesting areas damaged by
development, and its eggs eaten by an exotic species, these issues have to
be addressed as an integral part of a reestablishment program. Simply releasing captive-bred birds into the wild without discussions with local people, a change in land use patterns, and control of exotic species would result in a recurrence of the original situation.

Three basic approaches have been used to establish new populations
of animals and plants. A **reintroduction program** involves releasing cap-

tive-bred or wild-collected individuals into an area of their historic range where the species no longer occurs. The principal objective of a reintroduction program is to create a new population in the original environment. For example, a recently implemented plan to reintroduce gray wolves into Yellowstone National Park aims to restore the equilibrium of predators and herbivores that existed prior to human intervention in the region. Individuals frequently are released at the site where they or their ancestors were collected to ensure genetic adaptation to the site. Individuals are also sometimes released elsewhere within the range of the species when a new protected area has been established, when an existing population is under a new threat and will no longer be able to survive in its present location, or when natural or artificial barriers to the normal dispersal tendencies of the species exist. Unfortunately there is confusion among the terms denoting the reintroduction of populations, and sometimes these programs are also called "reestablishments," "restorations," or "translocations."

Two other distinct types of release programs are also being used. An **augmentation program** involves releasing individuals into an existing population to increase its size and gene pool. These released individuals may be wild individuals collected elsewhere or individuals raised in captivity. One special example of augmentation is a "headstarting" approach in which marine turtle hatchlings are raised in captivity during their vulnerable young stage, and then are released into the wild. An **introduction program** involves moving animals and plants to areas outside their historic range in the hope of establishing new populations (Conant 1988). Such an approach may be appropriate when the environment within the historic range of a species has deteriorated to the point at which the species can no longer survive there or when the factor causing the original decline is still present, making reintroduction impossible. An introduction of a species to new sites needs to be carefully thought out to ensure that the species does not damage its new ecosystem or harm populations of any local endangered species. Care must also be taken to ensure that released individuals have not acquired diseases while in captivity that could spread to and decimate wild populations.

Considerations for successful programs

Programs to establish new populations are often expensive and difficult; they require a serious, long-term commitment. The programs implemented to capture, raise, monitor, and release California condors, peregrine falcons, and black-footed ferrets, for instance, have cost millions of dollars and required years of work. When the animals are long-lived, the program itself may have to last for many years before its outcome is known. Decisions on initiating reintroduction programs can also become highly emotional public issues, as evidenced by the California condor, black-footed ferret, grizzly bear, and gray wolf programs (Lipske 1991;

Luoma 1992). Programs can be attacked as a waste of money ("Millions of dollars for a few ugly birds!"), unnecessary ("Why do we need wolves here when there are so many elsewhere?"), poorly run ("Look at all of the ferrets that died of disease in captivity!"), or unethical ("Why can't the last animals just be allowed to live out their lives in peace without being captured and put into zoos?"). The answer to all of these criticisms is straightforward: well-run, well-designed captive breeding and reintroduction programs are the best hope for preserving a species that is about to become extinct in the wild or is in severe decline. A crucial element in many reintroduction programs will be public relations efforts to explain the need for and the goals of the program to local people and convince them to support it, or at least not oppose it (Reading and Kellert 1993). Providing incentives to the local community as part of the program often is more successful than rigid enforcement of restrictions and laws.

Released animals may require special care and assistance during and immediately after release; this approach is known as "soft release." Animals may have to be fed and sheltered at the release point until they are able to subsist on their own, or they may need to be caged temporarily at the release point and released gradually, so that they can become familiar with the area (Figure 3.13). Social groups abruptly released from captivity (a "hard release") may explosively disperse in different directions and away from the protected area, resulting in a failed establishment effort. Intervention may be necessary if the animals appear to be unable to survive,

3.13 Cages within exclosures allow black-footed ferrets (*Mustela nigrepes*) to become familiar with the range where they will eventually be released. The ferrets' caretaker is wearing a mask to reduce the chance of the ferrets being exposed to human disease. (Photograph by LuRay Parker, Wyoming Game and Fish Department.)

particularly during episodes of drought or low food abundance. In such cases a decision has to be made whether it is better to give the animals occasional temporary help to get them established or to force them to survive on their own. Reintroduction efforts often involve a long-term commitment to conservation, extending over decades.

Successful reintroduction programs often have considerable educational value. In Brazil, efforts to preserve the golden lion tamarin through conservation and reintroduction have become a rallying point in attempts to protect the last remaining fragments of the Atlantic Coast forest. In Oman, captive-bred Arabian oryx were successfully reintroduced into desert areas, creating an important national symbol and a source of employment for the local Bedouins who run the program (Figure 3.14; Stanley Price 1989). Attempts are also under way to establish new populations of endangered insects, which is appropriate considering that there are so many species of insects, only some of which are well known to the public (Ravenscroft 1990; Samways 1994).

Establishment programs for common game species have always been widespread and have contributed a great deal of knowledge to the new programs being developed for threatened and endangered species. A detailed study that examined 198 bird and mammal establishment programs conducted between 1973 and 1986 found a number of significant generalizations (Griffith et al. 1989). The reported success of programs in establishing new populations was:

- Greater for game species (86%) than for threatened, endangered, and sensitive species (44%)

- Greater for release in excellent quality habitat (84%) than in poor quality habitat (38%)

- Greater in the core of the historic range (78%) than at the periphery of and outside the historic range (48%)

- Greater with wild-caught (75%) than with captive-bred animals (38%)

- Greater for herbivores (77%) than for carnivores (48%)

For these bird and mammal species, the probability of establishing a new population increased with the number of animals being released up to about 100 animals. Releasing more than 100 animals did not further enhance the probability of success.

A second survey of projects (Beck et al. 1994) used a more restricted definition of reintroduction: the release of captive-born animals within the historical range of the species. A program was judged a success if there was a self-maintaining population of 500 individuals. Using these precise definitions, only 16 out of 145 reintroduction projects were judged successful—a dramatically *lower* rate of success than the earlier survey. Ac-

3.14 The Arabian oryx (*Oryx leucoryx*), almost extinct in the wild, is being reintroduced to places in its former range, such as Oman. (Photograph by Ron Garrison, San Diego Zoo.)

cording to Beck et al., the key to success involves releasing large numbers of animals over many years. Clearly, monitoring and evaluating ongoing and future programs are crucial in order to determine whether efforts to establish new populations are achieving their stated goals.

Social behavior of released animals

Successful reintroduction, augmentation, and introduction programs need to consider the social organization and behavior of the animals that are being released. When social animals, particularly mammals and some birds, grow up in the wild, they learn about their environment and how to interact socially from other members of their species. Animals raised in captivity may lack the skills needed to survive in their natural environment, as well as the social skills necessary to find food cooperatively, sense

3.15 Captive golden lion tamarins (*Leontopithecus rosalia*) must learn skills needed for life in the wild; in this case, the animals must find food inside a complicated puzzle box. (Photograph by Jessie Cohen, National Zoological Park, Smithsonian Institution.)

danger, find mating partners, and raise young. To overcome these socialization problems, captive-raised mammals and birds may require extensive training before as well as after their release into the environment. Captive chimpanzees, for instance, have been taught how to use twigs to feed on termites and how to build nests. Red wolves are taught how to kill live prey. Golden lion tamarins are given complex food boxes to teach them skills that will be useful for opening wild fruits (Figure 3.15; Kleiman 1989). Captive animals are taught to fear potential predators by being frightened in some way when a dummy predator is shown.

Social interaction is one of the most difficult behaviors for people to teach to captive-bred mammals and birds because, for most species, the subtleties of social behavior are poorly understood. Nevertheless, some successful attempts have been made to socialize captive-bred mammals. In some cases, humans mimic the appearance and behavior of wild individuals. This method is particularly important when dealing with very young animals, which need to learn to identify with their own species rather than with a foster species or with humans. Captive-bred California condor hatchlings were originally unable to learn the behaviors of their wild relatives because they had imprinted on their human keepers. Newly hatched condors are now fed with condor hand puppets and kept from the sight of zoo visitors (Figure 3.16). In other cases, wild individuals are used as "instructors" for captive individuals of the same species. Wild golden lion tamarins are caught and held with captive-bred tamarins to form social groups that are then released together, in the hope that the captive-bred tamarins will learn from the wild ones (Kleiman 1989). When

3.16 California condor chicks (*Gymnogyps californianus*) raised in captivity are fed by researchers using hand puppets that look like adult birds. Conservation biologists hope that minimizing human contact with the birds will improve their chances of survival when they are returned to the wild. (Photograph by Mike Wallace, The Los Angeles Zoo.)

captive-bred animals are released into the wild, they sometimes join existing social groups or mate with wild animals and thereby gain some knowledge of their environment. The development of social relationships with wild animals may be crucial to the success of the captive-bred animals once they have been released.

Establishing new plant populations

Efforts at establishing new populations of rare and endangered plant species are fundamentally different from attempts using terrestrial vertebrate animal species. Animals can disperse to new locations and actively seek out the microsite conditions that are most suitable for them. In the case of plants, seeds are dispersed to new sites by such agents as wind, animals, and water (Guerrant 1992; Primack and Miao 1992). Once a seed lands on the ground, it is unable to move farther, even if a suitable microsite exists just a few centimeters away. The immediate microsite is crucial for plant survival: if the environmental conditions are too sunny, too shady, too wet, or too dry, either the seed will not germinate or the resulting seedling will die. Disturbance in the form of fire or blowdowns may also be necessary for seedling establishment in many species. As a result, a site may be suitable for seedling establishment only once every several years, making reintroductions difficult to carry out and hard to evaluate.

Populations of rare and endangered plant species typically fail to become established from introduced seeds at most sites that appear to be suitable for them. To increase their chances of success, botanists often germinate seeds in controlled environments and grow the young plants in protected conditions. Only after the plants are past the fragile seedling stage are they transplanted into the field. In other cases, plants are dug up from an existing wild population (usually either one that is threatened with destruction or one where removing a small percentage of the plants will not apparently harm the population), then transplanted into an unoccupied but apparently suitable site. While such transplantation methods have a good chance of ensuring that a species survives at its new location, they do not mimic a natural process, and new populations often fail to produce the seeds and seedlings needed to form the next generation (Allen 1987; Pavlik et al. 1993; Primack 1995). Plant ecologists are currently trying to work out new techniques to overcome these difficulties, such as fencing to exclude animals, removal of some of the existing vegetation to reduce competition, and mineral nutrient additions.

Reestablishment programs and the law

Reintroduction, introduction, and augmentation programs will increase in the coming years as the biological diversity crisis eliminates more species from the wild. Many of the reintroduction programs for endangered species will be mandated by official recovery plans set up by national governments (Tear et al. 1993). However, establishment programs, as well as research in general on endangered species, are increasingly being affected by legislation that restricts the possession and use of endangered species (New England Wild Flower Society 1992). If government officials rigidly apply these laws to scientific research programs, which was certainly not the original intent of the legislation, the creative insights and new approaches coming out of these programs could be stifled (Ralls and Brownell 1989). New scientific information is central to establishment programs and other conservation efforts. Conservation biologists must be able to explain the benefits of their research programs in a way that government officials and the general public can understand, and must address the legitimate concerns of those groups (Farnsworth and Rosovsky 1993). Government officials who block reasonable scientific projects may be doing a disservice to the organisms they are trying to protect. The harm to endangered species that could be caused by carefully planned scientific research is relatively insignificant in comparison with the actual massive loss of biological diversity being caused by habitat destruction and fragmentation, pollution, and overexploitation.

Experimental populations of rare and endangered species successfully created by introduction and reintroduction programs are sometimes given a degree of legal protection (Falk and Olwell 1992). Legislators and scientists alike must understand that the establishment of new populations through reintroduction programs in no way reduces the need to protect the original populations of endangered species; the original populations are more likely to have the most complete gene pool and the most intact interactions with other members of the biological community.

Ex Situ Conservation Strategies

The best strategy for the long-term protection of biological diversity is the preservation of natural communities and populations in the wild, known as **in situ** or **on-site preservation.** Only in the wild are species able to continue the process of evolutionary adaptation to a changing environment within their natural communities. However, for many rare species, in situ preservation is not a viable option in the face of increasing human disturbance. If a remnant population is too small to persist, or if all the remaining individuals are found outside of protected areas, then in situ preservation may not be effective. In such circumstances it is likely that the only way to prevent the species from becoming extinct is to maintain individuals in artificial conditions under human supervision (Conway 1980; Dresser 1988; Seal 1988). This strategy is known as **ex situ** or **off-site preservation.** Already a number of animal species are extinct in the wild but survive in captive colonies, such as the Père David's deer, *Elaphurus davidianus* (Figure 3.17). The beautiful Franklin tree (see Figure 2.1) grows only in cultivation and is no longer found in the wild.

Ex situ facilities for animal preservation include zoos, game farms, aquariums, and captive breeding programs. Plants are maintained in botanical gardens, arboretums, and seed banks. An intermediate strategy that combines elements of both ex situ and in situ preservation is the in-

3.17 Père David's deer (*Elaphurus davidianus*) has been extinct in the wild since about 1200 B.C. The species remained only in managed hunting reserves kept by Chinese royalty. (Photograph by Jessie Cohen, National Zoological Park, Smithsonian Institution.)

3.18 The rhinoceros is an example of an animal that is not amenable at present to ex situ conservation strategies; rhinos tend not to reproduce in captivity. Virtually all the rhinos seen in zoos, such as this pair of black rhinos (*Diceros bicornis*), were captured in the wild. (Photograph by Jessie Cohen, National Zoological Park, Smithsonian Institution.)

tensive monitoring and management of populations of rare and endangered species in small protected areas; such populations are still somewhat wild, but human intervention may be used on occasion to prevent population decline.

Ex situ conservation efforts are an important part of an integrated conservation strategy to protect endangered species (Falk 1991). Ex situ and in situ conservation strategies are complementary approaches (Kennedy 1987; Robinson 1992). Individuals from ex situ populations can be periodically released into the wild to augment in situ conservation efforts. Research on captive populations can provide insight into the basic biology of a species and suggest new conservation strategies for in situ populations. Ex situ populations that are self-maintaining can also reduce the need to collect individuals from the wild for display or research purposes. Finally, captive-bred individuals on display can help to educate the public about the need to preserve the species, and so protect other members of the species in the wild. In situ preservation of species, in turn, is vital to the survival of species that are difficult to maintain in captivity, such as the rhinoceros (Figure 3.18), as well as to the continued ability of zoos, aquariums, and botanical gardens to display new species. Ex situ conservation is not cheap; the cost of maintaining African elephants and black rhinos in zoos is 50 times greater than protecting the same number of individuals in East African national parks (Leader-Williams 1990). However, as Michael Soulé says, "There are no hopeless cases, only people without hope and expensive cases" (Soulé 1987).

Zoos

Zoos, along with affiliated universities, government wildlife departments, and conservation organizations, presently maintain over 700,000 individuals representing 3000 species of mammals, birds, reptiles, and amphibians (Groombridge 1992). While this number of captive animals may seem impressive, it is trivial in comparison to the numbers of domestic cats, dogs, and fish kept by people as pets. The emphasis zoos place on displaying "charismatic megafauna," such as pandas, giraffes, and elephants, tends to ignore the enormous threats to the huge numbers of insects and other invertebrates that form the majority of the world's animal species.

A current goal of most major zoos is to establish captive breeding populations of rare and endangered animals. Only about 10% of the 274 species of rare mammals kept by zoos worldwide currently have self-sustaining captive populations of sufficient size to maintain their genetic variation (Ralls and Ballou 1983; Groombridge 1992). To remedy this situation, zoos and affiliated conservation organizations have embarked on a major effort to build the facilities and develop the technology necessary to establish breeding colonies of rare and endangered animals, such as the snow leopard and the orangutan, and to develop new methods and programs for reestablishing species in the wild (Figure 3.19; Foose 1983; Dresser 1988). Some of these facilities are highly specialized, such as the

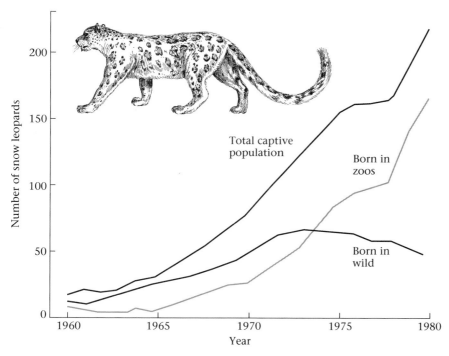

3.19 Snow leopards (*Panthera uncia*) reproduce well in captivity. Maintaining breeding colonies of these animals can reduce zoos' need to capture individuals from the declining wild population. Since 1974, the majority of snow leopards in zoos have been born in captivity. (Data from Foose 1983.)

International Crane Foundation in Wisconsin, which is attempting to establish captive breeding populations of all crane species.

The success of captive breeding programs has been enhanced by several programs that collect and disseminate knowledge about rare and endangered species. The Species Survival Commission Conservation Breeding Specialist Group of IUCN-The World Conservation Union provides zoos with the information necessary for proper care and handling of these species, including data on nutritional requirements, anaesthetic techniques, optimal housing conditions, and vaccinations and antibiotics. Central data bases of breeding records and stud books are being developed to prevent matings among close relatives and the resulting higher offspring mortality associated with genetic drift and inbreeding depression. One of the most important is the International Species Inventory System (ISIS), which provides information on 4200 kinds of animals at 395 zoological institutions in 39 countries.

A wide range of innovative techniques are being developed to increase the reproductive rates of captive species. Some of these come directly from human and veterinary medicine, while others are novel methods developed for particular species. These techniques include **cross-fostering**, having mothers of common species raise the offspring of rare species; **artificial insemination** when adults show no interest in mating or are living in different locations; **artificial incubation** of eggs in ideal hatching conditions; and **embryo transfer**, the implanting of fertilized eggs of rare species into surrogate mothers of common species (Figure 3.20).

When scientists decide to use these methods to preserve a species, they must address a series of ethical questions. First, how necessary and how effective are these methods for a particular species? Is it better to let the last few individuals of a species live out their days in the wild, or to start a captive population that may be unable to readapt to wild conditions? Second, does a population of a rare species that has been raised in captivity and does not know how to survive in its own natural environment really represent survival for the species? Third, are species held in captivity for their own benefit or for the benefit of zoos?

Even when the answers to these questions indicate that ex situ management is appropriate, it is not always feasible to create ex situ populations of rare animal species. A species may have been so severely reduced in numbers that it has low breeding success and high infant mortality due to inbreeding depression. Certain animals, particularly marine mammals, are so large or require such specialized environments that the facilities for maintaining and handling them are prohibitively expensive. Many invertebrates have complex life cycles in which their diets change as they grow and in which their environmental needs vary in subtle ways. Many of these species are not possible to raise with our present knowledge. Finally, certain species are simply difficult to breed, despite the best efforts of scientists. Two prime examples are many parrot species and the Sumatran

3.20 This bongo calf (*Tragelaphus euryceros*, an endangered species) was produced by embryo transfer using an eland (*Taurotragus oryx*) as a surrogate mother at the Cincinnati Zoo Center for Reproduction of Endangered Wildlife. (Photograph © Cincinnati Zoo.)

rhino, which have low reproductive rates in the wild and have not reproduced well in captivity despite a considerable effort to find effective breeding methods.

Aquariums

To deal with the threats to aquatic species, ichthyologists, marine mammalogists, and coral reef experts who work for public aquariums are increasingly working cooperatively with colleagues in marine research institutes, government fisheries departments, and conservation organizations to develop programs for the conservation of rich natural communities and species of special concern. At present, approximately 580,000 fish species are maintained in aquariums, with most of these collected from the wild (Olney and Ellis 1991). Major efforts presently are being made to develop breeding techniques so that rare species can be maintained in aquariums, sometimes for release back into the wild, and so that wild specimens do not have to be collected (Kaufman 1988). Many of the techniques used in fish breeding were originally developed by fisheries biologists for large-scale stocking operations involving trout, bass, salmon, and other commercial species. Other techniques were discovered in the aquarium pet

3.21 Breeding bottle-nosed dolphins (*Tursiops truncatus*) in captivity has provided aquarium personnel with valuable experience that can be applied to endangered cetacean species. Shown here are a mother and calf. (Photograph courtesy of Sea World.)

trade as dealers attempted to propagate tropical fish for sale. These techniques are now being applied to such endangered freshwater fauna as the desert pupfishes of the American Southwest, stream fishes of the Tennessee River Basin, and cichlids of the African Rift lakes. Programs for breeding endangered marine fishes and coral species are still in an early stage, but this is an area of active research at the present time.

Aquariums have a particularly important role to play in the conservation of endangered cetaceans. Aquarium personnel often respond to public requests for assistance in dealing with whales stranded on beaches or disoriented in shallow waters. The aquarium community potentially can use the lessons learned from working with common captive species, such as the bottle-nosed dolphin, to develop programs to aid endangered species (Figure 3.21).

Botanical gardens and arboretums

The world's 1500 botanical gardens contain major collections of living plants and represent a crucial resource for plant conservation efforts. The botanical gardens of the world are currently growing at least 35,000 species of plants, approximately 15% of the world's flora (IUCN/WWF 1989; Given 1994); perhaps double that number of species are being grown in greenhouses, subsistence gardens, hobby gardens, and other such situations (though often with very few individuals per species). The world's largest botanical garden, the Royal Botanical Gardens of England at Kew, has an estimated 25,000 plant species under cultivation—about 10% of the world's total—of which 2700 are endangered or threatened. Botanical gardens need to increase the number of individuals grown for every species in order to protect the range of genetic variability found in each.

3.22 The New England Wild Flower Society's Garden in the Woods in Massachusetts. Such botanical gardens offer great pleasure and enjoyment to visitors as well as preserving rare plant species. (Photograph by John A. Lynch.)

Botanical gardens increasingly focus on the cultivation of rare and endangered plant species, and many specialize in particular types of plants. The Arnold Arboretum of Harvard University grows hundreds of different temperate tree species. The New England Wild Flower Society has a collection of hundreds of perennial temperate herbs at its Garden in the Woods (Figure 3.22). In California, a specialized pine arboretum grows 72 of the world's 110 species of pines, while South Africa's leading botanical garden has 25% of that country's many plant species growing under cultivation.

Botanical gardens are in a unique position to contribute to conservation efforts because their living collections and their associated herbaria of dried plant collections represent one of the best sources of information on plant distribution and habitat requirements. The staff of botanical gardens are often recognized authorities on plant identification and conservation status. Expeditions sent out by botanical gardens discover new species and make observations on known species, while over 250 botanical gardens maintain nature reserves that serve as important conservation areas in their own right. In addition, botanical gardens are in a position to educate the public about conservation issues because an estimated 150 million people per year visit them.

At the international level, the Botanical Gardens Conservation Secretariat (BGCS) of IUCN-The World Conservation Union is organizing and coordinating conservation efforts by the world's botanical gardens (BGCS 1987). The priorities of this program include the development of a world-wide database system for coordinating collecting activity and identifying important species that are underrepresented or absent from living collections. A problem with the distribution of botanical gardens is that most of them are located in the temperate zone, even though most of the world's plant species are found in the tropics. While a number of major gardens exist in such places as Singapore, Sri Lanka, Java, and Colombia, establishing new botanical gardens in the tropics should be a priority for the international conservation community, along with training local plant taxonomists to fill staff positions.

Seed banks

In addition to growing plants, botanical gardens and research institutes have developed collections of seeds, sometimes known as **seed banks**, collected from the wild and from cultivated plants. The seeds of most plant species can be stored in cold, dry conditions in these seed banks for long periods of time and then later germinated. The ability of seeds to remain dormant is extremely valuable for ex situ conservation efforts because it allows the seeds of large numbers of rare species to be frozen and stored in a small space, with minimal supervision, and at a low cost. More than 50 major seed banks exist in the world, many of them in developing countries, with their activities coordinated by the Consultative Group on International Agricultural Research (CGIAR).

3.23 Endangered species of plants can often be propagated in large numbers using modern tissue culture techniques. A new plant is growing inside each plastic container. The plants will later be transferred outside or into pots in a greenhouse. (Photograph by John A. Lynch.)

Even though seed banks have great potential for conserving species, they have certain problems as well. If power supplies fail or equipment breaks down, the entire frozen collection may be damaged. Even in cold storage, seeds gradually lose their ability to germinate due to exhaustion of their energetic reserves and the accumulation of harmful mutations. To overcome this gradual deterioration of seed quality, seed samples must be periodically germinated, adult plants grown to maturity, and new seed samples stored. For seed banks with large collections, this testing and rejuvenation of seed samples can be a formidable task.

Approximately 15% of the world's plant species have "recalcitrant" seeds that either lack dormancy or do not tolerate low-temperature storage conditions, and consequently cannot be stored in seed banks. Seeds of these species must germinate right away or die. Species with recalcitrant seeds are much more common in the tropical forest than in the temperate zone; the seeds of many economically important tropical fruit trees, timber trees, and plantation crops, such as cocoa and rubber, cannot be stored (BGCS 1987). Intensive investigations are under way to find ways of storing recalcitrant seeds; one possible means may be storing only the embryo after removing the surrounding seed coat, endosperm, and other tissues. Some plant species can also be maintained in tissue culture in controlled conditions or propagated by cuttings from a parent plant, though these processes are currently more expensive than growing plants from seeds (Figure 3.23).

Seed banks have been embraced by the international agricultural community as an effective way of preserving the genetic variability that exists in agricultural crops (Figure 3.24). Often genes for resistance to a particular disease or pest are found in only one variety of a crop, known as a **landrace,** that is grown in only one small area of the world. This genetic vari-

3.24 The genetic variation in corn (*Zea mays,* also known as maize) is evident in its variety of cob shapes, seed (kernel) shapes, and color patterns. (Photograph © Steven King.)

ability is often crucial to the agricultural industry in its efforts to maintain and increase the high productivity of modern crops and to respond to changing environmental conditions, such as acid rain, changing weather patterns, and soil erosion. Researchers are in a race against time to preserve this genetic variability because traditional farmers throughout the world are abandoning their local crop varieties in favor of standard, high-yielding varieties (Altieri and Anderson 1992; Cleveland et al. 1994). This worldwide phenomenon is illustrated by Sri Lankan farmers, who grew 2000 different varieties of rice until the late 1950s, when they switched over to just 5 high-yielding varieties (Rhoades 1991). So far, over 2 million collections of seeds have been acquired by agricultural seed banks. Many of the major food crops, such as wheat, corn (maize), oats, and potatoes, are well represented in seed banks, and other important crops such as rice, millet, and sorghum are being intensively collected as well (Plucknett et al. 1987). However, crops of only regional significance, medicinal plants, fiber plants, and other useful plants are not as well represented in seed banks. Also, species with recalcitrant seeds are not represented in seed collections, yet these species have major significance to the economies of tropical countries and the diets of local people. Wild relatives of crop plants are not adequately represented in seed banks even though these species are extremely useful in crop improvement programs.

A major controversy over the development of seed banks is who owns and controls the genetic resources of crop plants. The genes of local landraces of crop plants and wild relatives of crop species provide the building blocks needed to develop advanced "elite" high-yielding varieties suitable for modern agriculture. An estimated 96% of the genetic variability necessary for modern agriculture comes from the developing countries of the world, such as India, Ethiopia, Peru, Mexico, Indonesia, and Egypt (Figure 3.25), yet the breeding programs for "elite" strains frequently take place in the industrialized countries of North America and Europe. In the past, international seed banks freely collected seeds and plant tissue from developing countries and gave them to research stations and seed companies. Once seed companies developed new "elite" strains through sophisticated breeding programs and field trials, however, they sold their seeds at a high price to make a profit. Developing countries are now questioning this system, arguing that it is not equitable and is possibly even a "holdover colonial mentality of maintaining ignorance" in which "dependent nations are robbed of diversity" (Goldstein, cited in Shulman 1986). From their perspective, the developing countries question why they should share their genetic resources freely but then have to pay for advanced seeds based on those genetic resources. One solution proposed is for developed countries and seed companies to pay for genetic resources that they obtain from developing countries (Vogel 1994). Another, perhaps overly idealistic, alternative is for all seed samples, including those developed by seed companies, to be shared freely.

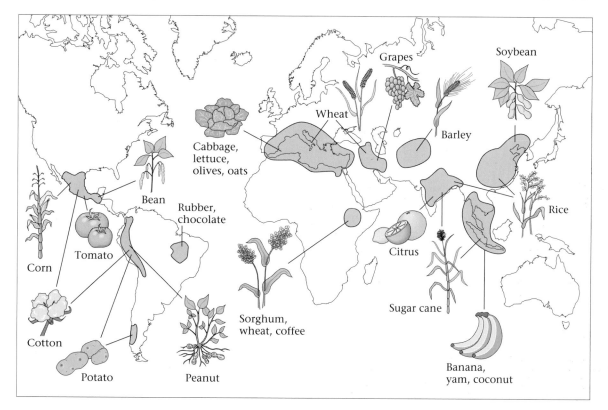

Cabbage,
lettuce,
olives, oats

Wheat

Grapes

Soybean

Barley

Bean

Rubber,
chocolate

Rice

Corn

Tomato

Citrus

Cotton

Sorghum,
wheat, coffee

Sugar cane

Potato

Peanut

Banana,
yam, coconut

3.25 Crop species show high genetic diversity in certain areas of the world, often the area where the species was first domesticated or where it is still grown in traditional agricultural settings. (Courtesy of Garrison Wilkes.)

Sampling strategies for wild species. In establishing seed banks, strategies for collecting seeds from endangered and rare wild plants must take into consideration the distribution of genetic variability: species that are more genetically variable may require more extensive sampling to acquire the majority of their alleles than species that are more genetically uniform. The Center for Plant Conservation (1991) has developed a set of seed sampling guidelines for conserving the genetic variability of endangered plant species; these guidelines could be modified for animals and other taxa.

1. The highest priorities for collecting should be species that (*a*) are in danger of extinction—that is, species showing a rapid decline in numbers of individuals or numbers of populations; (*b*) are evolutionarily or taxonomically unique; (*c*) can be reintroduced into the wild; (*d*) have the potential to be preserved in ex situ situations; (*e*) have potential economic value for agriculture, medicine, forestry, or industry.
2. Seeds should be collected from up to five populations per species to ensure that most of the important genetic variation is sampled.

Where possible, populations should be selected so as to cover the full geographical and environmental range of the species.

3. Seeds should be collected from 10–50 individuals per population. Sampling fewer than 10 individuals may miss alleles that are common in the population.

4. The number of seeds (or cuttings, bulbs, etc.) collected per plant is determined by the viability of the species' seeds; that is, the ability of seeds to germinate and grow into new plants when given the proper conditions. If seed viability is high, then only a few seeds need to be collected per individual.

5. If individual plants of a species have a low reproductive output, collecting many seeds in one year may have a negative effect on the sampled populations. A better strategy would be to spread the collecting over several years.

As the CPC (1991) concludes: "Conservation collections are only as good as the diversity that they contain. Thus the forethought and methods that go into sampling procedures play a critical role in determining the ultimate quality of the collection, as well as its usability for purposes such as reintroduction and restoration. In the long run, the real significance of collections in biological conservation is their role in reinforcing the management and maintenance of natural populations. Collectors should view themselves not as 'preserving' static entities, but as providing a stepping-stone on the pathway to survival and evolution."

Conservation of tree genetic resources

To conserve the genetic resources of commercially important tree species, foresters have used cuttings and families of closely related seeds to establish plantations of superior genetic varieties, known as "clone banks" (Ledig 1988). Selected trees are then used to establish seed orchards for producing commercial seeds. Eight thousand clones of loblolly pine (*Pinus taeda*) alone are being grown in clone banks in the southeastern United States. Storage of seeds is difficult for many important genera of trees, such as oaks (*Quercus*) and poplars (*Populus*). Even pine seeds cannot be stored indefinitely and must eventually be grown out as trees. Preservation of natural areas where commercial species occur is increasingly being considered as a way of protecting the genetic variability needed for forestry. International cooperation is needed in forestry research and conservation because commercial species are often grown far from their countries of origin; for example, loblolly pine and slash pine (*Pinus elliottii*) from the United States are planted on 2.8 million ha of land in Africa, Asia, and Latin America, and Monterey pine (*Pinus radiata*) from the United States is planted on 3 million ha in Chile, New Zealand, Australia, and Spain.

Conservation Categories of Species

To highlight the status of rare species for conservation purposes, IUCN-The World Conservation Union has established the following five conservation categories (IUCN 1984, 1988); species in categories 2–4 are considered to be "threatened" with extinction. These categories have proved useful at the national and international levels by directing attention toward species of special concern and by identifying species threatened with extinction for protection through international agreements such as the Convention on International Trade in Endangered Species (CITES).

1. **Extinct:** Species (and other taxa, such as subspecies and varieties) that are no longer known to exist in the wild. Searches of the localities where they were once found and of other possible sites have failed to detect these species.
2. **Endangered:** Species that have a high likelihood of going extinct in the near future. Included are species whose numbers have been reduced to the point that the survival of the species is unlikely if present trends continue.
3. **Vulnerable:** Species that may become endangered in the near future because their populations are decreasing in size throughout their range. The long-term viability of vulnerable species is not certain.
4. **Rare:** Species that have small total numbers of individuals, often due to limited geographical ranges or low population densities. Although these species may not face any immediate danger, their small numbers make them likely candidates to become endangered.
5. **Insufficiently known:** Species that probably belong in one of the conservation categories but are not sufficiently well known to be assigned to a specific category.

Using the IUCN categories, the World Conservation Monitoring Centre (WCMC) has evaluated and described the threats to about 60,000 plant and 2000 animal species in its series of Red Data Books (Table 3.1; IUCN 1990). The great majority of the species on these lists are plants, reflecting the recent trend of listing plant species in threatened habitats. However, there are also numerous listed species of fish (343), amphibians (50), reptiles (170), invertebrates (1355), birds (1037), and mammals (497). The IUCN system has been applied to specific geographical areas as a way of highlighting conservation priorities. Malaysia provides an example (Kiew 1991):

• Of 2830 tree species in peninsular Malaysia, 511 species are considered threatened.

- A large number of Malaysian herb species are endemic to single localities, such as mountaintops, streams, waterfalls, or limestone outcrops. These species are threatened with extinction if their habitat is destroyed.

- All five species of sea turtles in Malaysia are considered endangered due to a combination of habitat loss, egg collecting, hunting, pollution of marine waters, unregulated tourism, and entanglement in fishing nets.

- Thirty-five Malaysian bird species are listed as threatened, and many more species have experienced population declines associated with habitat destruction.

- Over 80% of Malaysian Borneo's primate species are under some threat, due to a combination of habitat destruction and hunting.

To help focus attention on the threatened species most in need of immediate conservation efforts, IUCN issues lists of the world's "most threatened" plants and animals (Cahn and Cahn 1985). These lists include species of unique conservation value. Among the animals are the kago, a rare flightless bird that is the symbol of New Caledonia; the komprey, a primitive wild ox from Southeast Asia that has been hunted to near extinction; and the Orinoco River crocodile, which has been decimated by illegal trade in hides.

The IUCN categories and WCMC Red Data Books are an excellent first step toward protecting the world's species; however, certain difficulties exist in using the category system (Fitter and Fitter 1987). First, each listed species must be studied to determine its population size and the

Table 3.1
Percentage of species in some temperate countries that are threatened with global extinction

Country	Mammals Number of species	Mammals Percent threatened[a]	Birds Number of species	Birds Percent threatened[a]	Reptiles Number of species	Reptiles Percent threatened[a]	Amphibians Number of species	Amphibians Percent threatened[a]	Plants Number of species	Plants Percent threatened[a]
Argentina	255	10.2	927	1.9	204	3.4	124	0.8	9,000	1.7
Canada	163	4.9	434	1.6	32	3.1	40	0	3,220	0.3
Japan	186	4.8	632	3.0	85	2.4	58	1.7	4,022	9.8
South Africa	279	7.2	774	1.7	299	1.0	95	1.1	23,000	5.0
United States[b]	367	10.3	1,090	6.1	368	4.6	222	6.3	20,000	8.5

Source: Data from WRI/IIED 1988; Groombridge 1992.
[a] Threatened species include those in the IUCN categories endangered, vulnerable, and rare.
[b] Includes Pacific and Caribbean islands.

trend in its numbers. Such studies can be difficult, expensive, and time-consuming. Second, a species must be studied over its whole range, which may present logistical difficulties. Third, the IUCN categories are not suitable for most tropical insect species, which are poorly known taxonomically and biologically, yet are threatened with extinction as rain forests are cut down. Fourth, species are often listed as endangered even if they have not been seen for many years, presumably on the assumption that they will be relocated if a thorough search is made. As an example, a survey of the natural history of the Indonesian island of Sulawesi showed that many endemic fish and bird species had not been seen for several decades; their status was unknown and they were not listed in the Red Data Books (Whitten et al. 1987). In such situations, species that have not been seen for many years and whose habitats have been heavily damaged by human activity should probably be listed as extinct or endangered until field studies have been undertaken to determine their true status (Diamond 1987).

The most serious problem with the IUCN system is that the criteria for assigning species to particular categories are subjective. With greater numbers of people and organizations involved in assigning and evaluating threat categories, there is a potential for species to be arbitrarily assigned to particular categories. To remedy this situation, Mace and Lande (1991) have proposed a three-level system of classification based on the probability of extinction:

1. *Critical species* have a 50% or greater probability of extinction within 5 years or 2 generations.
2. *Endangered species* have a 20–50% probability of extinction within 20 years or 10 generations.
3. *Vulnerable species* have a 10–20% probability of extinction within 100 years.

The criteria for assigning these categories are based on the developing methods of population viability analysis and focus particularly on population trends and habitat condition. For example, a critical species has two or more of the following characteristics: a total breeding population size of fewer than 50 individuals, fewer than two populations containing more than 25 breeding individuals, more than a 20% decline in population numbers within 2 years or 50% within one generation, or a population that is subject to catastrophic crashes every 5–10 years in which half or more of the population dies. Species can also be assigned critical status as a result of observed or predicted habitat loss, ecological imbalance, or commercial exploitation. Using this approach, as many as 43% of all vertebrate species can be considered to be under some degree of extinction threat (Mace 1994). The advantage of this proposed system is that it provides a standard method by which decisions can be reviewed and evaluated by other scientists according to accepted quantitative criteria and using whatever information is available. However, this method can still become arbitrary when decisions have to be made without sufficient data.

Legal Protection of Species

National laws

Legal means can be used at the local, national, and international levels to protect all aspects of biological diversity. Many national laws are specifically targeted toward preserving species. In the United States, the principal law protecting species is the Endangered Species Act of 1973 (Endangered Species Coalition 1992). This legislation has been a model for other countries, though its implementation has often been controversial (Rohlf 1989, 1991; Clark et al. 1994; Chadwick 1995).

The Endangered Species Act was created by the U.S. Congress to "provide a means whereby the ecosystems upon which endangered species and threatened species depend may be conserved (and) to provide a program for the conservation of such species." Species are protected under the Act if they are placed on an official list of endangered and threatened species. As defined by the law, endangered species are those likely to become extinct, as a result of human activities or natural causes, in all or a major portion of their range, while threatened species are those likely to become endangered in the near future. The Secretary of the Interior, acting through the U.S. Fish and Wildlife Service, and the Secretary of Commerce, acting through the National Marine Fisheries Service (NMFS), can add and remove species from the list based on information available to them. In addition, a recovery plan is required for each listed species. More than 900 species in the United States have been placed on the list, as well as about 500 species from elsewhere in the world. The Act requires all U.S. government agencies to consult with the Fish and Wildlife Service and the NMFS to determine whether their activities will affect listed species, and prohibits activities that will harm those species or their habitat. The law also prevents private individuals, businesses, and local governments from harming or "taking" listed species, and prohibits all trade in listed species.

In the two decades since its enactment, the Endangered Species Act has become increasingly important as a conservation tool. The Act has provided the legal basis for protecting some of the most significant animal species in the United States, such as the grizzly bear, the bald eagle, the whooping crane, and the gray wolf. Because the law protects the ecosystems in which endangered species live, entire biological communities and thousands of other species have in effect been protected at the same time (Orians 1993). The Act has also become a source of contention between conservation and business interests in the United States. The protection afforded to listed species is so strong that business interests often lobby vigorously against the listing of species in their area. At the present time 3700 species are candidates for listing; while awaiting official decisions, some of these species have probably become extinct (Horton 1992). One reason that business leaders are reluctant to allow new species to be added to the list is the difficulty of rehabilitating species to the point at which they can be removed from the list. So far only 5 of 749 listed species have been taken off the list, the most notable successes being the brown pelican and the American alligator. In 1994 the bald eagle was moved from the highly regulated "endangered" category to the less critical "threatened" category in recognition that its numbers had increased from 400 breeding pairs in the 1960s to the current 4000. The difficulty of implementing recovery plans is often not primarily biological, but to a large extent political, administrative, and ultimately financial. The U.S. Fish and Wildlife Service annually spends less than $50 million on activities related to the Act, but a recent estimate suggests that over $4 billion is needed to remove the threat of extinction from all listed species.

Pro-business groups have been formed that use environmental-sounding rhetoric to argue against the Endangered Species Act and for the "wise use" of natural resources. In an attempt to find compromises between the economic interests of the country and conservation priorities, the Endangered Species Act was amended in 1978 to allow a Cabinet-level committee, the so-called "God Squad," to exclude areas from protection. The clash of interests is illustrated dramatically by the controversy over the designation of 2.8 million ha of old-growth forest in the Pacific Northwest, potentially worth billions of dollars, as critical protected habitat for the northern spotted owl (Figure 3.26). Limitations on logging in this region, strongly advocated by environmental organizations, have been fiercely resisted by business and citizen groups as well as by many politicians. After years of negotiations, legal maneuvering, and political lobbying, a solution to this ongoing controversy still has not been found. Recognition that intact watersheds are needed to maintain salmon populations and the valuable commercial and sport fisheries they support may eventually tip the balance toward the preservation of these forests.

Concerns about the implications of the Endangered Species Act have often forced business organizations, conservation groups, and governments to develop compromise habitat conservation plans that reconcile conservation and business interests (Clark et al. 1994). In one such case, an innovative program in Riverside County, California, allows developers to build within the historic range of the endangered Stephen's kangaroo rat if they contribute to a fund that will be used to buy wildlife sanctuaries. Already, more than $25 million has been raised by this program, which has an eventual goal of $100 million. Large tracts of pine forest in the southeastern United States, formerly managed primarily for wood production, now have the conservation of the endangered red-cockaded

3.26 The northern spotted owl (*Strix occidentalis caurina*) is at the center of a conflict between the survival of species and ecosystems and economic interests. The owl's primary habitat is old-growth forest in the Pacific Northwest—a habitat coveted by the logging industry for its rich timber resources. This bird was photographed in a protected reserve in Mendocino, California. (Photograph by Jon Mark Stewart/Biological Photo Service.)

woodpecker as an additional management objective. Specific management strategies include protecting nesting trees and old-growth stands of preferred tree species and opening up the mid-canopy to make foraging easier for the birds. In these cases and others, the result is a compromise in which economic activities proceed but pay a higher cost to support conservation activities.

An analysis of the U.S. Endangered Species Act shows a number of revealing trends. The great majority of species listed under the Act are plants and vertebrates, despite the fact that most species are insects and other invertebrates. About half of the 300 freshwater mussel species found in the United States are declining, in danger of extinction, or already extinct, yet only 56 species are listed under the Act (Stolzenburg 1992; Chadwick 1995). Clearly, greater efforts must be made to study the various invertebrate groups and extend listing to endangered species whenever necessary. Another study of species covered by the Act has shown that animals have only about 1000 remaining individuals at the time of listing, and plants have fewer than 120 individuals remaining (Wilcove et al. 1993). Populations this small may encounter the genetic and demographic problems associated with small population size that can prevent recovery. At the extreme were 39 species listed when they had 10 or fewer individuals remaining, and a freshwater mussel that was listed when it had only a single remaining population that was not reproducing. Endangered species probably should be given protection under the Act before they decline to the point at which recovery becomes difficult. An earlier listing of a declining species might allow it to recover and become a candidate for de-listing more quickly. There is certainly potential for the Endangered Species Act to be used more widely and more effectively to protect biological diversity. Despite its value and success, business and political groups are actively working to weaken the Endangered Species Act, remove its funding, and even block its renewal. If this happens, it will represent a tremendous setback for species threatened with extinction.

International agreements

The protection of biological diversity needs to be addressed at multiple levels of government. While the major control mechanisms that presently exist in the world are based within individual countries, agreements at the international level are increasingly being used to protect species and habitats. International cooperation is an absolute requirement for several crucial reasons. First, species often migrate across international borders. Conservation efforts to protect migratory bird species in northern Europe will not work if the birds' overwintering habitat in Africa is destroyed.

Second, international trade in biological products can result in the overexploitation of species to supply the demand. Control and management of the trade are required at the points of both export and import.

Third, the benefits of biological diversity are of international importance. Wealthy countries of the temperate zone that benefit from tropical biological diversity need to be willing to help the less wealthy countries of the world that preserve it.

Finally, many of the problems that threaten species and ecosystems are international in scope and require international cooperation to solve. Such threats include overfishing and overhunting, atmospheric pollution and acid rain, pollution of lakes, rivers, and oceans, global climate change, and ozone depletion.

The single most important treaty protecting species at an international level is the Convention on International Trade in Endangered Species (CITES), established in 1973 in association with the United Nations Environmental Programme (UNEP) (Wijnstekers 1992; Hemley 1994). The treaty is currently endorsed by more than 120 countries. CITES establishes lists of species whose international trade is to be controlled; the member countries agree to restrict trade in and destructive exploitation of those species (Fitzgerald 1989). Appendix I of the treaty includes approximately 675 animals and plants whose commercial trade is prohibited, and Appendix II includes about 3700 animals and 21,000 plants whose international trade is regulated and monitored. Among plants, Appendixes I and II cover such important horticultural species as orchids, cycads, cacti, carnivorous plants, and tree ferns; increasingly they cover timber species as well. Among animals, closely regulated groups include parrots, large cat species, whales, sea turtles, birds of prey, rhinoceroses, bears, primates, species collected for the pet, zoo, and aquarium trades, and species harvested for their fur, skin, or other commercial products.

International treaties such as CITES are implemented when a country signing the treaties passes laws making it a criminal act to violate them. Once CITES laws are passed within a country, police, customs inspectors, wildlife officers, and other government agents can arrest and prosecute individuals possessing or trading in CITES listed species and seize the products or organisms involved. Technical advice to countries is provided by IUCN-The World Conservation Union Wildlife Trade Specialist Group, the World Wide Fund for Nature (WWF) TRAFFIC Network, and the World Conservation Monitoring Centre (WCMC) Wildlife Trade Monitoring Unit. The CITES treaty's most notable success has been a ban on the ivory trade, which was causing severe declines in African elephant populations (Figure 3.27).

Another international treaty is the Convention on Conservation of Migratory Species of Wild Animals, signed in 1979, with a primary focus on bird species. This convention serves as an important complement to CITES by encouraging international efforts to conserve bird species that migrate across international borders and by emphasizing regional approaches to research, management, and hunting regulations. The problems with this convention are that only 36 countries have signed it and that its budget is very limited. It also does not cover other migratory species, such as marine mammals and fish.

Other important international agreements that protect species include

- The Convention on Conservation of Antarctic Marine Living Resources

- The International Convention for the Regulation of Whaling, which established the International Whaling Commission

- The International Convention for the Protection of Birds and the Benelux Convention on the Hunting and Protection of Birds

- The Convention on Fishing and Conservation of Living Resources in the Baltic Sea

- Miscellaneous agreements protecting specific groups of animals, such as prawns, lobsters, crabs, fur seals, salmon, and vicuña

A weakness of these international treaties is that participation is voluntary; countries can withdraw from the convention to pursue their own interests when they find the conditions of compliance too difficult (French

3.27 African elephants were declining at an alarming rate in many African countries until trade in ivory was banned by the CITES treaty. Illegal trade continues to endanger the animals; these tusks were confiscated from smugglers by the Parks Board of Natal. (Photograph by R. de la Harpe/Biological Photo Service.)

1994). This flaw was highlighted recently when several countries walked out on the International Whaling Commission because of its ban on hunting (Ellis 1992). Persuasion and public pressure are necessary to induce countries to enforce the provisions of the treaties and prosecute violators.

Summary

1. Biologists have observed that small populations have a greater tendency to go extinct than large populations. The minimum viable population size (MVP) is the number of individuals necessary to ensure that a population has a high probability of surviving for the foreseeable future.

2. Small populations are subject to rapid extinction for three main reasons: loss of genetic variability and inbreeding depression, demographic fluc-

tuations; and environmental variation combined with natural catastrophes. The combined effects of these factors have been compared to a vortex that tends to drive small populations to extinction. Population viability analysis uses demographic, genetic, environmental, and natural catastrophe data to estimate a population's MVP and its probability of persistence in an environment.

3. Conservation biologists often determine whether an endangered species is stable, increasing, fluctuating, or declining by monitoring its populations. Often the key to protecting and managing a rare or endangered species is an understanding of its natural history. Some rare species are more accurately described as metapopulations in which a mosaic of temporary populations is linked by some degree of migration and recolonization.

4. New populations of rare and endangered species can be established in the wild using either captive-raised or wild-caught individuals. Mammals and birds raised in captivity may require social and behavioral training before release, and often require some degree of maintenance after release. Reintroduction of plant species requires a different approach because of their specialized environmental requirements at the seed and seedling stages.

5. Some species that are in danger of going extinct in the wild can be maintained in zoos, aquariums, and botanical gardens; this strategy is known as ex situ conservation. These captive colonies can sometimes be used later to reestablish species in the wild.

6. To highlight the status of species for conservation purposes, IUCN-The World Conservation Union has established five main conservation categories: extinct, endangered, vulnerable, rare, and insufficiently known. This system of classification is now widely used to evaluate the status of species and establish conservation priorities.

7. One of the most effective laws in the United States for protecting species is the Endangered Species Act of 1973. This law, the renewal of which is under debate, is often at the center of controversy between environmental interests and economic interests.

8. International agreements and conventions on the protection of biological diversity are needed because species migrate across borders, because there is an international trade in biological products, because the benefits of biological diversity are of international importance, and because the threats to diversity are often international in scope. The Convention on International Trade in Endangered Species (CITES) was enacted to regulate and monitor trade in endangered species.

Suggested Readings

Akçakaya, H. R. 1994. *RAMAS/GIS: Linking Landscape Data with Population Viability Analysis* (Version 1.0). Applied Biomathematics, Setauket, N.Y. Software that can be used to teach, demonstrate, and analyze mathematical aspects of conservation biology at the population and landscape levels.

Bowles, M. L. and C. J. Whelan (eds.). 1994. *Restoration of Endangered Species: Conceptual Issues, Planning, and Implementation.* Cambridge University Press, Cambridge. Good mixture of case studies, reviews, and analysis.

Chadwick, D. H. 1995. Dead or alive: The Endangered Species Act. *National Geographic* 187 (March): 2–41. History of the ESA, highlighting successes and controversies.

Clark, T. W. R. P. Reading and A. L. Clark. 1994. *Endangered Species Recovery: Finding the Lessons, Improving the Process.* Island Press, Washington, D.C. Administrative and political considerations are surprisingly important in the conservation of many high-profile species.

Given, D. 1994. *Principles and Practices of Plant Conservation.* Timber Press, Portland, OR. Review of current botanical approaches.

Goldsmith, B. (ed.). 1991. *Monitoring for Conservation and Ecology.* Chapman and Hall, New York. The purpose and methods of conservation monitoring, clearly explained.

Kleiman, D. G. 1989. Reintroduction of captive mammals for conservation. *BioScience* 39: 152–161. Outstanding outline of mammal reintroduction efforts, with many examples.

Loeschcke, V., J. Tomiuk and S. K. Jain (eds.). 1994. *Conservation Genetics.* Birkhauser Verlag, Basel. The current state of knowledge in this important field.

Primack, R. B. and P. Hall. 1992. Biodiversity and forest change in Malaysian Borneo. *BioScience* 42: 829–837. The conservation, policy, and management implications of tropical community studies. See also the other monitoring studies in the same issue.

Rhoades, R. E. 1991. World's food supply at risk. *National Geographic* 179 (April): 74–105. A beautifully illustrated popular account of the decline of traditional agricultural varieties and the need for seed banks.

Soulé, M. E. (ed.). 1987. *Viable Populations for Conservation.* Cambridge University Press, Cambridge. Leading authorities discuss the problems of small populations.

TRAFFIC USA. World Wildlife Fund, Washington, D.C. An informative newsletter covering the international trade in wildlife and wildlife products, with an emphasis on CITES activities.

CHAPTER 4

Conservation at the Community Level

P RESERVING INTACT BIOLOGICAL COMMUNITIES is the most effective way to preserve overall biological diversity. One could even argue that it is ultimately the only way to preserve species, because we have the resources and knowledge to maintain only a small minority of the world's species in captivity. Three means of preserving biological communities are the establishment of protected areas, the implementation of conservation measures outside protected areas, and the restoration of biological communities in degraded habitats.

Biological communities vary from a few that are virtually unaffected by human activities, such as communities found on the ocean floor or in the most remote parts of the Amazon rain forest, to those that are heavily modified by human activity, such as agricultural land, cities, and artificial ponds. But even in the most remote areas of the world, human influence is apparent in the form of rising carbon dioxide levels and the collection of valuable natural products, and even in the most modified of human environments there are often remnants of the original biota. Habitats with intermediate levels of disturbance present some of the most interesting challenges and opportunities for conservation biology because they often cover large areas. Considerable biological diversity may remain in selectively logged tropical forests, heavily fished oceans and seas, and grasslands grazed by domestic livestock (Western 1989). When a conservation area is established, the right compromise must be found between protecting biological diversity and ecosystem function and satisfying the immediate and long-term needs of the local human community and the national government for resources.

Protected Areas

One of the most critical steps in preserving biological communities is the establishment of legally designated protected areas. While legislation and purchases of land do not by themselves ensure habitat preservation, they represent an important starting point.

Protected areas can be established in a variety of ways, but the two most common mechanisms are government action (often at a national level, but also at a regional or local level) and purchases of land carried out by private individuals and conservation organizations. Governments can set aside land for protected areas and enact laws that allow varying degrees of commercial resource use, traditional use by local people, and recreational use in those areas. Many protected areas have also been established by private conservation organizations, such as The Nature Conservancy and the Audubon Society (Grove 1988). An increasingly common pattern is that of a partnership between the government of a developing country and international conservation organizations, multinational banks, and governments of developed countries; in such partnerships the conservation organizations often provide funding, training, and scientific and management expertise to assist the developing country in establishing a new protected area. The pace of this collaboration is accelerating due to the new funding provided by the Global Environment Facility (GEF) created by the World Bank and agencies of the United Nations (see Chapter 5).

Protected areas have also been established by traditional societies that wish to maintain their way of life. National governments have recognized traditional societies' rights to land in many countries, including the United States, Canada, Brazil, and Malaysia, though often not before conflict in the courts, in the press, and on the land under debate. In many cases, assertions of local rights to traditional lands have involved violent confrontations with the existing authorities seeking to develop the land, sometimes with loss of life (Poffenberger 1990; Gadgil and Guha 1992).

Once land comes under protection, decisions must be made regarding how much human disturbance will be allowed. IUCN-The World Conservation Union has developed a system of classification for protected areas that covers a range from minimal to intensive use of the habitat by humans (IUCN 1984, 1985; McNeely et al. 1994):

I. Strict nature reserves and wilderness areas are strictly protected areas maintained for scientific study, education, and environmental monitoring. These reserves allow populations of species to be maintained and ecosystem processes to continue in as undisturbed a state as possible.

II. National parks are large areas of scenic and natural beauty maintained to provide protection for one or more ecosystems and for scientific, educational, and recreational use; they are not usually used for commercial extraction of resources.

III. National monuments and landmarks are smaller reserves designed to preserve unique biological, geological, or cultural features of special interest.

IV. Managed wildlife sanctuaries and nature reserves are similar to strict nature reserves, but some human manipulation may be carried out to maintain the characteristics of the community. Some controlled harvesting may be permitted.

V. Protected landscapes and seascapes allow nondestructive traditional uses of the environment by resident people, particularly where these uses have produced an area of distinctive cultural, aesthetic, and ecological characteristics. Such places provide special opportunities for tourism and recreation.

VI. Resource reserves are areas in which natural resources are preserved for the future and in which resource use is controlled in ways compatible with national policies.

VII. Natural biotic areas and anthropological reserves allow traditional societies to continue to maintain their way of life without outside interference. Often these people hunt and extract resources for their own use and practice traditional agriculture.

VIII. Multiple-use management areas allow for sustainable uses of natural resources, including water, wildlife, grazing for livestock, timber, tourism, and fishing. Often the preservation of biological communities is compatible with these activities.

Of these categories, the first five can be considered truly **protected areas,** with the habitat managed primarily for biological diversity. Areas in the last three categories are not managed primarily for biological diversity, though this may be a secondary management goal. These **managed areas** may be particularly significant because they are often much larger than protected areas, because they still may contain many or even most of their original species, and because protected areas are often embedded in a matrix of managed areas.

Existing protected areas

As of 1993, a total of 8,619 protected areas had been designated worldwide, covering a total of 7,922,660 km^2 (Table 4.1; WRI/UNEP/UNDP 1994). The world's largest single park is in Greenland and covers 700,000 km^2. Although this amount of protected area may seem impressive, it rep-

Table 4.1

Protected and managed areas in the world's geographical regions

Region	Protected areas (IUCN categories I–V)			Managed areas (IUCN categories VI–VIII)		
	Number of areas	Size (km^2)	Percent of land area	Number of areas	Size (km^2)	Percent of land area
Africa	704	1,388,930	4.6	1,562	746,360	2.5
Asia[a]	2,181	1,211,610	4.4	1,149	306,290	1.1
North and Central America	1,752	2,632,500	11.7	243	161,470	0.7
South America	667	1,145,960	6.4	679	2,279,350	12.7
Europe	2,177	455,330	9.3	143	40,350	0.8
U.S.S.R. (former)	218	243,300	1.1	1	4,000	0
Oceania[b]	920	845,040	9.9	91	50,000	0.6
World[c]	8,619	7,922,660	5.9	3,868	3,588,480	2.7

Source: WRI/UNEP/UNDP 1994.

[a] Not including the former U.S.S.R.

[b] Australia, New Zealand, and the Pacific Islands.

[c] Not including Antarctica.

resents only 5.9% of the Earth's land surface. Only 3.5% of the Earth's land surface is in the strictly protected categories of scientific reserves and national parks. Coverage by protected areas is greatest in North and Central America and Oceania, and least in the former Soviet Union. The proportion of land in protected areas varies dramatically among countries, with high proportions of land protection in countries such as Germany (24.6%), Austria (25.3%), and the United Kingdom (18.9%), but surprisingly low proportions in others, including Russia (1.2%), Greece (0.8%), and Turkey (0.3%). The figures for individual countries and continents are only approximations because sometimes the laws protecting national parks and wildlife sanctuaries are not actually enforced, and sometimes sections of resource reserves and multiple-use management areas are carefully protected in practice. Examples of the latter are the sections within U.S. National Forests designated as wilderness areas.

Protected areas will never cover more than a small percentage of the Earth's land surface—perhaps 7%–10% or slightly more—due to the perceived needs of human society for natural resources. The establishment of new protected areas peaked in the 1970–1975 period and has been declining since then, probably because remaining land has already been designated for other purposes (McNeely et al. 1994). Many protected areas are located on land considered to be of little economic value. This limited area of protected habitat emphasizes the biological significance of the land that is managed for resource production. In the United States, the Forest Service and the Bureau of Land Management together manage 23.5% of the land, while in Costa Rica about 17% of the land is managed as forest and Indian reserves.

The effectiveness of protected areas

If protected areas cover only a small percentage of the Earth, how effective will they be at preserving the world's species? Concentrations of species occur at particular places in the landscape: along elevational gradients, at places where different geological formations are juxtaposed, in areas that are geologically old, and at places that have an abundance of critical natural resources (e.g., water holes; salt licks) (Terborgh 1986; Bibby et al. 1992; Carroll 1992). Often a landscape contains large expanses of a fairly uniform habitat type and only a few small areas of rare habitat types. Protecting biological diversity in this case will probably not depend so much on preserving large areas of the common habitat type as on including representatives of all the habitat types in a system of protected areas. The following examples illustrate the potential effectiveness of protected areas of limited extent.

- The Indonesian government plans to protect populations of all native bird and primate species within its system of national parks and reserves (IUCN/UNEP 1986). This goal will be accomplished by increasing the extent of protected areas from 3.5% to about 10% of Indonesia's land area.

- In most of the large tropical African countries, the majority of the native bird species have populations inside protected areas (Table 4.2). For example, Zaire has over 1000 bird species, and 89% of them occur in the 3.9% of the land area under protection. Similarly, 85% of Kenya's birds are protected in the 5.4% of the land area included in parks (Sayer and Stuart 1988).

- A dramatic example of the importance of small protected areas is Santa Rosa Park in northwestern Costa Rica. This park covers only 0.2% of the area of Costa Rica, yet it contains breeding populations of 55% of the country's 135 species of sphingid moths. Santa Rosa Park is included within the new 82,500 ha Guanacaste National Park, which is predicted to contain populations of almost every sphingid moth (Janzen 1988b).

These examples clearly show that well-selected protected areas can include many, if not most, of the species in a country. However, the long-term future of many species in these reserves remains in doubt. Popula-

Table 4.2
Percentage of bird species found within protected areas for
selected African nations

Country	Percentage of national land area protected	Number of bird species	Percentage of bird species found in protected areas
Cameroon	3.6	848	76.5
Côte d'Ivoire	6.2	683	83.2
Ghana	5.1	721	77.4
Kenya	5.4	1064	85.3
Malawi	11.3	624	77.7
Nigeria	1.1	831	86.5
Somalia	0.5	639	47.3
Tanzania	12.0	1016	82.0
Uganda	6.7	989	89.0
Zaire	3.9	1086	89.0
Zambia	8.6	728	87.5
Zimbabwe	7.1	635	91.5

Source: From Sayer and Stuart 1988.

tions of many species may be so reduced in size that their eventual fate is
extinction (Janzen 1986b). Consequently, while the number of species existing in a relatively new park is important as an indicator of the park's
potential, the real value of the park is its ability to support viable long-
term populations of species. In this regard, the size of the park and the
way it is managed are critical.

Establishing Priorities for Protection

In a crowded world with limited funding, priorities must be established
for conserving biological diversity and, most importantly, individual
species. While some conservationists would argue that no species should
ever be lost, the reality is that species are being lost every day. The real
question is how this loss of species can be minimized given the financial
and human resources available. The interrelated questions that must be
addressed by conservation planners are: *What* needs to be protected, *where*
should it be protected, and *how* should it be protected (Erwin 1991; Johnson, in press). Three criteria can be used in setting conservation priorities
for the protection of species and communities.

 1. **Distinctiveness.** A biological community is given higher priority
    for conservation if it is composed primarily of rare endemic species
    than if it is composed primarily of common, widespread species. A

4.1 Whooping cranes, which number only 155 individuals, are of greater conservation concern than sandhill cranes, which number about 500,000. One experimental strategy for preserving whooping cranes involved placing "extra" whooping crane eggs in the nests of wild sandhill cranes (the gray birds) at the Bosque del Apache Refuge in New Mexico. The whooping cranes (the white bird) grew to healthy adulthood, but failed to learn the species-specific behaviors they needed to mate with other whooping cranes and raise their own young. (Photograph © Art Wolfe.)

   species is often given more conservation value if it is taxonomically unique—that is, the only species in its genus or family—than if it is a member of a genus with many species (Faith 1994: Vane-Wright et al. 1994).

2. **Endangerment.** Species in danger of extinction are of greater concern than species that are not threatened with extinction; thus the whooping crane, with only about 155 individuals, is of greater concern than the sandhill crane, with approximately 500,000 individuals (Figure 4.1). Biological communities threatened with imminent destruction are also given priority.

3. **Utility.** Species that have present or potential value to people are given more conservation value than species of no obvious use to people. For example, wild relatives of wheat, which are potentially useful in developing improved cultivated varieties, are given a higher priority than species of grass that are not known to be related to any economically important plant.

The Komodo dragon of Indonesia (Figure 4.2) is an example of a species that would be a conservation priority using all three criteria: it is the world's largest lizard (distinctive); it occurs on only a few small islands of a rapidly developing nation (endangered); and it has major potential as

4.2 The carnivorous Komodo dragon of Indonesia is the largest living monitor lizard; many people feel it has unique status, and that protecting this endangered species is a conservation priority. (Photograph by Jessie Cohen, National Zoological Park, Smithsonian Institution.)

a tourist attraction, as well as being of great scientific interest (utility). Using these criteria, several priority systems have been developed at both national and international scales to target both species and communities (Johnson, in press). These approaches are generally complementary, with each one giving a different perspective.

Species approaches

Protected areas can be established to conserve unique species. Many national parks have been created to protect the "charismatic megafauna" that capture public attention, have symbolic value, and are crucial to ecotourism. In the process of protecting these species, whole communities that may consist of thousands of other species are also protected. For example, Project Tiger in India was started in 1973 after a census revealed that the Indian tiger was in imminent danger of extinction. Project Tiger has helped to provide attention, funding, and a management philosophy for national parks in India. The establishment of 18 Project Tiger reserves, combined with strict protection measures, has halted the decline in the number of tigers (Panwar 1987; Ward 1992).

Identification of high-priority species is the first step in developing survival plans for individual species. In the Americas, the Natural Heritage Programs and Conservation Data Centers associated with government agencies are acquiring data on the past and present distribution and ecology of rare and endangered species from all 50 U.S. states, 3 Canadian provinces, and

13 Latin American countries (Master 1991). This information is being used to target new localities for conservation. Another important program is the IUCN Species Survival Commission's Action Plans. About 2000 scientists have been organized into 80 specialist groups to provide evaluations and recommendations for mammals, birds, invertebrates, reptiles, fishes, and plants (Stuart 1987; Species Survival Commission 1990). One group, for example, produced an Action Plan for Asian primates, in which priority rankings were developed for 64 species based on degree of threat, taxonomic uniqueness, and association with other threatened primates (Eudey 1987). Areas needed to protect these primates were highlighted for the benefit of policy makers and conservation organizations.

Community and ecosystem approaches

A number of conservationists have argued that communities and ecosystems, rather than species, should be the target of conservation efforts (McNaughton 1989; Scott et al. 1991; Reid 1992; Grumbine 1994b). Conservation of communities can preserve large numbers of species in a self-maintaining unit, whereas targeted species rescues are often difficult, expensive, and ineffective. Spending $1 million on habitat protection and management might preserve more species in the long run than spending the same amount on an intensive effort to save just one conspicuous species.

Global priorities for new protected areas in developing countries need to be established so that resources and personnel are directed to the most critical needs. Such an allocation process might reduce the tendency of international funding agencies, tropical scientists, and development officers to cluster together in a few politically stable, accessible countries with high-profile conservation projects. Establishing global conservation priorities is more important now than ever because the amount of money available to acquire and manage new national parks is increasing substantially as a result of the creation of the Global Environment Facility and new conservation trust funds. The GEF is providing $1.2 billion over three years for environmental projects, with about a third of these funds allocated for biodiversity projects. Conservation biologists can play a valuable role in the allocation process by using their field experience to identify and recommend new areas suitable for preservation.

The placement of new protected areas should try to ensure that representatives of as many types of biological communities as possible are protected. Determining which areas of the world have adequate conservation protection and which urgently need additional protection is critical to the world conservation movement. Resources, research, and publicity must be directed to areas of the world that require additional protection. Regions throughout the world are being evaluated for the current percentage of area under protection, threats, need for action, and conservation importance (McNeely et al. 1994).

Gap analysis. One way to determine the effectiveness of ecosystem and community conservation programs is to compare biodiversity priorities with existing and proposed protected areas (Scott et al. 1991). This comparison can identify "gaps" in biodiversity preservation that need to be filled with new protected areas. On an international scale, this means protecting representative examples of all of the world's seven terrestrial biogeographic regions and 193 biological provinces. Although all seven biogeographic regions of the world have some protected areas (see Table 4.1), 10 of the 193 provinces have no protected areas, and 38 of the provinces have less than 1% of their area under protection (McNeely et al. 1994).

Establishment of priorities for marine conservation has lagged behind terrestrial conservation efforts. Urgent efforts are being made throughout the world to protect marine biological diversity in a way comparable to the terrestrial parks by establishing marine parks (Salm and Clark 1984; Kenchington and Agardy 1990), such as the Hol Chan Marine Reserve in Belize, which is proving invaluable to the rapidly growing ecotourism industry. The El Nido Marine Reserve along the coast of Palawan Island in the Philippines provides protection for the sea cow (also called the dugong), the hawksbill sea turtle, and the Ridley sea turtle. Worldwide, 977 marine and coastal protected areas have been established, protecting over 2 million km^2 (WRI/UNEP/UNDP 1994). About one-fourth of the 300 internationally recognized biosphere reserves worldwide include coastal or estuarine habitats (Ray and Gregg 1991). Protection of the nursery grounds of commercial species and recreational diving are among the main reasons for establishing these reserves (Moyle and Leidy 1992). Unfortunately, many of these reserves exist only on maps and receive little actual protection from overharvesting and pollution.

At the national level, biological diversity is protected most efficiently by ensuring that all major ecosystem types are included in a system of protected areas. In the United States, various federal and state agencies, often led by personnel from the Natural Heritage Programs, are involved in an intensive "bottom-up" effort to survey and classify ecosystems on a local level as part of a program to protect biological diversity. An alternative, "top-down" approach is to compare a detailed vegetation map with a map of lands under government protection (Crumpacker et al. 1988). In the United States, the most comprehensive ecosystem mapping has been based on the potential natural vegetation (PNV) system of Küchler (1964). PNV is defined as "the vegetation that would exist today if man were removed from the scene and if plant succession after his removal were telescoped into a single moment." The United States has 135 PNV types, such as spruce-cedar-hemlock forest and bluestem prairie. The distribution of these PNV types was compared with the 348 million ha of land owned and managed by U.S. government agencies, based on a map produced by the National Geographic Society. Nine of the 135 PNV types are not represented on federal lands, and 11 others are represented only by small areas; these types are either naturally rare or have been largely destroyed. Most of the unrepresented ecosystems are in central or southern Texas (e.g., mesquite savannah) and in Hawaii (e.g., mixed guava forest). These community types should be highlighted in conservation efforts and included if possible in new protected areas.

Geographic Information Systems (GIS) represent the latest development in gap analysis technology, using computers to integrate the wealth of data on the natural environment with information on species distributions (Scott et al. 1991; Sample 1994; Wright et al. 1994). GIS analyses make it possible to highlight critical areas that need to be included within national parks and areas that should be avoided by development projects. The basic GIS approach involves storing, displaying, and manipulating many types of mapped data, such as vegetation types, climate, soils, topography, geology, hydrology, and species distributions (Figure 4.3). This approach can highlight correlations among the abiotic and biotic elements of the landscape, help plan parks that include ecosystem diversity, and even suggest potential sites in which to search for rare species. Aerial

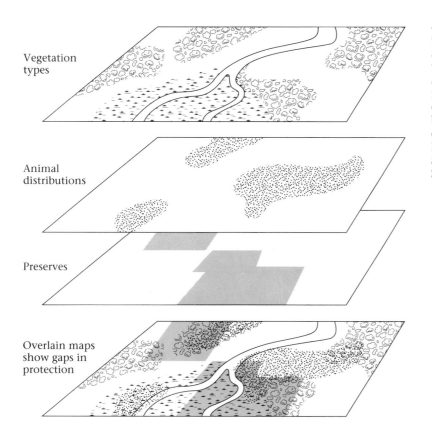

Vegetation types

Animal distributions

Preserves

Overlain maps show gaps in protection

4.3 Geographic Information Systems (GIS) provide a method for integrating a wide variety of data for analysis and display on maps. In this example, vegetation types, animal distributions, and preserved areas are overlapped to highlight areas that need additional protection. (After Scott et al. 1991.)

(A)

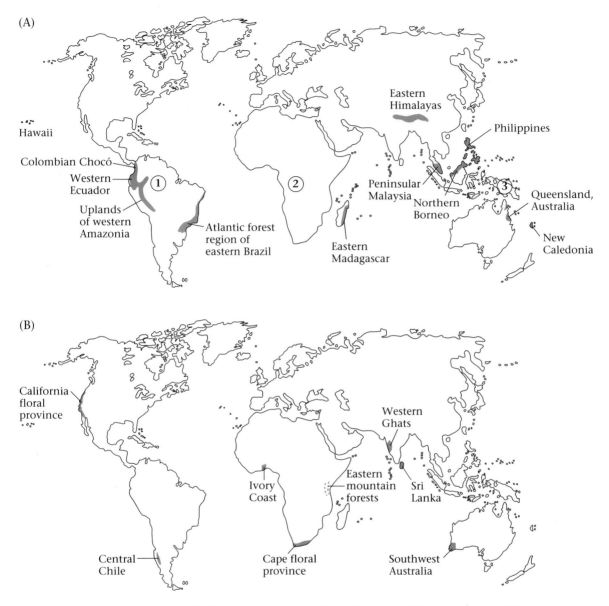

4.4 (A) Twelve tropical rain forest "hotspots"(shaded areas) of high endemism and significant threat of imminent extinctions. The circled numbers indicate the only three remaining tropical rain forest wilderness areas of any extent. (B) Eight "hotspots" in other climatic ecosystems. (Data from Myers 1988a, 1991a and Conservation International 1990.)

photographs and satellite imagery are additional sources of data for GIS analysis. In particular, a series of images taken over time can reveal patterns of habitat destruction that need prompt attention.

Centers of biodiversity. In order to establish priorities for conservation efforts, attempts have been made by IUCN-The World Conservation Union, the World Conservation Monitoring Centre, and others to identify key areas of the world that have great biological diversity and high levels of endemism and are under immediate threat of species extinctions and habitat destruction: so-called "hotspots" for preservation (Figure 4.4; Table 4.3). Using these criteria for rain forest plants, Myers (1988a) identified twelve tropical hotspots that together include 14% of the world's plant species in only 0.2% of its total land surface. This analysis was later expanded (Myers 1991a) to include eight nonforest habitats, four in the tropics and four outside of the tropics in Mediterranean-type climates. One such notable area is southern Africa, including South Africa, Lesotho, Swaziland, Namibia, and Botswana, which has 23,200 plant species, 80% of which are endemic to the region. Another valuable approach has been to identify twelve "megadiversity" countries that together contain 60%–70% of the world's biological diversity: Mexico, Colombia, Brazil, Peru, Ecuador, Zaire, Madagascar, Indonesia, Malaysia, India, China, and Australia. These countries are possible targets for increased funding and conservation attention (Table 4.4; Mittermeier 1988; Mittermeier and Werner 1990).

Table 4.3
Tropical rain forest "hotspots"

Hotspot	Original extent of forest (× 1000 ha)	Present extent of forest (× 1000 ha)	No. of plant species in original forest	Endemic species in original forest (percent)
New Caledonia	1,500	150	1,580	89
Madagascar	6,200	1,000	6,000	82
Atlantic Coast forest, Brazil	100,000	2,000	10,000	50
Philippines	25,000	800	8,500	44
Eastern Himalayas	34,000	5,300	9,000	39
Northern Borneo	19,000	6,400	9,000	39
Peninsular Malaysia	12,000	2,600	8,500	28
Western Ecuador	2,700	250	10,000	25
Colombian Chocó	10,000	7,200	10,000	25
Western Amazonia	10,000	3,500	20,000	25

Source: From Myers 1988a.

Table 4.4
"Top ten" countries with the largest number of species of selected well-known groups of organisms

Rank	Mammals	Birds	Amphibians	Reptiles	Swallowtail butteflies	Flowering plants[a]
1	Indonesia 515	Colombia 1721	Brazil 516	Mexico 717	Indonesia 121	Brazil 55,000
2	Mexico 449	Peru 1701	Colombia 407	Australia 686	China 99–104	Colombia 45,000
3	Brazil 428	Brazil 1622	Ecuador 358	Indonesia ca. 600	India 77	China 27,000
4	Zaire 409	Indonesia 1519	Mexico 282	Brazil 467	Brazil 74	Mexico 25,000
5	China 394	Ecuador 1447	Indonesia 270	India 453	Myanmar 68	Australia 23,000
6	Peru 361	Venezuela 1275	China 265	Colombia 383	Ecuador 64	So. Africa 21,000
7	Colombia 359	Bolivia ca. 1250	Peru 251	Ecuador 345	Colombia 59	Indonesia 20,000
8	India 350	India 1200	Zaire 216	Peru 297	Peru 58	Venezuela 20,000
9	Uganda 311	Malaysia ca. 1200	U.S.A. 205	Malaysia 294	Malaysia 55	Peru 20,000
10	Tanzania 310	China 1195	{ Venezuela Australia 197	{ Thailand Papua New Guinea 282	Mexico 52	U.S.S.R. (former) 20,000

Source: After Conservation International; data from numerous sources. Swallowtail data from Collins and Morris 1985. Data on flowering plants from Davis et al. 1986.
[a] Numbers of species given for flowering plants are estimates.

International priorities and global hotspots overlap considerably. There is general agreement on the need for increased conservation efforts in the following areas:

- *Latin America:* The coastal forests of Ecuador; the Atlantic Coast forest of Brazil

- *Africa:* The mountain forests of Tanzania and Kenya; the large lakes throughout the continent; the island of Madagascar

- *Asia:* Southwestern Sri Lanka; the eastern Himalayas; Indochina (Myanmar, Thailand, Cambodia, Laos, Vietnam, and southeastern China); the Philippines

- *Oceania:* New Caledonia

Additional priorities include the eastern and southern Brazilian Amazon, the uplands of the western Amazon, Colombia, Cameroon, equatorial West Africa, the Sudanian zone, Borneo, Sulawesi, Peninsular Malaysia, Bangladesh/Bhutan, eastern Nepal, and Hawaii.

Certain organisms can be used as biological diversity indicators when specific data about whole communities are unavailable. Diversity in birds, for example, is considered a good indicator of the diversity of a community. Several analyses have put this principle into practice. The IUCN Plant Conservation Office in England is identifying and documenting about 250 global centers of plant diversity with large concentrations of species (Groombridge 1992). The International Council for Bird Protection (ICBP) is identifying localities with large concentrations of birds that have restricted ranges (Bibby et al. 1992). To date 221 such localities, containing 2484 bird species, have been identified; 20% of these localities are not covered by protected areas. Many of them are islands and isolated mountain ranges that also have many endemic species of lizards, butterflies, and trees, and thus represent priorities for conservation.

Wilderness areas. Large areas of wilderness are important priorities for conservation efforts. Large blocks of land that have been minimally affected by human activity, that have a low human population density, and are not likely to be developed in the near future are perhaps the only places on Earth where the natural processes of evolution can continue. These wilderness areas can potentially remain as controls showing what natural communities are like with minimal human influence. In the United States, proponents of the Wildlands Project are advocating the management of whole ecosystems to preserve viable populations of large carnivores, such as grizzly bears, wolves, and large cats (Noss and Cooperrider 1994). Three tropical wilderness areas also have been identified and established as conservation priorities (see Figure 4.4A; McCloskey and Spaulding 1989; Conservation International 1990).

- *South America:* One arc of wilderness, containing rain forest, savannah, and mountains—but few people—runs through the southern Guianas, southern Venezuela, northern Brazil, Colombia, Ecuador, Peru, and Bolivia.

- *Africa:* A large area of equatorial Africa, centered on the Zaire basin, has a low population density and undisturbed habitat. This area includes large portions of Gabon, the Republic of the Congo, and Zaire.

- *New Guinea:* The island of New Guinea has the largest tracts of undisturbed forest in the Asian Pacific region, despite the effects of logging, mining, and transmigration programs. The eastern half of the island is the independent nation of Papua New Guinea, with 3.9 million people in 462,840 km^2. The western half of the island, Irian Jaya, is a state of Indonesia and has a population of only 1.4 million people in 345,670 km^2.

International agreements

Habitat conventions at the international level complement species conventions, such as CITES, by emphasizing unique ecosystem features that need to be protected. Within these habitats, multitudes of individual species can be protected. Three of the most important such conventions are the Ramsar Convention on Wetlands of International Importance Especially as Waterfowl Habitat, the Convention Concerning the Protection of the World Cultural and Natural Heritage, and the UNESCO Biosphere Reserves Programme (McNeely et al. 1990, 1994).

The Ramsar Convention on Wetlands was established in 1971 to halt the continued destruction of wetlands, particularly those that support migratory waterfowl, and to recognize the ecological, scientific, economic, cultural, and recreational values of wetlands (Kusler and Kentula 1990). The Ramsar Convention covers freshwater, estuarine, and coastal marine habitats, and includes more than 590 sites with a total area of over 37 million ha. The 61 signing countries agreed to conserve and protect their wetland resources and to designate for conservation purposes at least one wetland site of international significance.

The Convention Concerning the Protection of the World Cultural and Natural Heritage is associated with UNESCO, IUCN, and the International Council on Monuments and Sites (Thorsell and Sawyer 1992). This convention has received unusually wide support, with 109 countries participating, among the most of any conservation convention. The goal of the convention is to protect natural areas of international significance through its World Heritage Site program. The convention is unusual because it emphasizes the cultural as well as the biological significance of natural areas and recognizes that the world community has an obligation to support the sites financially. Included in the list of 100 World Heritage Sites are some of the world's premier conservation areas: Serengeti National Park (Tanzania), Sinharaja Forest Reserve (Sri Lanka), Iguaçu (Brazil), Manu National Park (Peru), Queensland Rain Forest (Australia), and Great Smokies National Park (U.S.).

UNESCO's Man and the Biosphere Program (MAB) created an international network of Biosphere Reserves in 1971. Biosphere Reserves are designed to be models demonstrating the compatibility of conservation efforts with sustainable development for the benefit of local people (see below). As of 1994, a total of 312 reserves had been created in more than 70 countries, covering about 1.7 million km², and including 44 reserves in the United States (Figure 4.5). The success of the Biosphere Reserve concept will depend on whether the sites can be successfully organized into a network that can address larger ecosystem and biodiversity questions at a regional and landscape level (Dyer and Holland 1991).

These three conventions establish an overarching consensus regarding appropriate conservation of general habitat types. More limited agreements protect unique ecosystems and habitats in particular regions, in-

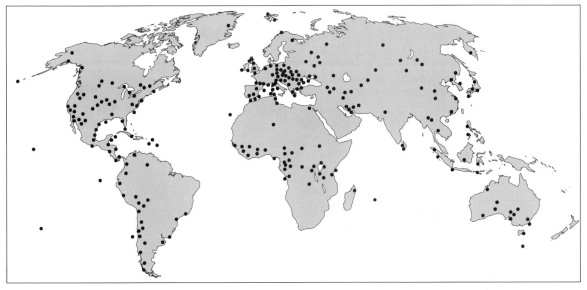

4.5 Locations of recognized Biosphere Reserves (dots). A lack of reserves is apparent in such biologically important regions as New Guinea, the Indian subcontinent, South Africa, and Amazonia. (Data from Groombridge 1992.)

cluding the Western Hemisphere, the Antarctic flora and fauna, the South Pacific, Africa, and European wildlife and natural habitat (WRI/UNEP /UNDP 1994). Other international agreements have been signed to prevent or limit pollution that poses regional and international threats to the environment. The Convention on Long-Range Trans-Boundary Air Pollution in the European Region recognizes the role that long-range transport of air pollution plays in acid rain, lake acidification, and forest dieback. The Convention on the Protection of the Ozone Layer was signed in 1985 to regulate and discourage the use of chlorofluorocarbons, which have been linked to the destruction of the ozone layer and a resulting increase in the levels of harmful ultraviolet light.

Marine pollution is another key area of concern because of the extensive areas of international waters not under national control and the ease with which pollutants released in one area can spread to another area (Norse 1993). Agreements covering marine pollution include the Convention on the Prevention of Marine Pollution by Dumping of Wastes and Other Matters, and the Regional Seas Conventions of the United Nations Environmental Programme (UNEP). Regional agreements cover the northeastern Atlantic, the Baltic, and other specific locations, particularly in the North Atlantic region.

Designing Protected Areas

The sizes and placement of protected areas throughout the world are often determined by the distribution of people, potential land values, and the

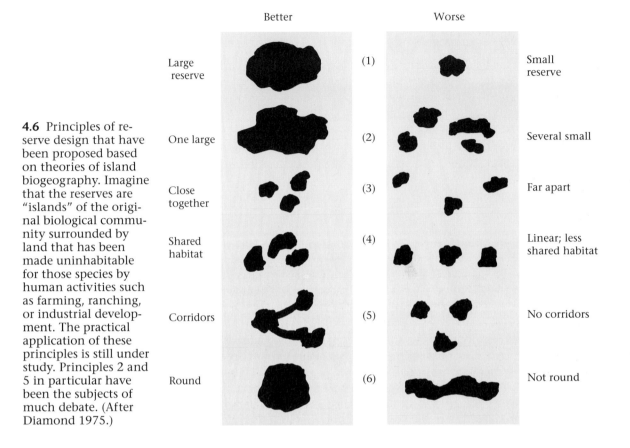

Better   Worse

Large reserve   (1)   Small reserve

One large   (2)   Several small

Close together   (3)   Far apart

Shared habitat   (4)   Linear; less shared habitat

Corridors   (5)   No corridors

Round   (6)   Not round

4.6 Principles of reserve design that have been proposed based on theories of island biogeography. Imagine that the reserves are "islands" of the original biological community surrounded by land that has been made uninhabitable for those species by human activities such as farming, ranching, or industrial development. The practical application of these principles is still under study. Principles 2 and 5 in particular have been the subjects of much debate. (After Diamond 1975.)

political efforts of conservation-minded citizens. In many cases, land is set aside for conservation protection because it has no immediate commercial value; these parks are sited on "the lands that nobody wanted" (Runte 1979; Pressey 1994). Although most parks and conservation areas have been acquired and created in this haphazard fashion, depending on the availability of money and land, a considerable body of ecological literature has been developed addressing the most efficient ways to design conservation areas to protect biological diversity (Figure 4.6; Shafer 1990; Murphy and Noon 1992). Many of the conclusions are derived from equilibrium theory, often using the island biogeographical model of MacArthur and Wilson (1967; see Chapter 2). The guidelines developed from this research have proved to be of great interest to governments, corporations, and private landowners who are being urged and mandated to manage their properties for both the commercial production of natural resources and biological diversity. However, conservation biologists have also been cautioned against trying to provide simple, general guidelines for designing nature reserves because every conservation situation requires special consideration (Ehrenfeld 1989). Key questions conservation biologists attempt to address include:

1. How large should nature reserves be to protect species?
2. Is it better to create a single large reserve or many smaller reserves?
3. How many individuals of an endangered species must be protected in a reserve to prevent extinction?
4. What is the best shape for a nature reserve?
5. When several reserves are created, should they be close together or far apart, and should they be isolated from one another or connected by corridors?

Reserve size

An early debate within conservation biology occurred over whether species richness is maximized in one large nature reserve or in several smaller ones of an equal total area (Diamond 1975; Simberloff and Abele 1976, 1982; Terborgh 1976); this is known in the literature as the "SLOSS debate" (single *large* or *several small*). For example, is it better to set aside one reserve of 10,000 ha, or four reserves of 2500 ha each? The proponents of large reserves argue that only large reserves can contain sufficient numbers of large, wide-ranging, low-density species (such as large carnivores) to maintain long-term populations (Figure 4.7). Also, a large reserve minimizes edge effects, encompasses more species, and has greater habitat diversity than a small reserve. These advantages of large parks follow from island biogeographical theory and have been demonstrated in numerous surveys of animals and plants in parks. There are three practical implications to this viewpoint. First, when a new park is being established, it should be made as large as possible in order to preserve as many species as possible. Second, when possible, additional land adjacent to nature reserves should be acquired in order to increase the area of existing parks. And finally, if there is a choice of creating a new small park or a new large park in similar habitat types, the large park should be created. On the other hand, once a park is larger than a certain size, the number of new species added with each increase in area starts to decline. In such a situation, creating a second large park some distance away may be a better strategy for preserving additional species than adding to the existing park.

The extreme proponents of large reserves argue that small reserves should not be maintained because their inability to support long-term populations gives them little value for conservation purposes. Opposing this viewpoint, other conservation biologists argue that well-placed small reserves are able to include a greater variety of habitat types and more populations of rare species than would one large block of the same area (Simberloff and Gotelli 1984). Also, creating more reserves, even if they are small ones, prevents the possibility of a single catastrophic force, such

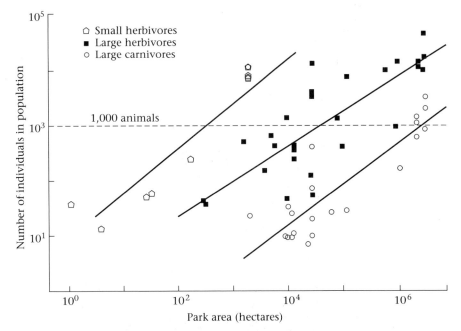

4.7 Population studies show that large parks and protected areas in Africa contain larger populations of each species than small parks; only the largest parks may contain long-term viable populations of many vertebrate species. Each symbol represents an animal population. If the viable population size of a species is 1000 (10^3; dashed line) individuals, parks of at least 100 (10^2) ha will be needed to protect small herbivores (e.g., rabbits, squirrels); parks of more than 10,000 (10^4) ha will be needed to protect large herbivores (e.g., deer, zebras, giraffes); and parks of at least a million (10^6) ha will be needed to protect large carnivores (e.g., lions, wolves). (After Schonewald-Cox 1983.)

as an exotic animal, a disease, or fire, destroying an entire population located in a single large reserve. In addition, small reserves located near populated areas can make excellent conservation education and nature study centers, furthering the long-range goals of conservation biology by developing a public awareness of important issues.

The consensus now seems to be that strategies on reserve size depend on the group of species under consideration as well as the scientific circumstances (Soulé and Simberloff 1986). It is accepted that large reserves are better able than small reserves to maintain many species because of the larger population sizes and greater variety of habitats they contain. However, well-managed small reserves also have value, particularly for the protection of many species of plants, invertebrates, and small vertebrates (Lesica and Allendorf 1992). Often there is no choice other than to accept the challenge of managing species in small reserves because no additional land around the small reserves is available for conservation purposes. This is particularly true in places that have been intensively cultivated and settled for centuries, such as Europe, China, and Java. For example, Sweden has 1200 small nature reserves that average about 350 ha each, and small reserves account for 30%–40% of the protected area of the Netherlands (McNeely et al. 1994).

Minimizing edge and fragmentation effects

It is generally agreed that parks should be designed to minimize harmful edge effects. Conservation areas that are rounded in shape minimize the edge-to-area ratio, and the center of such a park is farther from the edge than in other park shapes. Long, linear parks have the most edge, and all points in the park are close to the edge. Using these same arguments for parks with four straight sides, a square park is a better design than an elongated rectangle of the same area. These ideas have rarely, if ever, been implemented. Most parks have irregular shapes because land acquisition is typically a matter of opportunity rather than a matter of completing a geometric pattern.

Internal fragmentation of reserves by roads, fences, farming, logging, and other human activities should be avoided as much as possible because of the many negative effects fragmentation can have on species and populations (see Chapter 2). The forces promoting fragmentation are powerful, because protected areas are often the only undeveloped land available for new projects, such as agriculture, dams, and residential areas. Government planners often locate transportation networks and other infrastructure in protected areas because they encounter less political opposition than if they choose to locate the projects on privately owned land. In the eastern United States many parks near cities are crisscrossed by roads, railroad tracks, and power lines that divide large areas of habitat like pieces of a roughly cut pie.

Strategies exist for aggregating small nature reserves into larger conservation blocks. Nature reserves are often embedded in a larger matrix of habitat managed for resource extraction, such as timber forest, grazing land, or farmland. If the protection of biological diversity can be included as a secondary priority in the management of the production areas, then larger areas can be included in conservation management plans and the effects of fragmentation can be reduced. Whenever possible, nature reserves should be managed as a regional system to facilitate gene flow and migration among populations and to ensure adequate representation of species and habitats (Figure 4.8). Cooperation among public and private landowners is particularly important in developed metropolitan areas, where there are often numerous small, isolated parks under the control of a variety of different government agencies and private organizations (Salwasser et al. 1987).

Whenever possible, protected areas should include an entire ecosystem (such as a watershed, a lake, or a mountain range), because the ecosystem is the most appropriate unit of management. Damage to an

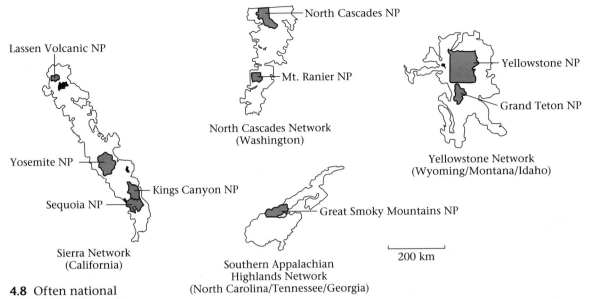

4.8 Often national parks (shaded areas) are adjacent to other public lands (unshaded) that are managed by different agencies. The United States government is considering managing large blocks of land that include national parks, national forests, and other federal lands as networks of natural areas in order to maintain populations of large and scarce wildlife. This illustration shows four of ten such networks that have been proposed. Privately owned land is shown in black. (After Salwasser et al. 1987.)

unprotected portion of the ecosystem could threaten the health of the whole. Controlling the whole ecosystem allows park managers to defend it more effectively against destructive outside influences (Peres and Terborgh 1995).

Habitat corridors

One intriguing suggestion for managing a system of nature reserves has been to link isolated protected areas into one large system through the use of **habitat corridors**: strips of protected land running between the reserves (Simberloff et al. 1992). Such habitat corridors, also known as conservation corridors or movement corridors, could allow plants and animals to disperse from one reserve to another, facilitating gene flow and colonization of suitable sites. Corridors might also help to preserve animals that must migrate seasonally among a series of different habitats to obtain food; if these animals were confined to a single reserve, they could starve. This principle was put into practice in Costa Rica to link two wildlife reserves, the Braulio Carillo National Park and La Selva Biological Station. A 7700 ha corridor of forest several kilometers wide, known as La Zona Protectora, was set aside to provide an elevational link that allows at least 35 species of birds to migrate between the two large conservation areas (Wilcove and May 1986). A similar corridor has been proposed to allow herds of large herbivores to migrate between two national parks in Tanzania (Figure 4.9).

Although the idea of corridors is intuitively appealing, it has some potential drawbacks. Corridors could facilitate the movement of pest species and disease, so that a single infestation could quickly spread to all of the connected nature reserves and cause the extinction of all populations of a rare species. Also, animals dispersing along corridors might be exposed to greater risks of predation because human hunters, as well as animal predators, tend to concentrate on routes used by wildlife. At present, the empirical evidence to support the value of corridors is very limited. In general, the value of habitat corridors should be evaluated on a case-by-case basis.

4.9 A game corridor has been proposed to allow herds to migrate between Lake Manyara and Tarangire National Parks in northeastern Tanzania. Many of the animals living in this area need to migrate to follow the seasonal availability of good grazing. Current cropland is indicated by diagonal hatching. The horizontally hatched area between the lake and the proposed corridor is an area used by tribespeople for dry-season grazing of their herds. A proposed "buffer zone" (dark shading) would allow additional areas for grazing. (After Mwalyosi 1991.)

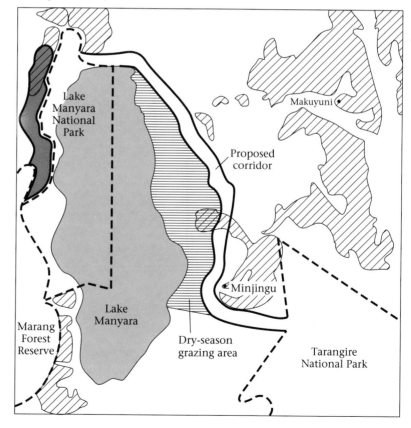

Corridors are most obviously needed along known migration routes. In some cases, leaving small clumps of original habitat between large conservation areas may also serve to facilitate movement by a "stepping-stone" process. Where corridors already exist, they should be preserved. Many of the corridors that currently exist are along watercourses and may be biologically important habitats themselves.

All of these theories of reserve design have been developed mainly with land vertebrates, higher plants, and large invertebrates in mind. The applicability of these ideas to aquatic nature reserves, where dispersal mechanisms are largely unknown, requires further investigation.

Landscape ecology and park design

The interaction of actual land use patterns and conservation theory is evident in the discipline of **landscape ecology**. Landscape ecology investigates patterns of habitat types on a regional scale and their influence on species distribution and ecosystem processes (Urban et al. 1987; Hansson et al. 1995). A landscape is defined by Forman and Godron (1986) as an "area where a cluster of interacting stands or ecosystems is repeated in similar form" (Figure 4.10). Landscape ecology has been more intensively studied in the human-dominated environments of Europe than in North America, where research in the past has emphasized single habitat types.

Landscape ecology is important to the protection of biological diversity because many species are not confined to a single habitat, but move between habitats or live on borders where two habitats meet. For these species, the patterns of habitat types on a regional scale are of critical importance. The presence and density of many species may be affected by the size of habitat patches and their degree of linkage. For example, the population size of a rare animal species will be different in two 100 ha parks, one with an alternating checkerboard of 100 patches of field and forest, each 1 ha in area, the other with a checkerboard of 4 patches, each 25 ha in area. These alternative landscape patterns may have very different effects on microclimate (wind, temperature, humidity, and light), pest outbreaks, and animal movement patterns.

To increase the number and diversity of animals, wildlife managers often attempt to create the greatest amount of landscape variation possible within the confines of their management unit (Yahner 1988). Fields and meadows are created and maintained, small thickets are encouraged, fruit trees and crops are planted on a small scale, small patches of forests are periodically cut, small ponds and dams are developed, and numerous trails and dirt roads meander across and along all of the patches. The result is a park transformed into a mass of edges, where transition zones abound. In one textbook of wildlife management, managers are advised to "develop as much edge as possible" because "wildlife is a product of the places where two habitats meet" (Yoakum and Dasmann 1971).

(A) Scattered patch landscapes

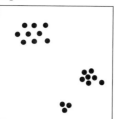

Open clearings
in a forest

Groves of trees
in a field

(B) Network landscapes

Network of roads
in a large plantation

Riparian network of
rivers and tributaries
in a forest

(C) Interdigitated landscapes

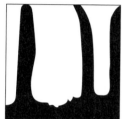

Tributary streams
running into a lake

Shifting
forest–grassland
borders

(D) Checkerboard landscapes

Farmland under
cultivation for
different crops

Lots in a residential
development

4.10 Four renditions
of landscape types in
which interacting
ecosystems or other
land uses form repeti-
tive patterns. The dis-
cipline of landscape
ecology focuses on
such interactions
rather than on a single
habitat type. (After
Zonneveld and For-
man 1990.)

The conservation biologist's goal, however, is not just to include as many species as possible within nature reserves, but also to protect those species most in danger of extinction as a result of human activity. Small reserves broken up into many small habitat units within a compressed landscape may have a large number of species, but these are likely to be principally "weedy" species—species that depend on human disturbance—and non-native species. A park that contains the maximum amount of edge may lack many rare species that inhabit only large blocks of undisturbed habitat.

To remedy this localized approach, biological diversity needs to be managed on the regional landscape level, at which the size of the landscape units—such as entire watersheds or groups of hills—more closely approximates the natural units prior to human disturbance (Grumbine 1994b; Noss and Cooperrider 1994). An alternative to creating a miniature landscape of contrasting habitats on a small scale is to link all parks in an area in a regional plan so that larger habitat units can be created. Some of these larger habitat units would then be large enough to protect rare species that are not able to tolerate human disturbance.

Managing Protected Areas

Once a protected area has been legally established, it must be effectively managed if biological diversity is to be maintained. The conventional wisdom that "nature knows best" and that there is a "balance of nature" leads some people to the conclusion that biodiversity is best served when there is no human intervention. The reality is often very different: in many cases humans have already modified the environment so much that the remaining species and communities need human intervention in order to survive (Blockhus et al. 1992; Spellerberg 1994). The world is littered with "paper parks" that have been created by government decree but not effectively managed on the ground. These parks have gradually—or sometimes rapidly—lost species, and their habitat quality has been degraded. In some countries, people do not hesitate to farm, log, and mine in protected areas because government land is owned by "everyone," "anybody" can take whatever they want, and "nobody" is willing to intervene. The crucial point is that parks must sometimes be actively managed to prevent deterioration. However, decisions on park management can usually be made most effectively when information is provided by a research program and funds are available to implement management plans.

It is also true that sometimes the best management involves doing nothing; management activities are sometimes ineffective or even detrimental (Chase 1986). For example, active management to promote the abundance of game species, such as deer, has frequently involved eliminating top predators, such as wolves and cougars. Removal of top predators can result in an explosion of game populations (and, incidentally, rodents). The result is overgrazing, habitat degradation, and a collapse of the animal and plant communities. Overenthusiastic park managers who remove fallen trees and underbrush to "improve" a park's appearance may unwittingly remove a critical resource needed by certain animal species for nesting and overwintering. In many parks, fire is part of the ecology of the area. Attempts to suppress fire completely are expensive and unnatural, eventually leading to massive, uncontrolled fires such as those that occurred in Yellowstone National Park in 1988.

Many good examples of park management come from Britain, where there is a history of scientists and volunteers successfully monitoring and managing small reserves, such as the Monks Wood and Castle Hill Nature Reserves (Usher 1975; Peterken 1994). At these sites, the effects of different grazing methods (sheep vs. cattle, light vs. heavy grazing) on populations of wildflowers, butterflies, and birds are closely followed. In a symposium called *The Scientific Management of Animal and Plant Communities for Conservation* (Duffey and Watt 1971), Morris concluded, "There is no inherently right or wrong way to manage a nature reserve...the aptness of any method of management must be related to the objects of management for

4.11 Tern nesting habitat in the Cape Cod National Seashore and at nearby beaches is extremely vulnerable to the "wear and tear" that is inevitable in a heavily visited recreation area. Management is needed to reduce the impact of recreational uses on the birds. (Photograph by David C. Twitchell.)

any particular site. ...Only when objects of management have been formulated can results of scientific management be applied."

Many government agencies and conservation organizations have clearly articulated the protection of rare and endangered species as one of their top priorities. These priorities are often outlined in mission statements, which allow managers to defend their actions. For example, at the Cape Cod National Seashore in Massachusetts, protecting tern nesting habitat has been given priority over the use of the area by off-road vehicles and the "right" of sport fishermen to fish (Figure 4.11). A "hands-off" policy by park managers, ostensibly allowing nature to take its course, would result in the rapid destruction of the tern colonies.

Dealing with threats to parks

In 1990, the World Conservation Monitoring Centre and UNESCO conducted a survey of 89 World Heritage Sites to gain an idea of the management problems there (WRI 1992). Threats to protected areas were generally greatest in South America and least in Europe. The most serious management problems in Oceania (Australia, New Zealand, and the Pacific Islands) were introduced plant species, while illegal wildlife harvesting, fire, grazing, and cultivation were the major threats in both South America and Africa. Inadequate park management was a particular problem in the developing countries of Africa, Asia, and South America. The greatest threats faced by parks in industrialized countries were internal and external threats associated with economic activities such as mining, logging, agriculture, and water projects. Although these general patterns give an overview, any single park has its own unique problems, such as illegal logging and hunting in many Central American parks, or the vast numbers of tourists who crowd into Yellowstone National Park in July and August.

Assessing the threats to parks does not necessarily mean attempting to eliminate their presence; in many cases it is nearly impossible to do so. For example, exotic species may already be present inside the park, and new exotic species may be invading along the park boundaries. If these species are allowed to increase unchecked, native species and even entire communities may be eliminated from the park. Where an exotic species threatens native species, it should be removed if possible, or at least reduced in frequency (Temple 1990). An exotic species that has just arrived and has known noxious tendencies should be aggressively removed while it is still at low densities. Once an exotic species becomes established in an area, however, it may be difficult (if not impossible) to eliminate it.

Habitat management

A park may have to be aggressively managed to ensure that the original habitat types are maintained. Many species occupy only a specific habitat or a specific successional stage of a habitat. When land is set aside as a protected area, the pattern of disturbance and human use may change so markedly that many species previously found on the site fail to persist (Gomez-Pompa and Kaus 1992). Natural disturbances, including fires, grazing, and tree falls, are key elements in the presence of certain rare species. In small parks, the full range of successional stages may not be present, and many species may be missing for this reason; for example, in an isolated park dominated by old-growth trees, species characteristic of the early successional herb and shrub stage may be missing. Park managers sometimes must actively manage sites to ensure that all successional stages are present. One common way to do this is to periodically set localized, controlled fires in grasslands, shrublands, and forests to re-initiate the successional process. In some wildlife sanctuaries, open fields are maintained by mowing, disking, or grazing livestock. For example, many of the unique wildflowers of Nantucket Island off the coast of Massachusetts are found in the scenic heathland areas. These heathlands were previously maintained by sheep grazing; they must now be burned every few years to prevent scrub oak forest from taking over the area and shading out the wildflowers (Figure 4.12A). In other situations, parts of protected areas must be carefully managed to minimize human disturbance and provide the conditions required by old-growth species (Figure 4.12B). For example, certain ground beetle species are found only in mature stands of boreal forest and disappear from lands managed under a system of clear-cut harvesting (Niemelä et al. 1993).

Wetlands management is a particularly crucial issue. The maintenance

(A)

(B)

4.12 Conservation management: intervention versus leave-it-alone. (A) Heathland in protected areas of Nantucket Island is burned on a regular basis in order to maintain the open vegetation habitat and protect wildflowers and other rare species. (Photograph by P. Dunwiddie.) (B) Sometimes management involves keeping human disturbance to an absolute minimum. This old-growth stand in the Olympic National Forest, Washington, is the result of many years of solitude. (Photograph by Thomas Kitchin/Tom Stack and Associates.)

of wetlands is necessary to preserve populations of water birds, fish, amphibians, aquatic plants, and a host of other species (Moyle and Leidy 1992). Yet parks may become direct competitors for water resources with irrigation projects, flood control schemes, and hydroelectric dams in places such as the floodplains of India (Pandit 1991) and the Florida Everglades (Holloway 1994). Wetlands are often interconnected, so a decision affecting water levels and quality in one place has repercussions in other areas. Park managers may have to become politically sophisticated and effective at public relations to ensure that the wetlands under their supervision continue to receive the clean water they need to survive.

The need for habitat management to maintain populations of rare species is illustrated by the example of Crystal Fen in northern Maine, recognized for its numerous rare plant species (Jacobson et al. 1991). An apparent drying of the fen (a type of wet meadow) and an increase in woody vegetation were attributed by some biologists to the construction of a railroad in 1893 and a drainage ditch in 1937; there was concern that the fen community might be lost. Subsequent studies using aerial photography, vegetation history, and dated fossil remains from peat layers collectively showed that the construction of the railroad bed had allowed the wetland to *expand* in area by impeding drainage. The fen also increased in area following fires started by cinder-producing locomotives. Today, the large area of fen in which rare plants occur is primarily a product of human activity. The construction of the drainage ditch and the decrease in fires following the change to diesel-powered locomotives are allowing the vegetation to return to its original state. If the goal is to maintain the current extent of the fen and the populations of rare species, management practices such as periodic burning, removing woody plants, and manipulating drainage patterns are necessary.

In managing parks, attempts should be made to preserve and maintain keystone resources on which many species depend (see Chapter 1). If it is not possible to keep these keystone resources intact, attempts can be made to reconstruct them. For example, an artificial salt lick could be built in place of one that has been destroyed, or artificial pools could be built in streambeds to provide replacement water supplies. Keystone resources and keystone species could conceivably be enhanced in managed conservation areas to increase the populations of species whose numbers have declined. For example, by planting fruit trees, building an artificial pond, and providing salt licks, it might be possible to maintain vertebrate species in a smaller conservation area at higher densities than would be predicted based on studies of species distribution in undisturbed habitat. Another example is the provision of nesting boxes for birds as a substitute resource when few dead trees with nesting cavities are available. In this way a viable population of a rare species might be established, whereas without such interventions the population size might be too small for it to persist. In each case a balance must be struck between establishing nature reserves free from human influence and creating seminatural gardens in which the plants and animals are dependent on people.

Park management and people

Human use of the landscape is a reality that must be dealt with in park design. People have been a part of virtually all the world's ecosystems for thousands of years, and excluding humans from nature reserves can have unforeseen consequences (Gomez-Pompa and Kaus 1992). For example, a savannah protected from fires set by people may change to forest, with a subsequent loss of the savannah species. However, excluding local people from protected areas may be the only option when resources are being overharvested to the point at which the integrity of the biological communities is being threatened. Such a situation could result from overgrazing by cattle, excessive collection of fuelwood, or hunting with guns. It is better if compromises can be found before this point is reached.

The use of parks by local people and outside visitors must be a central part of any management plan, in both developed and developing countries (MacKinnon et al. 1992; Wells and Brandon 1992; Western et al. 1994). People who have traditionally used products from inside a nature reserve and are suddenly not allowed to enter the area will suffer from their loss of access to the basic resources that they need to stay alive. They will be understandably angry and frustrated, and people in such a position are unlikely to be strong supporters of conservation. Many parks flourish or are destroyed depending on the degree of support, neglect, hostility, or exploitation they receive from the people who use them. If the purpose of a protected area is explained to local residents, and if most residents agree with the objectives and respect the rules of the park, then the area may maintain its natural communities. In the most positive scenario, local people become involved in park management and planning, are trained and employed by the park authority, and benefit from the protection of biodiversity and regulation of activity within the park. At the other extreme, if there is a history of bad relations and mistrust between local people and the government, or if the purpose of the park is not explained adequately, the local people may reject the park concept and ignore park regulations. In this eventuality, the local people will come into conflict with park personnel, to the detriment of the park.

There is now increasing recognition that the involvement of local people is the crucial missing element in conservation management strategies. "Top-down" strategies, in which governments try to impose conservation plans, need to be integrated with "bottom-up" programs, in which villages and other local groups are able to formulate and reach their own development goals (Clay 1991). As explained by Lewis et al. (1990):

> If any lesson can be learned from past failures of conservation in Africa, it is that conservation implemented solely by government for the presumed benefit of its people will probably have limited success, especially in coun-

Opening conservation to man

Is the best way to protect a natural area to seal it off in a "closed jar" from the outside human world? Sooner or later such a policy can destroy the area it was intended to protect. Ecological and sociological pressures - both inside and outside - eventually may shatter the reserve.

Almost all natural areas have been modified by man: creating a reserve by excluding man can upset the ecological balance. Boundaries may not coincide with territorial areas and feeding grounds. Pressure builds up within the reserve. Jammed inside, some animals overbreed, others "eat themselves to starvation"

In some cases, nature reserves are created by excluding the local inhabitants from their traditional grazing and hunting areas. They have difficulty in accepting that these areas are only accessible to tourists. Gradually illicit hunting, grazing and cropping may encroach upon and eradicate the reserve.

MAB emphasizes man's partnership with nature. A reserve is open and interacts with its region. The local people can be its guardians.

It is not suggested that the traditional policy of conservation should be changed everywhere. Certainly some areas must remain untouched. But there are fewer and fewer natural areas left to conserve and certain reserves are being destroyed by these internal and external pressures. Opening conservation to man does not only apply to the Kenyan situation here but to many other countries. It may be a longer term solution.

The diagram (right) illustrates how a Kenyan specialist envisages integrating wildlife conservation, tourism and traditional land use through zonation into different use areas, research for rational management and participation of the local population. The term "biosphere reserve" was coined to identify reserves putting the "open" concept into practice.

MAN AND THE BIOSPHERE (MAB) PROGRAMME, UNESCO

4.13 Past policies have often attempted to protect natural areas by sealing them off from outside influences. The MAB program is an attempt to integrate the needs and cultures of local people in park planning and protection. (Poster from "Ecology in Action: An Exhibit," UNESCO, Paris, 1981.)

tries with weakened economies. Instead, conservation for the people and by the people with a largely service and supervisory role delegated to the government could foster a more cooperative relationship between government and the residents living with the resource. This might reduce the costs of law enforcement and increase revenues available to other aspects of wildlife management, which could help support the needs of conservation as well as those of the immediate community. Such an approach would have the added advantage of restoring to local residents a greater sense of traditional ownership and responsibility for this resource. Convincing proof that such a partnership is possible has yet to be demonstrated and has therefore been more theoretical than practical.

The United Nations Educational, Scientific, and Cultural Organization (UNESCO) has pioneered one such approach with its Man and the Biosphere (MAB) Program. This program has designated a number of Biosphere Reserves worldwide in an attempt to integrate human activities, research, and protection of the natural environment at a single location (Figure 4.13; Dyer and Holland 1991). The Biosphere Reserve concept involves a core area in which biological communities and ecosystems are strictly protected, surrounded by a buffer zone in which traditional human activities, such as collection of thatch, medicinal plants, and small fuelwood, are monitored and nondestructive research is carried out. Surrounding the buffer zone is a transitional zone in which some forms of sustainable development, such as small-scale farming, and some extraction of natural resources, such as selective logging, as well as experimental research are allowed (Figure 4.14).This general strategy of surrounding core conservation areas with buffer and transitional zones can have several desirable effects. First, the local people may be encouraged to support the goals of the protected area. Second, certain desirable features of the landscape created by human use may be maintained. And third, the buffer zones may facilitate animal dispersal and gene flow between highly protected core conservation areas and human-dominated transitional and unprotected areas.

Conservation Outside Protected Areas

A crucial element in conservation strategies must be the protection of biological diversity outside as well as inside protected areas. A danger of relying on parks and reserves alone is that this strategy can create a "siege mentality," in which species and communities inside the parks are to be rigorously protected while those outside can be freely exploited. If the areas surrounding the parks are degraded, however, biological diversity within the parks will decline as well, with the loss of species being most severe in small parks (Table 4.5). This decline will occur because many species must migrate across park boundaries to gain access to resources be-

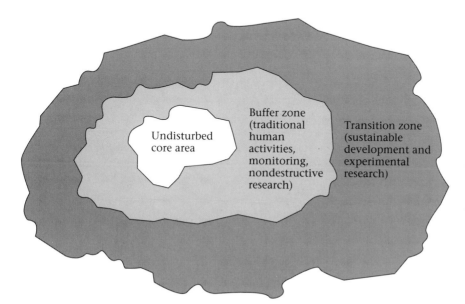

Undisturbed core area

Buffer zone (traditional human activities, monitoring, nondestructive research)

Transition zone (sustainable development and experimental research)

4.14 The general pattern of an MAB reserve includes a core protected area, surrounded by a buffer zone in which traditional human activities are monitored and managed and research is carried out, which in turn is surrounded by a transition zone of sustainable development and experimental research.

Table 4.5
The number of large herbivore species currently in East African national parks, and the number expected to remain if areas outside the parks become unavailable to wildlife

National park	Area (× 1000 ha)	Number of species in park	
		Now	If areas outside parks exclude wildlife[a]
Serengeti, Tanzania	1,450	31	30
Mara, Kenya	181	29	22
Meru, Kenya	102	26	20
Amboseli, Kenya	39	24	18
Samburu, Kenya	30	25	17
Nairobi, Kenya	11	21	11

Source: Data from Western and Ssemakula 1981.
[a] Estimated number of species that will remain if areas outside the protected parks exclude wildlife due to agriculture, hunting, herding, or other human activities.

yond what the park itself can provide. Also, the number of individuals of any one species contained within park boundaries may be lower than the minimum viable population size. As stated by Western (1989), "If we can't save nature outside protected areas, not much will survive inside."

More than 90% of the world's land will remain outside of protected areas, according to even the most optimistic predictions. Strategies for reconciling human needs and conservation interests in these unprotected areas are critical to the success of conservation plans. The majority of unprotected lands are not used intensively by humans and still harbor some of their original biota. Because the majority of the land area in most countries will never be in protected areas, numerous rare species will inevitably occur outside protected areas. In Australia, for example, 79% of the endangered and vulnerable plant species occur outside protected areas (Leigh et al. 1982). The majority of the species listed under the U.S. Endangered Species Act are found on private land.

Conservation strategies in which private landowners are educated and encouraged to protect rare species are obviously the key to the long-term survival of many species. Government endangered species programs in many countries inform road builders and developers of the locations of rare species and assist them in modifying their plans to avoid damage to the sites. Forests that are selectively logged on a long cutting cycle or are used for traditional shifting cultivation by a low density of farmers can maintain a considerable percentage of their original biota (Johns 1987; Thiollay 1992). In Malaysia, the majority of bird species are still found in rain forests 25 years after selective logging when undisturbed forest is available nearby to act as a source of colonists (Wong 1985).

Native species can often continue to live in unprotected areas when those areas are set aside or managed for some other purpose that is not harmful to the ecosystem. Security zones surrounding government installations are some of the most outstanding natural areas in the world. In the United States, excellent examples of natural habitat occur on the sites of military reservations such as Fort Bragg in North Carolina; nuclear processing facilities such as the Savannah River site in South Carolina; and watersheds adjacent to metropolitan water supplies such as the Quabbin Reservoir in Massachusetts. Although dams, reservoirs, canals, dredging operations, port facilities, and coastal development destroy and damage aquatic communities, some species are capable of adapting to the altered conditions, particularly when the water itself is not polluted. In estuaries and seas managed for commercial fisheries, many of the native species remain, because commercial and noncommercial species alike require that the chemical and physical environment not be damaged.

Other areas that are not protected by law may retain biological diversity because their human population density and degree of utilization are typically very low. Border areas such as the demilitarized zone between North and South Korea often have an abundance of wildlife because they remain undeveloped and depopulated. Mountain areas are often too steep and inaccessible for development. These areas are frequently managed by governments as watersheds for their value in producing a steady supply of water and preventing flooding, yet they also harbor natural communities. Likewise, desert communities may be at less risk than other unprotected communities because desert regions are considered marginal for human habitation and use. In many parts of the world, wealthy individuals have acquired large tracts of land for their personal estates and for private hunting. These private estates frequently are used at a very low intensity, often in a deliberate attempt by the landowner to maintain large wildlife populations. Some estates in Europe that have been owned and protected for hundreds of years by royal families have preserved unique old-growth forests.

Large parcels of government-owned land in many countries are designated for multiple use. In the past, such uses have included logging, mining, grazing, wildlife management, and recreation. Increasingly, multiple-use lands are also being valued and managed for their ability to protect species, biological communities, and ecosystems (Figure 4.15; Norse et al. 1986; Johnson and Cabarale 1993; Noss and Cooperrider 1994). Laws and court systems are now being used by conservation biologists to halt government-approved activities on public lands that threaten the survival of endangered species there (Mlot 1992).

Ecosystem management

Many land managers around the world are expanding their goals to include the health of ecosystems. The developing concept of **ecosystem management** is described by Grumbine (1994a) as follows: "Ecosystem

4.15 Longleaf pine forest in the southeastern United States, including areas of South Carolina, North Carolina, and Georgia, that has traditionally been managed by the U.S. Forest Service for timber production is now also being managed to protect the endangered red-cockaded woodpecker and the groves of old trees the birds need for breeding. Heavily logged areas lack older trees with the nesting holes that the woodpecker requires; in managed forests, artificial nesting holes are drilled in the trees. Here a young woodpecker leaves the nest for its first flight. (Photograph © Derrick Hamrick.)

management integrates scientific knowledge of ecological relationships within a complex sociopolitical and values framework toward the general goal of protecting native ecosystem integrity over the long term." Resource managers increasingly are being urged to expand their traditional emphasis on the maximum production of goods (such as volume of timber harvested) and services (such as the number of visitors to parks) and instead take a broader perspective that includes the conservation of biological diversity (Grumbine 1994b; Noss and Cooperrider 1994). Not all ecologists have accepted the paradigm of ecosystem management, however; some consider it unlikely to change the human-oriented management practices that lead to the overexploitation of natural resources (Stanley 1995).

Important themes in ecosystem management include:

1. Seeking connections among all levels and scales in the ecosystem hierarchy; for example, from the individual organism to the species, to the community, to the ecosystem.

2. Managing at the appropriate scale, not just according to the artificial political boundaries and administrative priorities set up by governments. The goal of regional management should be to ensure viable populations of all species, representative examples of all biological communities and successional stages, and healthy ecosystem functions.

3. Monitoring significant components of the ecosystem (numbers of individuals of significant species, vegetation cover, water quality, etc.), gathering the needed data, and then using the results to adjust management practices in an adaptive manner.

4. Changing the rigid policies and practices of land management agencies, which often result in a piecemeal approach. Instead, interagency cooperation and integration at the local, regional, national, and international levels, and cooperation between public agencies and private organizations, should be encouraged.

5. Recognizing that humans are part of ecosystems and that human values influence management goals.

Case studies

Mountain sheep. Mountain sheep often occur in isolated populations in steep, open terrain surrounded by large areas of apparently unsuitable habitat (see Figure 3.10). Recent studies using radiotelemetry have revealed that mountain sheep often move well outside their normal territories and even show considerable ability to move across inhospitable terrain between mountain ranges. These observations emphasize the need to protect not only the land presently occupied by mountain sheep but also the managed habitat and private lands between populations that can act as "stepping stones" for dispersal, colonization, and gene flow. Fences and other artificial barriers to movement will reduce the ability of mountain sheep to maintain their populations.

The Florida panther. The Florida panther is an endangered subspecies of puma in South Florida with probably no more than 50 individuals remaining (Maehr 1990). Half of the present range of the panther is in private hands, and all animals tracked with radio collars have spent at least some of their time on private lands (Figure 4.16). Acquiring the 400,000 ha of private land occupied by the panther would be financially and politically impossible. Two other, more practical, possibilities are educating private owners about the value of conservation and making payments to landowners willing to practice management options that allow the continued existence of panthers.

Managed coniferous forests. The coniferous forests of the Pacific Northwest are managed primarily for timber production, but also contain numerous unique species (Hansen et al. 1991). In this ecosystem, the conflict between timber production and the conservation of biodiversity has

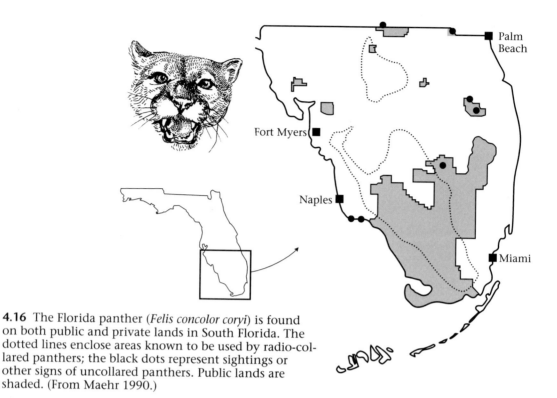

4.16 The Florida panther (*Felis concolor coryi*) is found on both public and private lands in South Florida. The dotted lines enclose areas known to be used by radio-collared panthers; the black dots represent sightings or other signs of uncollared panthers. Public lands are shaded. (From Maehr 1990.)

become a highly emotional and political issue, cast in terms of "owls versus jobs" (see Chapter 3). In managed forests in the Pacific Northwest, the current practice of clear-cutting staggered patches of timber produces a landscape pattern that is a mosaic of forest fragments of different but uniform ages. Current research suggests that managed forests can contain considerable biological diversity and suggests specific ways in which conifer forests can be managed both to produce timber and to maintain a greater number of species. These lessons are being incorporated into the concept of "new forestry" being advocated for the Pacific Northwest (Gillis 1990). This still untested method involves a modified type of clear-cutting that leaves a low density of large live trees, in addition to some standing dead trees and some fallen trees, to serve as habitat for animal species in the next successional cycle (Figure 4.17). This practice would particularly benefit birds such as the spotted owl that nest only in the cavities of large, old trees. However, the "new forestry" requires a reduced harvest of timber at the time of cutting and a somewhat longer cutting cycle, resulting in lower profitability for the timber industry. It remains to be seen whether the industry and the society are willing to pay the costs of these new forestry practices that could potentially enhance biological diversity.

African wildlife outside parks. East African countries such as Kenya are famous for the large wildlife species found in their national parks, which are the basis of a valuable ecotourism industry. Despite the fame of these parks, about three-fourths of Kenya's 2 million large animals live in areas outside of the parks, often sharing rangeland with domestic cattle (Western 1989). The rangelands of Kenya occupy 700,000 km², or about 40% of the country. Among the well-known species found predominantly outside the parks are giraffes (89%), impalas (72%), Grevy's zebras (99%), oryx (73%), and ostriches (92%). Only rhinoceroses, elephants, and wildebeest are found predominantly inside the parks; rhinos and elephants are concentrated in the parks because poachers seeking ivory, horns, and hides have virtually eliminated external populations of these animals. The large herbivores found in the parks often graze seasonally outside of the parks; many of these species would be unable to persist if they were restricted to

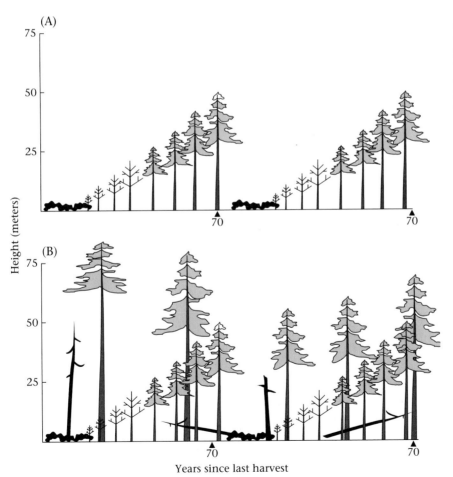

4.17 (A) Conventional clear-cutting methods remove all trees from an area on a 70-year cycle, thus reducing the structural diversity of the forest. (B) Proposed new practices would better maintain the structural diversity by leaving behind some old, standing dead trees, and fallen trees. (From Hansen et al. 1991.)

Height (meters)

Years since last harvest

the limits of the parks by fencing, poaching, and agricultural development.

The main factors affecting the continued existence of wild species of large mammals in unprotected African lands appear to be a stable social structure and secure land tenure in the local human population (Western 1989). These factors tend to be characteristic of both traditional societies and highly developed modern societies. In these situations, use of resources is regulated by a recognized authority and current wants can be deferred to enhance future production of resources.

Within Kenya, there is a movement to create a new government policy to allow rural communities and landowners to profit directly from the presence of large game animals on unprotected land (Baskin 1994b). With assistance from international donor agencies, local ecotourist businesses (including hiking, photography, canoeing, and horseback safaris) would be established. Where the land is adequately stocked with animals, trophy hunting could be allowed for high fees. This revenue could be shared between the local communities and the national government; meat and hides from hunting expeditions could also be sold for additional shared revenue. Communities receiving such revenue would have a strong incentive to protect wildlife and prevent poaching.

Restoration Ecology

An important opportunity for conservation biologists is the chance to participate in the restoration of damaged or degraded ecosystems (Jordan et al. 1990; Lieth and Lohmann 1993). Rebuilding damaged ecosystems has great potential for enlarging and enhancing the current system of protected areas. **Ecological restoration** is defined as "the process of intentionally altering a site to establish a defined, indigenous, historic ecosystem. The goal of this process is to emulate the structure, function, diversity and dynamics of the specified ecosystem" (Society for Ecological Restoration 1991). Restoration ecology has its origins in older applied technologies that restore ecosystem functions of known economic value: wetland replication to prevent flooding, mine site reclamation to prevent soil erosion, range management to ensure the production of grasses, and forest management for timber and amenity value (Bradshaw and Chadwick 1980; Bradshaw 1990; Kusler and Kentula 1990). However, these technologies sometimes produce only simplified communities, or communities that cannot maintain themselves. With the emergence of biological diversity as an important societal concern, the reestablishment of species assemblages and entire communities has been included as a major goal in restoration plans.

Ecosystems can be damaged by natural phenomena such as lightning-caused fires, volcanoes, and storms, but they typically recover their original biomass, community structure, and even a similar species composition through the process of succession. Some ecosystems damaged by human activity, however, are so degraded that their ability to recover is severely limited. Recovery is unlikely when the damaging agent is still present in the ecosystem. For example, restoration of degraded savannah woodlands in western Costa Rica and the western United States is not possible as long as the land continues to be overgrazed by introduced cattle; reduction of the grazing pressure is obviously the key starting point in restoration efforts (Fleischner 1994). Recovery is also unlikely when many of the original species have been eliminated over a large area, so that there is no source of colonists. For example, prairie species were eliminated from huge areas of the midwestern United States when the land was converted to agriculture. Even when an isolated patch of land is no longer cultivated, the original community does not become reestablished because there is no source of seeds or colonizing animals of the original species. In addition, recovery is unlikely when the physical environment has been so altered that the original species can no longer survive at the site; examples of this situation include mine sites, where the restoration of natural communities may be delayed by decades or even centuries due to the poor structure, heavy metal toxicity, and low nutrient status of the soil (Figure 4.18).

In certain cases entirely new environments are created by human activity, such as reservoirs, canals, landfills, and industrial sites. If these sites are neglected, they often become dominated by exotic and weedy species, resulting in biological communities that are unproductive, not typical of

4.18 To speed the recovery of this devastated coal mine site in Wyoming, crews planted 120,000 shrubs. Mining sites often need a great deal of human help in order to recover even a semblance of biodiversity. (From Jordan et al. 1990.)

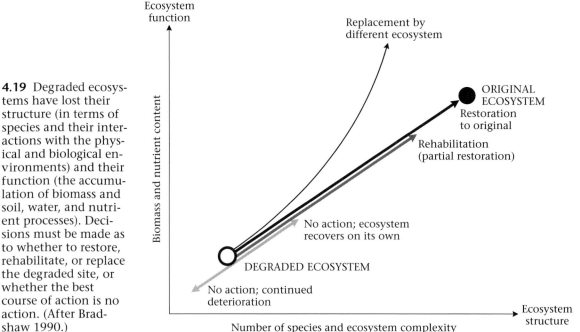

4.19 Degraded ecosystems have lost their structure (in terms of species and their interactions with the physical and biological environments) and their function (the accumulation of biomass and soil, water, and nutrient processes). Decisions must be made as to whether to restore, rehabilitate, or replace the degraded site, or whether the best course of action is no action. (After Bradshaw 1990.)

the surrounding areas, valueless from a conservation perspective, and aesthetically unappealing. If these sites are properly prepared and native species are reintroduced, native communities can be successfully restored.

Restoration ecology provides the theory and techniques to address these various types of degraded ecosystems. Four main approaches are available in restoring biological communities and ecosystems (Figure 4.19; Cairns 1986; Bradshaw 1990).

1. **No action** because restoration is too expensive, because previous attempts at restoration have failed, or because experience has shown that the ecosystem will recover on its own. The last situation is typical of old fields in eastern North America, which return to forest within a few decades after being abandoned for agriculture.
2. **Restoration** of the area to its original species composition and structure by an active program of reintroduction; in particular, by planting and seeding of the original plant species.
3. **Rehabilitation** to restore at least some of the ecosystem functions and some of the original species; for example, replacing a degraded forest with a tree plantation.
4. **Replacement** of a degraded ecosystem with another productive ecosystem type; for example, replacing a degraded forest area with a productive pasture.

Civil engineers and others involved in major development projects deal with the restoration of degraded habitats in a practical, technical manner. Their goals are to find economical ways to permanently stabilize land surfaces, prevent soil erosion, make the site look better to neighbors and the general public, and if possible, restore the productive value of the land. Ecologists contribute to these restoration efforts by developing ways to restore the original communities in terms of species diversity, species composition, vegetation structure, and ecosystem function. Practitioners of restoration ecology must have a clear grasp of how natural systems work and what methods of restoration are feasible. To be practical, restoration ecology must also consider the speed of restoration, the cost, the reliability of the results, and the ability of the final community to persist with little or no further maintenance. Considerations such as the cost and availability of seeds, when to water plants, how much fertilizer to add, and how to prepare the surface soil may become paramount in determining the success of a project. Dealing with such practical details has not generally been attractive to academic biologists in the past, but they must be dealt with in restoration ecology.

Restoration ecology is valuable to the science of ecology because it provides a test of how well we really understand biological communities by challenging us to reassemble them from their component parts (Diamond 1990). As Bradshaw (1990) has said, "Ecologists working in the field of ecosystem restoration are in the construction business, and like their engineering colleagues, can soon discover if their theory is correct by whether the airplane falls out of the sky, the bridge collapses, or the ecosystem fails to flourish." In this sense, restoration ecology can be viewed as an experimental methodology that complements existing programs of basic research on intact systems. Restoration ecology provides an opportunity to completely reassemble communities in different ways, to see how well they function, and to test ideas on a larger scale than would otherwise be possible (Diamond 1990; Gilpin 1990).

Restoration ecology will play an increasingly valuable role in the conservation of biological communities if degraded lands and aquatic communities can be restored to their original species composition and added to the limited existing area under protection. Because degraded areas are unproductive and of little economic value, governments may be willing to restore them and increase their productive and conservation value. Restoration ecology is almost certain to become one of the major growth areas in conservation biology. However, conservation biologists in this field must take care to ensure that restoration efforts are legitimate, rather than just a public relations cover for industrial corporations intent on continuing their environmentally unsound practices (Falk and Olwell 1992; Holloway 1994). In particular, many development projects include efforts to create or restore wetlands to replace those destroyed or degraded by the project as part of the overall plan required before government approval for the project is given. The intent of this requirement is to ensure that there is no net loss of wetlands. However, the overwhelming majority of these new and restored wetlands must be considered failures because they do not have the same species composition or hydrological properties as the original wetland communities.

Efforts to restore ecological communities have focused extensively on lakes, prairies, wetlands, and forests. These environments have suffered severe alteration from human activities and are good candidates for restoration work.

Lakes

Attempts to restore eutrophic lakes have not only provided practical management information but have also provided insight into the basic science of limnology (the study of the chemistry, biology, and physics of fresh water) that otherwise would not be possible (Welch and Cooke 1990). One of the most common types of damage to lakes and ponds is cultural eutrophication, caused by excess mineral nutrients produced by human activity (see Chapter 2). The signs of eutrophication include increases in the algal population (particularly surface scums of blue-green algae), lowered water clarity, lowered oxygen content of the water, fish die-offs, and an eventual increase in the growth of floating plants and other water weeds. The effects on biological diversity are further compounded by the large number of exotic species that have been introduced into lakes and are highly competitive in this disturbed, nutrient-rich environment (Mills et al. 1994).

In many lakes, reducing the mineral nutrients entering the water— through better sewage treatment or by diverting polluted water—leads to a reversal of the eutrophication process and a restoration of the original conditions; this approach is known as "bottom-up" control. In other lakes, this improvement does not occur, suggesting that there are internal mechanisms within the lake that are recycling nutrients from the sediment to the water column and keeping the nutrient levels artificially high. One possible mechanism for the return of phosphorus to the water column is the role of fish, such as the carp (*Cyprinus carpio*) and the brown bullhead (*Ictalurus nebulosus*), that eat organic matter and excrete phosphorus. This hypothesis is supported by the declines in phosphorus concentrations that have been observed after carp populations have been reduced in eutrophic lakes. The composition of the fish community can also affect the eutrophication process through predator-prey relationships. In some eutrophic lakes, zooplanktonic invertebrates (such as the crustacean *Daphnia*) that eat algae are rapidly consumed by zooplanktivorous fish, allowing the algae to grow unchecked. If predatory fish are added to the lake, the population of zooplanktivorous fish often drops; an increasing crustacean population then reduces the abundance of algae, and water quality improves. Such improvements in water quality achieved through manipulations of fish populations are referred to as "top-down" control.

One of the most dramatic and expensive examples of lake restoration is that of Lake Erie (Makarewicz and Bertram 1991). Lake Erie was the most polluted of the Great Lakes in the 1950s and 1960s, and was characterized by deteriorating water quality, extensive algal blooms, declining indigenous fish populations, the collapse of commercial fisheries, and oxygen depletion in deeper waters. To address this problem, the United States and Canadian governments have invested more than $7.5 billion since 1972 in wastewater treatment facilities, reducing the annual discharge of phosphorus into the lake from 15,260 tons in 1972 to 2449 tons in 1985. Once water quality began to improve in the mid-1970s and 1980s, stocks of the native commercial walleye pike (*Stizostedion vitreum*), a predatory fish, began to increase on their own, and other predatory and game fish species were added to the lake by state agencies. As a result, both "bottom-up" and "top-down" control agents worked to improve water quality.

The 1980s have seen a continued improvement in Lake Erie's water quality, as shown by lower concentrations of phosphorus, lower algal abundance, and a shift in community composition toward higher relative numbers of algal-feeding zooplankton and predatory fish, with lower numbers of zooplankton-feeding fish. There is even some evidence of improvement in oxygen levels at the lower depths of the lake. Even though the lake will never return to its original condition because of its large numbers of exotic species and altered water chemistry, the combination of bottom-up and top-down controls—and the investment of billions of dollars—has resulted in a significant degree of restoration in this large, highly managed ecosystem.

Prairies

Many small parcels of former agricultural land in North America have been restored as prairies (Kline and Howell 1990). Prairies represent ideal subjects for restoration work because they are species-rich, are home to many beautiful wildflowers, and can be established within a few years. Also, the technology used for prairie restoration is similar to that of gardening and agriculture and is well suited to incorporating volunteer labor.

Some of the most extensive research on the restoration of prairies has been carried out in Wisconsin, starting in the 1930s. A wide variety of techniques have been used in these prairie restoration attempts. The basic method involves a light site preparation by disking, burning, and raking if prairie species are present, or elimination of all vegetation by plowing or herbicides if only exotics are present. Native plant species are then established by transplanting prairie sods obtained elsewhere, planting individuals grown from seed, or scattering prairie seed collected from the wild or from cultivated plants (Figure 4.20). The simplest method is gathering hay from a native prairie and sowing it on the prepared site. In summarizing five decades of Wisconsin experiments, Cottam (1990) observes:

4.20 (A) In the late 1930s, members of the Civilian Conservation Corps (one of the organizations created by President Franklin D. Roosevelt in order to boost employment during the Great Depression) participated in a University of Wisconsin project to restore the wild species of a Midwestern prairie. (B) The prairie as it looked 50 years later. (Photographs from the University of Wisconsin Arboretum and Archives.)

All of these methods work, but the success rate is highly variable and depends on the quantity of weeds present, the amount and timing of precipitation, the way the seeds are stratified, and a number of other variables both known and unknown. ...Why the plants distribute themselves as they do is not easily discerned, so at best a lot of guesswork and intuition goes into the actual planting of the species, and a large amount of background information increases the chance of success.

One of the most ambitious and controversial proposed restoration schemes involves re-creating a prairie ecosystem, or "buffalo commons," on about 380,000 km^2 of the American Plains states, from the Dakotas to Texas and from Wyoming to Nebraska (Popper and Popper 1991; Mathews 1992). This land is currently used for environmentally damaging and often unprofitable agriculture and grazing, which are supported by government subsidies. The human population of this region is declining as farmers and townspeople go out of business and young people move away. From an ecological, sociological, and even an economic perspective, the best long-term use of much of the region might be a restored prairie ecosystem. The human population of the region could potentially stabilize around nondamaging core industries such as tourism, wildlife management, and low-level grazing, leaving only the best lands in agriculture.

Tropical dry forests

Throughout the world, tropical forests are being degraded by logging, grazing, fire, shifting cultivation, and collection of fuelwood (see Chapter 2). These lands often become degraded to the point at which they have few remaining trees and little value to the local human population. In order to reverse these disastrous trends, governments, local people, and private organizations are involved in planting hundreds of millions of tree seedlings per year and in protecting remaining forests.

An exciting experiment in restoration ecology is currently taking place in northwestern Costa Rica. The tropical dry forests of Central America have suffered from large-scale conversion to cattle ranches and farms. Cattle grazing, fire, and clearing have reduced this diverse community to a few fragments. Even in these fragments, exotic grasses and hunting pressure threaten remaining native species. This destruction has gone on largely unnoticed as international scientific and public attention has focused on the more glamorous rain forests elsewhere. To reverse this trend, the American ecologist Daniel Janzen has been working with the Costa Rican government and local people to restore 75,000 ha of land in Guanacaste National Park (Allen 1988; Janzen 1988b). The plans for restoration include planting native trees, controlling fires, and banning hunting. Livestock grazing will be reduced to the minimum levels necessary for controlling exotic grasses, which fuel fires and prevent the regeneration of native plant species. The goal is to eliminate exotic species and reestablish a forest ecosystem within the next 100–300 years.

An innovative aspect of this restoration effort is the incorporation of local people into many aspects of park management and the intended role of the park in their cultural and educational life. Many of the farmers and ranchers living within the park borders were given the opportunity to be trained as park employees and to use their skills and knowledge of the area to develop the park. Those individuals showing initiative and ability are being trained as park managers and biologists. A key element in the restoration plan is what has been termed *biocultural restoration,* meaning that the park will serve as a center for teaching the 40,000 local residents about natural history and the principles of ecology and conservation. Janzen believes that in rural areas such as Guanacaste, providing opportunities for learning about nature can be one of the most valuable functions of national parks:

> The public is starving for and responds immediately to presentations of complexity of all kinds—biology, music, literature, politics, education, et cetera. ...The goal of biocultural restoration is to give back to people the understanding of the natural history around them that their grandparents had. These people are now just as culturally deprived as if they could no longer read, hear music, or see color.

To achieve this goal, educational and research programs have been designed to include local students at grade schools, high schools, and universities, as well as citizen groups. The hope is that if local people learn about natural history and understand the value of the park, they will become advocates both locally and nationally for the conservation of natural resources. Janzen continues,

> The most practical outcome is that this program will begin to generate an ongoing populace that understands biology. In 20 to 40 years, these children will be running the park, the neighboring towns, the irrigation systems, the political systems. When someone comes along with a decision to be made about conservation, resource management, or anything else, you want that person to understand the biological processes that are behind that decision because he or she knew about them since grade school. (Janzen, quoted in Allen 1988)

On a practical level, funding for land purchases and park management comes from the Costa Rican government and private international foundations. In the future, operating income will increasingly come from fees paid by foreign and Costa Rican scientists working at the park's biological field stations. Also, the proximity of the park to the Pan American Highway makes it an ideal location for ecotourism. Employment in these expanding research, tourist, and educational facilities will provide a significant source of employment for the local community, particularly for those who are interested in nature and education. A key element in the future success of Guanacaste National Park will be whether the plan for park development and management provides for the integration of community needs and restoration needs in a way that satisfactorily fulfills both objectives. In the final analysis, a crucial reason that this restoration effort has been so successful and has attracted so much media attention up to this point is the efforts of a single individual—Daniel Janzen—committing all his time and resources to a cause he passionately believes in.

The fine points of restoration ecology

Efforts to restore degraded terrestrial communities have emphasized the establishment of the original plant community. This emphasis is appropriate because the plant community typically contains the majority of the biomass and provides a structure for the rest of the community. However, more attention needs to be devoted to the other major components of the community. Mycorrhizal fungi and bacteria play a vital role in decomposition of organic matter and nutrient cycling (Miller 1990); soil invertebrates are important in creating soil structure; herbivorous animals are important in reducing plant competition and maintaining species diversity; and many vertebrates have vital functions as seed dispersers, insect predators, and soil diggers. Many of these non-plant species can be transferred to a restored site in sod samples; large animals and aboveground invertebrates may have to be deliberately caught in sufficient numbers and then released onto restored sites. If an area is going to be destroyed and then restored later, as might occur during strip mining, the top layer of soil, which contains the majority of buried seeds, soil invertebrates, and other soil organisms, could be carefully removed and stored for later use in restoration efforts.

Restoration efforts could also be used to re-create a threatened biological community in a new location. For example, degraded rangelands in Texas could be restored using species from a threatened savannah ecosystem in Africa. If the black rhinoceros and other wildlife are going to be hunted to extinction in Africa, their only hope might be preserving them in restored ecosystems elsewhere. This idea is not as far-fetched as it seems: rhinos occurred in Texas until about 10,000 years ago, when they were possibly eliminated by human activities. Whole groups of plants and animals could be moved from one continent to another, although this would have to be done cautiously: introduced species are, after all, one of the major problems that conservation biologists must contend with, and it would be important to ascertain that none of the transported species had the potential to become an invasive pest in its new home.

Summary

1. Protecting habitat is one of the most effective methods of preserving biological diversity. The area of legally protected habitats will probably never significantly exceed the current 5.9% of the Earth's land surface due to the perceived needs of human societies for natural resources. Well-selected protected areas can initially protect large numbers of species, but their long-term effectiveness remains in doubt.

2. Government agencies and conservation organizations are now setting national and worldwide priorities for establishing new protected areas based on the relative distinctiveness, endangerment, and utility of the species and biological communities occurring in a place. To be effective at preserving biological diversity, the Earth's protected areas need to include examples of all biological communities.

3. Principles of conservation biology need to be considered along with common sense and experience in designing new protected areas. In general, new parks should be as large as possible and should not be fragmented by roads, fences, and other human activities. Many endangered species require such undisturbed conditions for their continued existence.

4. Protected areas often must be managed in order to maintain their biological diversity because the original conditions of the area have been altered by human activities. Parts of protected areas may have to be periodically burned, dug up, or otherwise disturbed by people to maintain the habitat types and successional stages that certain species need.

5. Considerable biological diversity exists outside of protected areas, particularly in habitat managed for multiple-use resource extraction. Governments are increasingly including the protection of biological diversity as one of their management priorities for multiple-use land, a practice sometimes called ecosystem management.

6. Restoration ecology provides methods for reestablishing species, whole communities, and ecosystem functions in degraded habitat. Restoration ecology provides an opportunity to enhance biological diversity in habitats that have little other value to humans.

Suggested Readings

Edwards, P. J., R. M. May and N. R. Webb (eds.). 1994. *Large-Scale Ecology and Conservation Biology.* Blackwell Scientific Publications, Oxford. Leading authorities discuss how broad temporal and spatial scales apply to conservation issues.

Grumbine, R. E. 1994. What is ecosystem management? *Conservation Biology* 8:27–38. Argues for a new philosophy to manage lands in a more integrated manner.

Janzen, D. H. 1988. Tropical ecological and biocultural restoration. *Science* 239: 243–244. Unique integration of ecology and public education.

Jordan, W. R. III, M. E. Gilpin and J. D. Aber (eds.). 1990. *Restoration Ecology: A Synthetic Approach to Ecological Research.* Cambridge University Press, Cambridge. Papers outlining case studies and general approaches to restoration ecology.

Lieth, H. and M. Lohmann (eds.). 1993. *Restoration of Tropical Rainforest Ecosystems.* Kluwer Academic Publishers, Dordrecht. Efforts to rebuild tropical forests and restore biodiversity.

McNeely, J. A., J. Harrison and P. Dingwall (eds.). 1994. *Protecting Nature: Regional Reviews of Protected Areas.* IUCN, Gland, Switzerland. Authoritative reports on current status of protected areas throughout the world.

Noss, R. F. and A. Y. Cooperrider. 1994. *Saving Nature's Legacy: Restoring and Protecting Biodiversity.* Island Press, Washington, D.C. Practical advice on how to include the protection of biological diversity as a management objective.

Poffenberger, M. (ed.). 1990. *Keepers of the Forest.* Kumarian, West Hartford, CT. Local people often protect biological diversity; governments often favor overexploitation of resources.

Shafer, C. L. 1990. *Nature Reserves: Island Theory and Conservation Practice.* Smithsonian Institution Press, Washington, D.C. A comprehensive, well-illustrated review of the theories of reserve design that also presents evidence and counter-arguments.

Spellerberg, I. F. 1994. *Evaluation and Assessment for Conservation: Ecological Guidelines for Determining Priorities for Nature Conservation.* Chapman & Hall, London. Methods for developing a management plan for conservation areas.

Western, D. and M. Pearl (eds.). 1989. *Conservation for the Twenty-First Century.* Oxford University Press, New York. Essays by leading authorities, many of which are related to conservation outside of protected areas.

Zonneveld, I. S. and R. T. Forman (eds.). 1990. *Changing Landscapes: An Ecological Perspective.* Springer-Verlag, New York. Articles by landscape ecologists give a good overview of the field.

CHAPTER 5

Conservation and Sustainable Development

OST EFFORTS TO PRESERVE species and habitats rely on concerned citizens, conservation organizations, and government officials taking the initiative to act. This action may take many forms, but it begins with individual and group decisions to prevent the destruction of habitats and species in order to preserve something of perceived value. Governments and community organizations are often involved in these efforts because the environment is perceived to be a "public good," and public policy and public action often directly determine the optimal allocation of resources. As Peter Raven, director of the Missouri Botanical Garden, said regarding the loss of biological diversity: "You can think about it on a worldwide basis, and then it becomes discouraging and insoluble, or you can think about it in terms of specific opportunities, seize those opportunities, and reduce the problem to a more manageable size" (quoted in Tangley 1986).

Efforts to preserve biodiversity, however, sometimes come into conflict with perceived human needs (Figure 5.1). Increasingly, many conservation biologists are recognizing the need for **sustainable development**—economic development that satisfies both present and future human needs for resources and employment while minimizing its impact on biological diversity (WCED 1987; Lubchenco et al. 1991; WRI/IUCN/UNEP 1992). The concept of sustainable development has been applied in a variety of ways. As defined by some environmental economists, *development,* which refers to improvements in organization without increases in resource con-

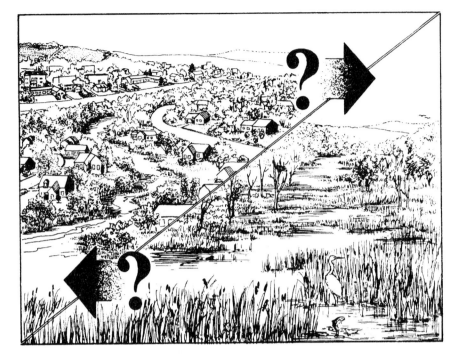

5.1   Decisions have to be made concerning compromises between development to meet human needs and the preservation of the natural world. (From Gersh and Pickert 1991; drawing by Tamara Sayre.)

sumption, is clearly distinguished from *growth,* that is, increases in the amounts of resources used (Costanza and Daly 1992). If sustainable development is to be a useful concept in conservation biology, it must emphasize development that occurs without growth in the use of natural resources. Investing in national park infrastructure to improve the protection of biological diversity and provide revenue opportunities to local people would be an example of sustainable development along these lines, as would an effort to develop less destructive logging or fishing practices.

Many large corporations, and the policy organizations that they fund, have tried to use and misuse the concept of sustainable development to "greenwash" their ongoing industrial activities without any change in their practices (Willers 1994). Can a plan to establish a huge mining complex in the middle of a forest wilderness justifiably be called "sustainable development" simply because a small percentage of the land area is set aside as a park? Some conservationists have been portrayed as going to the opposite extreme, advocating that vast areas of the world be kept off-limits to any development at all and allowed to remain or return to wilderness (Mann and Plummer 1993). As with all controversies, informed scientists and citizens must study the issues carefully, examine which groups are advocating which positions and why, and then make careful decisions that best meet the sometimes conflicting needs of human society and the protection of biological diversity.

Government Action

Local legislation

In modern societies, local (city and town) and regional (county, state, provincial) governments pass laws to provide protection for species and habitats (Caldwell 1985; Gross et al. 1991). Such laws are passed because citizens and political leaders feel that they represent the will of the majority and provide long-term benefits to the society. Conservation laws regulate activities that directly affect species and ecosystems. The most common kinds of conservation laws govern when and where hunting can occur, the size and number of animals that can be taken, the types of weapons, traps, and other equipment that can be used, and the species of animals that can be taken. In some settled areas and protected areas, hunting and fishing are banned entirely. Hunting and fishing restrictions are enforced through licensing requirements and patrols by game wardens. Similar laws affect the harvesting of plants, seaweeds, and shellfish.

Laws that control the manner in which land is used are another means of protecting biological diversity. These laws include restrictions on amount of use of or access to land, types of land use, and generation of pollution. For example, vehicles and even people on foot may be restricted from habitats and resources that are sensitive to damage, such as bird nesting areas, bogs, wildflower patches, and sources of drinking water. Uncontrolled fires may severely damage habitats, so practices contributing to accidental fires, such as campfires, are often rigidly controlled. Zoning laws sometimes prevent construction in sensitive areas such as barrier beaches and floodplains. Even where development is permitted, building permits increasingly are being reviewed to ensure that damage will not be done to endangered species or to wetlands. For major regional and national projects, environmental impact statements must be prepared that describe the damage that the project could cause.

One of the most powerful strategies for protecting biological diversity at the local level is the designation of biological communities as nature reserves. Governments often set aside public lands for various conservation purposes. In many countries, private conservation organizations are among the leaders in acquiring land for conservation efforts (Land Trust Exchange 1988; Elfring 1989). In the United States alone, over 800,000 ha of land are protected at a local level by land trusts, which are private, nonprofit corporations established to protect land and natural resources. At a national level, major organizations such as The Nature Conservancy and the Audubon Society have protected an additional 3 million ha. In Britain, the private County Nature Trusts own or lease about 2000 nature reserves covering 52,000 ha, and in the Netherlands, about half of the protected areas are privately owned (McNeely et al. 1994). Jean Hocker, executive director of the Land Trust Exchange, an association of land trust organizations, explains:

Different land trusts may save different types of land for different reasons. Some preserve farmland to maintain economic opportunities for local farmers. Some preserve wildlife habitat to ensure the existence of an endangered species. Some protect land in watersheds to improve or maintain water quality. Whether biologic, economic, productive, aesthetic, spiritual, educational, or ethical, the reasons for protecting land are as diverse as the landscape itself. (Elfring 1989)

In addition to outright purchases of land, both governments and conservation organizations protect land through **conservation easements.** Landowners are often willing to give up the right to develop, build on, or subdivide their property in exchange for a sum of money, a lower real estate tax, or a tax benefit. For many landowners, accepting a conservation easement is an attractive option because they receive a financial advantage while still keeping their land, and because they feel that they are assisting conservation objectives. Many landowners will voluntarily accept conservation restrictions without compensation. Another option that land trusts use is **limited development**, in which a landowner, a property developer, and a conservation organization reach a compromise allowing part of the land to be commercially developed while the remainder is protected by a conservation easement. Limited development projects are often successful because the developed lands typically have their value enhanced by being adjacent to conservation land. Limited development also allows the construction of necessary buildings for an expanding human society.

Local efforts by land trusts to protect land are sometimes criticized as elitist because they can provide tax breaks to those wealthy enough to take advantage of them as well as lowering the revenue collected from land and property taxes. Others argue that land in alternative uses, such as agriculture or shopping malls, is more productive. While land in trust may yield lower tax revenues, the loss of revenue from land acquired by a land trust is often offset by the increased value of property adjacent to the reserve. In addition, nature reserves, national parks, wildlife refuges, and other protected areas generate revenue throughout the local economy, which benefits the community (Power 1991). Finally, by preserving important features of the landscape and the natural communities, local nature reserves also preserve and enhance the cultural heritage of the local society.

National legislation

Throughout much of the modern world, national governments play a leading role in conservation activities (Bean 1983). The establishment of national parks is a common conservation strategy. National parks are the single largest source of protected lands in many countries. For example, Costa Rica's national parks protect over half a million hectares, or about 8% of the nation's land area (Tangley 1986; WRI/IUCN/UNEP 1992). Outside of the parks deforestation is proceeding rapidly, and soon the parks may represent the only undisturbed habitat in the country. The U.S. National Park system, with 357 sites, covers 32 million ha (Pritchard 1991).

National government agencies are the principal instrument for developing national standards on environmental pollution. Laws regulating aerial emissions, sewage treatment, waste dumping, and development of wetlands are often enacted to protect human health and property as well as natural resources such as drinking water, forests, and commercial and sport fisheries. The effectiveness with which these laws are enforced determines a nation's ability to protect its citizens and natural resources (Tobin 1990). At the same time, these laws protect biological communities that would otherwise be destroyed by pollution. The air pollution that exacerbates human respiratory disease also damages commercial forests and natural biological communities, and the pollution that ruins drinking water also kills terrestrial and aquatic species.

National governments can also have a substantial effect on the protection of biological diversity through their control of their borders, ports, and commerce. To protect forests and regulate their use, governments can restrict the export of logs, as was done in Indonesia, and penalize timber companies that damage the environment. To prevent the exploitation of rare species, governments can restrict the possession of certain species and control all imports and exports of the species. For example, the export of ivory from the rare rhinoceros hornbill bird, a valuable international commodity used for carving, is strictly controlled by the Malaysian government.

Finally, national governments can identify endangered species within their borders and take steps to conserve them, such as acquiring habitat for the species, controlling use of the species, developing a research program on the species, and implementing in situ and ex situ recovery plans.

Traditional Societies and Biological Diversity

A great deal of biodiversity exists in places where people have lived for many generations, using the resources of their environment in a sustainable manner. Local people practicing a traditional way of life in rural areas, with relatively little outside influence in terms of modern technology, are variously referred to as tribal people, indigenous people, native people, or traditional people (Dasmann 1991). These people often have established local systems of rights to natural resources, which are sometimes recognized by their governments. In most areas of the world, local people are increasingly coming into contact with the modern world, resulting in a changing belief system (particularly among the younger members of the society), and a greater use of outside manufactured goods. These established indigenous people need to be distinguished from settlers who have arrived more recently and may not be as concerned with the health of the biological community.

People have lived in nearly every terrestrial ecosystem of the world for thousands of years as hunters, fishermen, farmers, and gatherers. Even remote tropical rain forests that are designated as "wilderness" by governments and conservation groups often have a small, sparse human population. In fact, tropical areas of the world have had a particularly long association with human societies because the tropics have always been free of glaciation and are particularly amenable to human settlement. The great biological diversity of the tropics coexisted with human societies for thousands of years, and in most places, humans did not substantially damage the biological diversity of their surroundings (Gomez-Pompa and Kaus 1992). Traditional societies utilizing innovative irrigation methods and a mixture of crops were often able to support relatively high human population densities without destroying their environment or the surrounding biological communities. The present mixture and relative densities of plants and animals in many biological communities may reflect the historic activities of people in those areas, such as selective hunting of certain game animals, fishing, and planting of useful plant species (Dufour 1990; Redford 1992). The commonly practiced agricultural system known variously as swidden agriculture, shifting cultivation, and slash-and-burn agriculture has also affected forest structure and species composition by creating a mosaic of forest patches of different ages. In this system, the trees in an area are cut down, the fallen plant material is burned, and crops are planted in the nutrient-rich ash. After one or several harvests, the nutrients are washed out of the soil by the rain; the farmer then abandons the field and cuts down a new patch of forest for planting. This system works well and does not degrade the environment as long as human population density is low and there is abundant forest land.

Traditional societies have been viewed from a variety of perspectives by Western civilization. At one extreme, local people are viewed as destroyers of biological diversity who cut down forests and overharvest game. This destruction is accelerated when they acquire guns, chain saws, and outboard motors and a growing need for manufactured goods. It is also true that in some areas of the world, most notably seasonally dry areas such as Greece, people practicing traditional agriculture did severely degrade their environment. At the other extreme, traditional people are viewed as "noble savages" living in harmony with nature and minimally disturbing the natural environment. An emerging middle view is that traditional societies are highly varied, and that there is no one simple description of their relationship to their environment that fits all groups (Alcorn 1993). In addition, these societies are changing rapidly as they encounter outside influences, and there are often sharp differences between the older and younger generations.

Many traditional societies do have strong conservation ethics that are more subtle and less clearly stated than Western conservation beliefs, but which affect people's actions in their day-to-day lives (Gomez-Pompa and

5.2   River fish are the main source of protein for the Tukano people of the Amazon basin. (Photograph © Paul Patmore.)

Kaus 1992; Posey 1992). One well-documented example of such a conservation perspective is that of the Tukano Indians of northwestern Brazil (Chernela 1987). The Tukano live on a diet of root crops and river fish (Figure 5.2); they have strong religious and cultural prohibitions against cutting the forest along the Upper Río Negro, which they recognize as important to the maintenance of fish populations. The Tukano believe that these forests belong to the fish and cannot be cut by people. They have also designated extensive refuges for fish, and permit fishing along less than 40% of the river margin. Chernela observes, "As fishermen dependent upon river systems, the Tukano are aware of the relationship between their environment and the life cycles of the fish, particularly the role played by the adjacent forest in providing nutrient sources that maintain vital fisheries."

Local people can also manage their environment to maintain biological diversity, as shown by the traditional agroecosystems and forests of the Huastec Indians of northeastern Mexico (Alcorn 1984). In addition to

5.3 A Huastec Indian woman at a *te'lom,* an indigenous managed forest in northeastern Mexico. Here she collects sapote fruit (*Manilkara achras*) and cuttings of a frangipani tree (*Plumeria rubra*) for planting. (From Alcorn 1984; photograph by Janis Alcorn.)

maintaining permanent agricultural fields and practicing swidden agriculture, the Huastec maintain managed forests—known as *te'lom*—on slopes, along watercourses, and in other areas that are either fragile or unsuitable for intensive agriculture (Figure 5.3). These forests contain over 300 species of plants, from which the people obtain food, wood, and other needed products. Species composition in the forests is altered in favor of useful species by planting and periodic selective weeding. These forest resources provide Huastec families with the means to survive the failure of their cultivated crops. Comparable examples of intensively managed village forests exist in traditional societies throughout the world (Oldfield and Alcorn 1991; Nepstad and Schwartzman 1992; Redford and Padoch 1992).

Local people and their government

In the developing world, local people typically obtain the products they need—including food, fuelwood, and building materials—from their environment (MacKinnon et al. 1992). Without these products, some local people may not be able to survive. When a new national park is created, or when the boundaries of an existing park are rigidly enforced, people may be denied access to a resource that they have traditionally used or even protected. The common practice of disregarding the traditional rights and practices of local people in order to establish new conservation areas has been termed "ecocolonialism" because of its perceived similarity to the historic abuses of native rights by colonial powers of past eras (Cox and Elmqvist 1993). Most local people will react cautiously and even antagonistically when their traditional rights are curtailed (Clay 1991; Dasmann 1991). In order to survive, they will violate the park boundaries, which sometimes results in confrontations with park officers. In effect, the creation of a national park often makes local people into poachers, even though they have not changed their behavior. Even worse, if local people feel that the park and its resources no longer belong to them, but rather to an outside government, they may begin to exploit the resources of the park in a destructive manner. Park managers throughout the world frequently cite conflicts with local people as their most serious problem (Machlis and Tichnell 1985).

An extreme example of such a conflict occurred in 1989, when angry members of the Bodo tribe in Assam, India, killed twelve employees of the Manas National Park and opened the area for farming and hunting (McNeely et al. 1990). The Bodo justified their action on the basis that they were reclaiming their traditional lands that had been stolen from them by the British and not returned to them by the modern Indian government. The fact that Manas had been designated a World Heritage Site and contained such endangered species as the Indian rhinoceros and the pygmy hog was not relevant to the Bodo; the advantages of the national park were not apparent to them.

In the developing world, a rigid separation between lands used by local people to obtain natural resources and strictly protected national parks is often not possible (Wells and Brandon 1992; McNeely 1993a,b). Many examples exist in which people are allowed to enter protected areas periodically to obtain natural products. In Biosphere Reserves, local people are allowed to use resources in designated buffer zones. In another example, local people are allowed to collect canes and thatch from Chitwan National Park in Nepal (Figure 5.4; Lehmkuhl et al. 1988). Large game animals are legally harvested for meat in many African game reserves (Lewis et al. 1990). Through such compromises, the economic needs of local people are included in local conservation management plans, to the benefit of both the people and the reserve. Such compromises, known as **integrated conservation–development projects**, are increasingly being regarded as one of the best conservation strategies (Wells and Brandon 1992).

Local people sometimes even take the lead in protecting biological diversity from destruction by outside influences. The destruction of com-

5.4 Local residents collect cane grass and thatching materials from Chitwan National Park in Nepal. Park officials weigh the bundles in order to keep the harvest at a sustainable level. (Photograph © John E. Lehmkuhl.)

munal forests by government-sanctioned logging operations has been a frequent target of protests by traditional people throughout the world (Poffenberger 1990). In India, followers of the Chipko movement hug trees to prevent logging (Gadgil and Guha 1992). In Borneo, the Penan, a small tribe of hunter-gatherers, have attracted worldwide attention with their blockades of logging roads entering their traditional forests. In Thailand, Buddhist priests are working with villagers to protect communal forests and sacred groves from commercial logging operations (Figure 5.5). As stated by a Tambon leader in Thailand, "This is our community forest that was just put inside the new national park. No one consulted us. We protected this forest before the roads were put in. We set up a roadblock on the new road to stop the illegal logging. We caught the district police chief and arrested him for logging. We warned him not to come again" (Alcorn 1991). Empowering such local people and helping them to obtain legal title to their traditionally owned lands is often an important component of efforts to establish locally managed protected areas in developing countries (Davis and Wali 1994).

5.5 Buddhist priests in Thailand offer prayers and blessings to protect trees from commercial logging operations. (Photograph by Project for Ecological Recovery, Bangkok.)

Biological diversity and cultural diversity

Biological and cultural diversity are often linked. The rugged tropical areas of the world where the greatest concentrations of species are found are frequently the areas where people have the greatest cultural and linguistic diversity. The geographical isolation by mountain ranges and complex river systems that favors biological speciation also favors the differentiation of human cultures. The cultural diversity found in places such as Central Africa, Amazonia, New Guinea, and Southeast Asia represents one of the most valuable resources of human civilization, providing unique insights into philosophy, religion, music, art, resource management, and psychology (Denslow and Padoch 1988). The protection of these traditional cultures within their natural environment provides the opportunity to achieve the dual objectives of protecting biological diversity and preserving cultural diversity. In the words of Toledo (1988):

> In a country that is characterized by the cultural diversity of its rural inhabitants, it is difficult to design a conservation policy without taking into

account the cultural dimension; the profound relationship that has existed since time immemorial between *nature* and *culture*. …Each species of plant, group of animals, type of soil and landscape nearly always has a corresponding linguistic expression, a category of knowledge, a practical use, a religious meaning, a role in ritual, an individual or collective vitality. To safeguard the natural heritage of the country without safeguarding the cultures which have given it feeling is to reduce nature to something beyond recognition, static, distant, nearly dead.

Cultural diversity is strongly linked to the genetic diversity of crop plants. In mountainous areas in particular, the geographically isolated cultures develop local plant varieties known as landraces; these cultivars are adapted to the local climate, soils, and pests, and satisfy the tastes of the local people. The genetic variation in these landraces has global significance to modern agriculture because of its potential for the improvement of crop species (see Chapter 3).

Involving traditional societies in conservation efforts

Several strategies exist for integrating the protection of biological diversity, the customs of traditional societies, and the genetic variability of traditional crops. Many of them could be classified as Integrated Conservation–Development Projects (Wells and Brandon 1992).

Biosphere reserves. UNESCO's Man and the Biosphere Program (MAB) includes among its goals the maintenance of "samples of varied and harmonious landscapes resulting from long-established land use pattern" (UNESCO 1985; Gregg 1991). The MAB Program recognizes the role of people in shaping the natural landscape, as well as the need to find ways in which people can sustainably use natural resources without degrading the environment. The MAB research framework, applied in its worldwide network of designated Biosphere Reserves (see Chapter 4), integrates natural science and social science research. It includes investigations of how biological communities respond to different human activities, how humans respond to changes in their natural environment, and how degraded ecosystems can be restored to their former condition.

One valuable example of a Biosphere Reserve is the Kuna Yala Indigenous Reserve on the northeastern coast of Panama (Gregg 1991). In this protected area of 60,000 ha of tropical forest, 30,000 Kuna people in 60 villages practice traditional medicine, agriculture, and forestry, while documentation and research are carried out by scientists from outside institutions. The Kuna carefully regulate the levels of scientific research in the reserve, insisting on local training, presentation of reports before scientists leave the area, payment of research fees, and having local guides accompany the scientists. The Kuna people even control the type and rate of economic development in the reserve, with assistance from their own outside, paid advisors. The level of empowerment of the Kuna people is unusual and illustrates the potential for traditional people to take control of their destiny, their way of life, and their environment. However, as tradi-

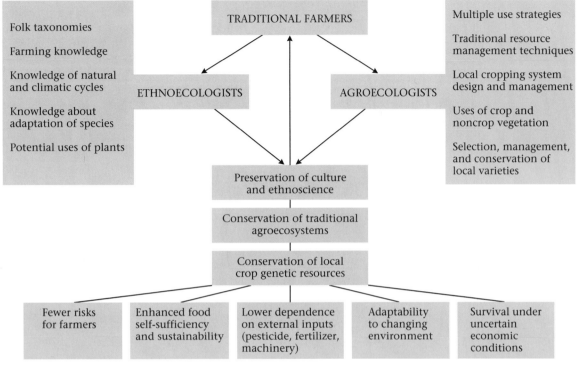

5.6 Traditional agricultural practices can be viewed from both a human cultural and an agricultural perspective. A synthesis of these viewpoints can lead to theoretical and methodological approaches toward the conservation of the environment, the culture, and the genetic variation found in these traditional agroecosystems. (After Altieri and Anderson 1992.)

tional conservation beliefs erode in the face of outside influences, younger Kuna are beginning to question the need to rigidly protect the reserve.

In situ agricultural conservation. In many areas of the world, local farmers cultivating locally adapted varieties of crop plants can preserve genetic variability in crop species (Figure 5.6). For example, thousands of distinct varieties of potatoes are grown by Andean farmers in South America. Often these farmers grow many varieties in one field to minimize the risk of crop failure and to produce different varieties for different uses. Similarly, traditional farmers in the Apo Kayan of Borneo may grow more than 50 varieties of rice. These local varieties often have unique genes for dealing with disease, nutrient deficiencies, pests, drought, and other environmental variations (Browning 1991; Cleveland et al. 1994). Moreover, these local varieties continue to evolve new genetic combinations, some of which may be effective in dealing with looming global environmental threats. However, farmers throughout the world are abandoning their traditional forms of agriculture with local landraces in order to grow high-yielding varieties using capital-intensive methods. In countries such as Indonesia, Sri Lanka, and the Philippines, over 80% of the farmers have adopted modern varieties (Brush 1989).

While an increased yield may be better in the short term for the individual farmer and his society, the long-term health of modern agriculture depends on the preservation of the genetic variability represented by local varieties. One innovative suggestion has been for an international agricultural body to subsidize villages to be in situ, or in place, "landrace custodians" (Nabhan 1985; Wilkes 1991; Altieri and Anderson 1992). Villagers in these zones would be paid to grow their traditional crops in a traditional manner, providing a crucial source of genes for modern crop improvement programs.

Programs incorporating in situ conservation practices have already been initiated in some places. In Mexico in particular, a number of development programs are attempting to integrate traditional agriculture, conservation, and research (Gliessman 1991; Toledo 1991). One example is the 140,000 ha Sierra de Manantlan Biosphere Reserve in western Mexico, which was established to preserve the only known populations of *Zea diploperennis,* a perennial relative of corn (maize) (Benz et al. 1990). This plant, occurring only in abandoned *milpas* (fields planted using traditional shifting agricultural methods), is of great potential value in efforts to preserve genes that may someday be used to protect the annual corn crop, valued at $55 billion per year. The long-term protection of *Z. diploperennis* in the wild depends on encouraging local farmers to remain on the land and continue their traditional cultivation practices.

A slightly different approach used in arid regions of the American Southwest involves linking traditional agriculture and genetic conservation (Nabhan 1985). A private organization, Native Seeds/SEARCH, collects the seeds of traditional crop cultivars for long-term preservation. The organization also encourages farmers to grow traditional crops, provides them with the seeds of traditional cultivars, and buys the farmers' unsold production. Countries have also established special reserves to conserve areas containing wild relatives of crops. Species reserves protect the wild relatives of wheat, oats, and barley in Israel (Browning 1991), and 127 such reserves were created in the former Soviet Union.

Extractive reserves. In many areas of the world, people have extracted products from biological communities for decades and even centuries. The sale and barter of these natural products are a major part of the livelihood of the people. The right to continue collecting natural products from the surrounding countryside is a major concern of local people. The establishment of a national park that excludes the traditional collection of products will meet with as much resistance from the local community as will a land-grab by outsiders that involves exploitation of the natural resources and conversion to other uses.

The Brazilian government is trying to address the legitimate demands of local citizens through a new type of protected area known as an **extractive reserve,** from which local people collect natural products such as rubber, resins, and nuts in a way that minimizes damage to the forest ecosystem (Fearnside 1989; Holloway 1993). Such areas, currently comprising about 3 million hectares, guarantee the ability of local people to continue their way of life and guard against possible conversion of the land to cattle ranching and farming. The government protection afforded to the local people also serves to protect the biological diversity of the area because the ecosystem remains basically intact (Nepstad et al. 1992). Populations of large animals in extractive reserves, however, may still decline due to subsistence hunting.

The real challenge for the local people and their Brazilian and international allies is to develop natural products that can be collected and sold at a good market price. If the local people cannot survive by collecting natural products, they could be forced to cut down their forests for timber and agriculture out of economic desperation.

Community-based initiatives. In many cases, local people already protect the forests, rivers, coastal waters, wildlife, and plants in the vicinity of their homes. Such protection is often enforced by village elders and is based on religious and traditional beliefs. Governments and conservation organizations can assist local conservation initiatives by providing help in obtaining legal title to traditional lands, access to scientific expertise, and financial assistance to develop needed infrastructure. One example of such a project is the Community Baboon Sanctuary in eastern Belize, created by a collective agreement among a group of villages to maintain the forest habitat required by the local population of howler monkeys (*Alouatta palliata*) (Horwich 1993). Ecotourists visiting the sanctuary must pay a fee to the village organization and additional fees if they stay overnight and eat meals with a local family. Conservation biologists working at the site have provided training for local nature guides, a body of scientific information on the wildlife, funds for a local natural history museum, and business training for the village leaders.

In the Pacific islands of Samoa, much of the rain forest land is under customary ownership by indigenous people (Cox and Elmqvist 1991). Villagers are under increasing pressure to sell logs from their forests to pay for schools and other necessities. Despite this situation, the local people have a strong desire to preserve the forests because of their religious and cultural significance, as well as their value as sources of medicinal plants and other products. A variety of solutions are being developed to meet these conflicting needs. In American Samoa, the U.S. government has agreed to lease forest and coastal land from the villages to establish a new national park. In this case, the villages will retain ownership of the land and traditional hunting and collecting rights. Village elders are also assigned places on the park advisory board. In Western Samoa, international conservation organizations and various donors agreed to build schools, medical clinics, and other public works projects that the villages needed in exchange for their stopping all commercial logging. Thus, each dollar donated did double service, both protecting the forest and providing humanitarian aid to the villages. A key element in the success of these projects was the ability to build on and work with stable, flexible local institutions. Conservation initiatives involving recent immigrants or demoralized local people are generally more difficult.

International Approaches to Conservation and Sustainable Development

The Earth Summit

Protecting the environment is both a local and a global task. Despite the continued destruction of key resources and ecosystems, significant strides have been made in adopting a global approach to sound environmental management. One of the most recent hallmarks of this progress was the Earth Summit, held for 12 days in June 1992 in Rio de Janeiro, Brazil. Known officially as the United Nations Conference on Environment and Development (UNCED), it included representatives from 178 countries, with over 100 heads of state, plus leaders of the United Nations and major nongovernmental and conservation organizations, in attendance. The purpose of the conference was to discuss ways of combining increased protection of the environment with more effective economic development in less wealthy countries (United Nations 1993a,b). The conference was successful in heightening awareness of the seriousness of the environmental crisis and placing the issue at the center of world attention (Haas et al. 1992). A noteworthy feature of the conference was the clear linkage perceived between the protection of the environment and the need to alleviate Third World poverty through increased levels of financial assistance from wealthier countries.

The conference participants discussed and eventually signed the five major documents described below and initiated many new projects. Aside from these specific achievements, the central accomplishment of the Earth Summit was the willingness of the participants to keep working together on long-term goals.

- *The Rio Declaration.* The Declaration provides general principles to guide the actions of both wealthy and poor nations on issues of the environment and development. The right of nations to utilize their own resources for economic and social development is recognized, as long as the environment elsewhere is not harmed. The Declaration affirms the "polluter pays" principle, according to which companies and governments take financial responsibility for the environmental damage that they cause.

- *Convention on Climate Change.* This agreement requires industrialized countries to reduce their emissions of carbon dioxide and other greenhouse gases and to make regular reports on their progress.

While specific emission limits were not decided upon, the convention states that greenhouse gases should be stabilized at levels that will not interfere with the Earth's climate.

- *Convention on Biodiversity.* The Convention on Biodiversity has three objectives: the protection of biological diversity; its sustainable use; and equitable sharing of the benefits of new products made with wild and domestic species. While the first two objectives are straightforward, the last recognizes that developing countries should receive fair compensation for the use made of species collected within their borders. The United States has not ratified this convention because of what are perceived to be potential restrictions on its enormous biotechnology industry.

- *Statement on Forest Principles.* An agreement on the management of forests proved to be difficult to negotiate due to strong differences of opinion between tropical and temperate countries. The final, non-binding treaty calls for the sustainable management of forests without making any specific recommendations.

- *Agenda 21.* This 800-page document is an innovative attempt to describe in a comprehensive manner the policies needed for environmentally sound development (United Nations 1993a). Agenda 21 shows the linkages between the environment and other issues that are often considered separately, such as child welfare, poverty, women's issues, technology transfer, and unequal divisions of wealth. Plans of action are described to address problems of the atmosphere, land degradation and desertification, mountain development, agriculture and rural development, deforestation, aquatic environments, and pollution. Financial, institutional, technological, and legal mechanisms for implementing these action plans are also described.

The most contentious issue was deciding how to fund the Earth Summit programs, particularly Agenda 21. The cost of these programs was estimated to be about $600 billion per year, of which $125 billion was to come from the developed countries as overseas development assistance (ODA). Because existing levels of ODA amount to $60 billion per year for all activities, this means that implementing Agenda 21 would require a tripling of the present foreign aid commitment. The major developed countries, known as the Group of Seven, did not agree to this increase in funding. Dr. Mahathir bin Mohamed, Prime Minister of Malaysia, eloquently summarized the developing countries' frustration at the lack of financial commitment on the part of the wealthy nations:

The poor countries of the world have been told to preserve their forests and other genetic resources on the off chance that at some future date something is discovered which might prove useful to humanity. But now they are told that the rich will not agree to compensate the poor for their sacrifices, arguing that the diversity of genes stored and safeguarded by the poor are of no value until the rich, through their superior intelligence, release the potential within.

In the end, the industrialized countries did announce $6 billion in new contributions, but only a portion of that amount has been received so far. Raising additional funds for the implementation of Agenda 21 will be an ongoing process. Also, questions on how this money is to be allocated have not been satisfactorily resolved, with major disagreements remaining between developing and developed countries over the control of the program (Haas et al. 1992; WRI/UNEP/UNDP 1994).

International funding and sustainable development

Increasingly, groups in the developed countries are realizing that if they want to preserve biological diversity in species-rich but cash-poor developing countries, they cannot simply provide advice: a financial commitment is also required. Institutions within the United States represent some of the largest sources of this financial assistance. The aid these organizations provide is substantial: in 1991, a total of 1410 projects receiving aid from U.S. institutions were identified in 102 developing countries, accounting for a total investment of $105 million (Abramovitz 1991, 1994). The predominant sources of funds were U.S. government agencies ($70 million) such as the Agency for International Development and the National Science Foundation, charitable foundations ($20 million) such as the Mellon Foundation, the MacArthur Foundation, the W. Alton Jones Foundation, and Pew Charitable Trusts, and nongovernmental organizations ($10 million) such as the World Wildlife Fund, Conservation International, and The Nature Conservancy. Investment by large foundations increased sevenfold between 1987 and 1991, and government funding tripled during this period, demonstrating that tropical conservation has clearly been targeted as a funding priority (Figure 5.7).

The projects funded by U.S. institutions were overwhelmingly concentrated in Latin America and the Caribbean, which received 54% of the funds (Abramovitz 1994). Funding was much lower in other regions of the world, with only four countries in Africa (Botswana, Kenya, Madagascar, and Tanzania) and five in Asia (Bhutan, India, Indonesia, the Philippines, and Thailand) receiving more than $1 million per year (Table 5.1). While funding levels for conservation in developing countries are increasing substantially, the amount of money being spent is still inadequate to protect the great storehouse of biological riches needed for the long-term prosperity of human society. In comparison with the billions of dollars allocated to other large U.S. science projects, such as the Human Genome Project and the space program, the $105 million per year being spent on biological diversity is meager indeed.

A major new source of funds for conservation and environmental activities in developing countries is the Global Environment Facility (GEF),

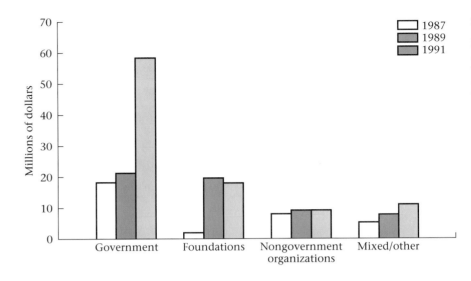

5.7 Funding from United States sources for biodiversity research and conservation efforts in developing countries, by type of funding organization: organizations and divisions of the U.S. government; charitable foundations and trusts; nongovernment organizations such as the World Wildlife Fund; and funding from multiple sources or from miscellaneous institutions (such as universities, zoos, and museums). (From Abramovitz 1994.)

created in 1991 by the World Bank along with the United Nations Development Programme (UNDP) and the U.N. Environmental Programme (UNEP). Most of the funds for the program were authorized and the projects approved by the time of the Earth Summit in June 1992. The GEF was established as a three-year pilot program with a budget of $1.2 billion, to be used for funding projects relating to global warming, biodiversity, international waters, and ozone depletion. Two recent evaluations of the GEF judged the first round of projects to be a mixed success, and identified lack of participation by community groups and government leaders as a major problem (Bowles and Prickett 1994; UNDP/UNEP/World Bank 1994). An additional problem was the mismatch of large-scale funding over short periods with the long-term needs of poor countries. Hopefully, the second round of funding currently under way will deal with these issues.

An increasingly important mechanism used to provide secure, long-term support for conservation activities in developing countries is the national environmental fund (NEF). NEFs are typically set up as conservation trust funds or foundations in which a board of trustees—composed of representatives of the host government, conservation organizations, and donor agencies—allocates the annual income from an endowment to support inadequately funded government departments, as well as nongovernment conservation organizations and activities. NEFs have been established in over 20 countries with funds contributed by the United States government and by such major organizations as the World Bank and the World Wildlife Fund (IUCN/TNC/WWF 1994; Mitikin and Osgood 1994).

One important early example of an NEF, the Bhutan Trust Fund for Environmental Conservation (BTF), was established in 1991 by the government of Bhutan in cooperation with the United Nations Development Pro-

Table 5.1
U.S. funding for tropical biodiversity conservation in 1991

Country	1991 funding ($U.S.)[a]	Land area (× 1000 ha)	Dollars per 1000 ha
Brazil	9,278,761	851,197	11
Mexico	7,948,514	195,820	41
Philippines	6,405,862	30,000	214
Costa Rica	5,079,758	5,110	994
Ecuador	4,576,125	28,356	161
Indonesia	3,260,962	190,457	17
Peru	2,397,939	128,522	19
Paraguay	2,357,722	40,675	58
Botswana	2,250,500	58,173	39
Madagascar	1,723,960	58,704	29
Tanzania	1,666,323	94,509	18
Jamaica	1,547,087	1,099	1,408
Belize	1,368,468	2,296	596
Bolivia	1,318,753	109,858	12
Kenya	1,293,816	58,037	22
Bhutan	1,272,220	4,700	271
Chile	1,127,156	75,695	15
India	1,084,009	328,726	3
Thailand	1,090,956	51,312	21

Source: Funding data from World Resources Institute Biodiversity Projects Database, in Abramovitz 1994.

[a] Table includes those countries that received more than $1,000,000.

gramme and the World Wildlife Fund. The BTF has already received about $14 million out of its goal of $20 million, with the Global Environment Facility being the largest donor. Activities include surveying the rich biological resources of this eastern Himalayan country, training foresters, ecologists, and other environmental professionals, promoting environmental education, establishing and managing protected areas, and designing and implementing integrated conservation development projects.

An innovative idea, the debt-for-nature swap, has been used as a vehicle for financing projects to protect biological diversity. Collectively, developing countries owe about $1.3 trillion to international financial institutions, which represents 44% of their combined gross national products (Hansen 1989; Dogsé and von Droste 1990). In some debt-for-nature swaps, the commercial banks that hold these debts sell them at a steep discount on the international secondary debt market, due to low expectations of repayment. An international conservation organization buys a developing country's discounted debt from a bank. The debt is then canceled in exchange for the developing country agreeing to make annual payments, in its own currency, for conservation activities such as land acquisition, park management, and public education.

In other "swaps," governments of developed countries owed money directly by developing countries may decide to cancel a certain percentage of the debt if the developing country will agree to contribute to a national environmental fund or other conservation activity. Such programs have converted debt valued at $1 billion for conservation and sustainable development activities in Colombia, Poland, Madagascar, and a dozen other countries.

The total amount of debt involved in debt-for-nature swaps is only about 0.1% of Third World debt, so their overall effect has been minimal so far. Debt swaps have also proved to be complex and difficult to negotiate due to the their novelty, the weak financial condition of many debtor governments, and shifting political climates. Although their application appears to be fairly limited, in particular situations debt-for-nature swaps can be one of many useful financing tools (Patterson 1990).

How are funds allocated to conservation projects? When a conservation need, such as protecting a species or establishing a nature reserve, is identified, this often initiates a complex process of project design, proposal writing, fund raising, and implementation that involves several different types of conservation organizations. Charitable foundations (e.g., the MacArthur Foundation) and government agencies (e.g., U.S. Agency for International Development) often provide money for conservation projects through direct grants to the institutions that implement the projects (e.g., Colorado State University, Missouri Botanical Garden). In other cases, foundations and government agencies give money to major nongovernmental conservation organizations (e.g., World Wildlife Fund, Wildlife Conservation International), which in turn provide grants to local conservation organizations. The major international conservation organizations are often active in establishing, strengthening, and funding local nongovernmental organizations, as well as government conservation programs, in the developing world. Working with local organizations in developing countries is an effective strategy because it provides training and support for groups of citizens within the country, who can then be advocates for conservation for many years to come.

International development banks and ecosystem damage

The rates of tropical deforestation, habitat destruction, and loss of aquatic ecosystems have sometimes been accelerated by poorly conceived projects financed by the international development agencies of major industrial nations, as well as by the four major **multilateral development banks** (MDBs) controlled by those nations: the World Bank, which lends to all regions of the globe, and the regional MDBs, the Inter-American Development Bank (IDB), the Asian Development Bank (ADB), and the African Development Bank (AFDB). The MDBs loan more than $25 billion per year to 151 countries to finance economic development projects (Rich 1990). While the goal of the MDBs and aid agencies ostensibly is economic development, the effect of many of the projects they support is to exploit natural resources for export to international markets. In many cases, these development projects have resulted in the destruction of ecosystems over a wide area.

Because the MDBs are controlled by the governments of the major developed countries, such as the United States, Japan, Germany, the United Kingdom, and France, the policies of the MDBs can be scrutinized by the elected representatives of the MDB member countries, the national media, and conservation organizations. In particular, as some of the ill-conceived projects of the World Bank have been publicly criticized, the World Bank has reacted by making the conservation of biological diversity part of its assistance policy and requiring new projects to be more environmentally responsible (Goodland 1992). However, it remains to be seen whether the MDBs will actually change their practices or only their rhetoric. It is also true that the MDBs have no enforcement authority; once the money is handed over, countries can choose to ignore the environmental provisions in the agreement, despite local and international protests.

How can multilateral development banks operate more responsibly? First, they can stop making loans for environmentally destructive projects (WRI/IUCN/UNEP 1992). This step would require the banks to analyze development projects using economic cost-benefit models that include the environmental and ecological effects of projects. An accurate analysis of a project would include all of its costs and benefits, including the effects of soil erosion, the loss of biological diversity, the impact of water pollution on the health and diets of local people, and the loss of income associated with the destruction of renewable resources (Daly and Cobb 1989; Repetto 1992). Programs that encourage land reform, reductions in rural poverty, establishment of new protected areas, and truly sustainable development should be encouraged. Also, banks need to encourage open public discussion among all groups in a country before projects are implemented. In particular, the banks should allow examination, independent evaluations, and discussions of environmental impact reports before a project is approved for funding.

Lending for development: some case studies

The following are some of the most highly publicized examples of the effects of lending for national economic development.

Indonesia. From the 1970s to the late 1980s, the World Bank loaned $560 million to the Indonesian government to resettle millions of people from the densely populated inner islands of Java, Bali, and Lombok on the sparsely inhabited, heavily forested outer islands of Borneo (Kalimantan), New Guinea (Irian Jaya), and Sulawesi (Rich 1990). These settlers were supposed to raise crops to feed themselves as well as cash crops, such as rubber, oil palm, and cacao, that could be exported to pay off the World Bank loan. This transmigration program has been an environmental and economic failure because the poor tropical forest soils on the outer islands are not suited to the intensive agriculture practiced by the settlers (Whitten 1987). As a result, many of the settlers have become impoverished and are forced to cut down forests to practice shifting agriculture. The production of export crops to pay off the World Bank loan has not materialized. In addition, at least 2 million and possibly up to 6 million ha of tropical rain forest, as well as adjacent aquatic ecosystems, has been destroyed by the settlers. Although this amount of land is enormous, it still represents only a small fraction of the forested area of the outer islands.

Brazil. The highway project in the Brazilian state of Rondonia is a classic example of a development program gone awry (Fearnside 1987, 1990; Anderson 1990). The World Bank and the Inter-American Development Bank have loaned hundreds of millions of dollars to Brazil since 1981 to build roads and settlement areas in this region. When a highway to Porto Velho, the capital of Rondonia, was opened, farmers from southern and northeastern Brazil, who had been displaced from their land by increasing mechanization and land ownership laws that favored the wealthy, flocked to Rondonia seeking free land. Much of the land in Rondonia was unsuitable for agriculture but was cleared to establish land claims; this practice was often facilitated by tax subsidies. As a result, Rondonia had one of the most rapid rates of deforestation in the world during the 1980s. At the peak of deforestation in 1987, 20 million hectares—2.5% of Brazil's total land area—was burned in one of the world's most massive episodes of environmental devastation. Agricultural, industrial, and transportation projects have consistently been launched in this area without environmental impact studies or land use studies to determine their feasibility. In its haste to develop the region, the Brazilian government also built roads across Amerindian reserves and biological reserves that were supposed to be completely protected, effectively opening up even these areas to deforestation. The result was environmental devastation with minor, fleeting economic benefits. With stricter controls on land clearing and an end to the subsidies, the rate of deforestation in Rondonia has now been reduced (Skole et al. 1994).

Dam projects. A major class of projects financed by development agencies and banks is dam and irrigation systems that provide water for agricultural activities and generate hydroelectric power (Figure 5.8; Goodland 1990). These projects often damage large aquatic ecosystems by changing water depth and current patterns, increasing sedimentation, and creating barriers to dispersal. As a result of these changes, many species are no longer able to survive in the altered environment.

Ironically, research indicates that the long-term success of some of the large international dam projects that threaten aquatic ecosystems may depend on preserving the forest ecosystem surrounding the project site. The

5.8 A hydroelectric dam on the Volta River in Ghana. The watersheds around such dams must be protected if the dams are to operate efficiently. (Photograph courtesy of FAO.)

loss of plant cover on the slopes above water projects often results in soil erosion and siltation, with resulting losses of efficiency, higher maintenance costs, and damage for irrigation systems and dams. Protecting the forests and other natural vegetation in the watersheds is now widely recognized as an important and relatively inexpensive way to ensure the efficiency and longevity of water projects, while at the same time preserving large areas of natural habitat. In one study of irrigation projects in Indonesia, it was found that the cost of protecting watersheds ranged from only 1% to 10% of the total cost of the project, in contrast to an estimated 30%–40% drop in efficiency due to siltation if the forests were not protected (MacKinnon 1983). One of the most successful examples of an effective environmental investment was the $1.2 million loan made by the World Bank to assist in the development and protection of Dumoga–Bone National Park in northern Sulawesi, Indonesia (McNeely 1987). A 278,700 ha primary rain forest, which included the catchment area on the slopes above a $60 million irrigation project also financed by the World Bank, was converted into a national park (Figure 5.9). In this particular case, the World Bank was able to protect its original investment through environmental funding representing less than 2% of the project's cost, and create a significant new national park in the process.

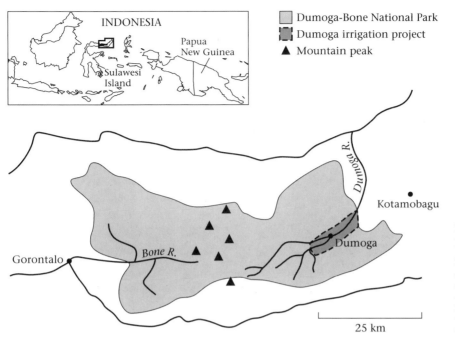

INDONESIA

Papua
New Guinea

Sulawesi
Island

☐ Dumoga-Bone National Park
▨ Dumoga irrigation project
▲ Mountain peak

Dumoga R.

Kotamobagu

Bone R.

Gorontalo

Dumoga

25 km

5.9 The Dumoga–
Bone National Park on
the northern arm of
Sulawesi Island, In-
donesia, protects the
watershed above the
Dumoga Irrigation
Project. (After Wells
and Brandon 1992.)

An Agenda for the Future

People at all levels of society must learn that it is in their own interest to
work for conservation and to halt the ongoing worldwide loss of species
and biological communities. If conservationists can demonstrate that the
protection of biological diversity has more value than the destruction of
biological diversity, then people and their governments may be willing to
take positive action.

There is a consensus among conservation biologists that a number of
major problems are involved in preserving biological diversity, and that
certain changes in policies and practices are needed.

Problem: Protecting biological diversity is difficult when most of the
world's species remain undescribed by scientists, and entire biological
communities remain undiscovered.

Response: More scientists and enthusiastic nonscientists need to be
trained to identify, classify, and monitor species, and funding should be
increased in this area, particularly biological exploration in remote regions
of the world and unusual habitats.

Problem: Many conservation issues are global in scope, involving many
countries.

Response: Countries are increasingly willing to discuss international conservation issues, as shown by the 1992 Earth Summit, as well as to sign and implement treaties such as the recent Convention on Biodiversity and CITES. International conservation efforts are expanding, and further participation in these activities by conservation biologists and the general public should be encouraged. Citizens and governments of developed countries must become aware that they bear a direct responsibility for the destruction of biological diversity through their overconsumption of the world's resources. Widespread changes in lifestyle, reduced use of resources, and alternative markets for "green" products can all have a positive effect on the environment.

Problem: Developed countries often place a greater emphasis on the preservation of biological diversity than do the poorer Third World countries that have the most biological diversity.

Response: Developed countries and international conservation organizations should provide secure, long-term financial support to developing countries that establish and maintain national parks and other protected areas. Related economic and social problems must be resolved at the same time.

Problem: Economic analyses often paint a falsely encouraging picture of development projects that are environmentally damaging.

Response: New types of cost-benefit analyses and "green accounting" that include environmental and human costs, such as the costs of soil erosion, water pollution, loss of natural products, loss of traditional knowledge with potential economic value, loss of tourist potential, loss of species of possible future value, and loss of home sites, must be developed and used. Environmental impact analyses also need to include comparative studies of similar projects completed elsewhere, and the probabilities and costs of possible worst-case scenarios.

Problem: Ecosystem services do not receive the recognition they deserve in economic analyses.

Response: Economic activities should be linked with the maintenance of ecosystem services through fees, penalties, and land acquisition. The "polluter pays" principle, in which industries and governments pay for cleaning up the environmental damage their activities have caused, must be adopted. A step in this direction is the recent initiative by electric power companies to plant trees in the tropics to absorb the excess carbon dioxide that their power plants produce.

Problem: Much of the destruction of the world's biological diversity is caused by people who are desperately poor and are simply trying to survive.

Response: Conservation biologists and charitable and humanitarian organizations need to assist local people in organizing and developing suitable economic activities that do not damage biological diversity. Foreign assistance programs need to be carefully planned so that they help to alleviate rural poverty rather than primarily benefiting urban elites. Programs promoting smaller families and reducing human population growth should be closely linked to efforts aimed at improving economic opportunities and halting environmental degradation (Dasgupta 1995).

Problem: Decisions on land conversion and the establishment of protected areas are often made by central governments with little input from people in the region being affected. Consequently, local people sometimes feel alienated from conservation projects and do not support them.

Response: Local people have to believe that they will benefit from a conservation project and that their involvement is important. To achieve this goal, environmental impact statements and other project information should be publicly available to encourage open discussion at all steps of a project. Decision-making mechanisms should be established to ensure that the rights and responsibilities of management of conservation projects are shared between government agencies and local communities (Western et al. 1994).

Problem: The revenues, business activities, and scientific research associated with national parks often do not directly benefit surrounding communities.

Response: Whenever possible, local people should be trained and employed in parks as a way of utilizing local knowledge and providing local income. Also, a portion of park revenues can be used to fund community projects such as schools and clinics. Conservation biologists working in national parks should periodically explain the purpose and results of their work to nearby communities and school groups, and listen to what the local people have to say.

Problem: National parks and conservation areas in developing countries have inadequate budgets to pay for conservation activities. Revenues that they collect are often returned to government treasuries.

Response: Funds for park management can often be raised from foreign tourists and scientists by charging them "international rates" for admission, lodging, or meals. Making sure that these revenues and profits remain at the park and in the surrounding area is important. Also, zoos and conservation organizations in the developed world can make direct financial contributions to conservation efforts in developing countries, strengthening the most significant programs.

Problem: People cut down tropical forests and graze grasslands to establish title to the land, even on lands that are not suitable for agriculture. Timber companies that lease forests and ranchers who rent grassland from the government often damage the land and reduce its productive capacity in pursuit of short-term profits.

5.10 Business interests and governments are often unwilling to acknowledge and deal with environmental problems. Citizen activism is sometimes needed to convince businesses and governments that concern for biological diversity often makes economic as well as ecological sense. (Drawing by Dana Fradon; © The New Yorker Magazine, Inc.)

"Sir, would you take this latest warning of ecological disaster and pooh-pooh it for me?"

Response: Laws should be changed so that people and companies can obtain titles and leases to harvest trees and use grasslands only so long as the health of the biological community is maintained.

Problem: In some countries, governments are inefficient, slow-moving, and bound by excessive regulation, and consequently are ineffective at protecting biological communities.

Response: Local nongovernmental conservation organizations, villages, and neighborhood groups are often the most effective agents for dealing with conservation issues and should be encouraged and supported politically, scientifically, and financially. Bringing together all of the stakeholders for discussions, meetings, and planning sessions is crucial so that local people, in particular, feel that their involvement is important.

Problem: Many businesses, banks, and governments are uninterested in and unresponsive to conservation issues (Figure 5.10).

Response: Lobbying efforts may be effective at changing the policies of institutions that want to avoid bad publicity. Petitions, rallies, letter-writing campaigns, press releases, and economic boycotts all have their place when reasonable requests for change are ignored (Figure 5.11). In many situations, radical environmental groups, such as Greenpeace and Earth-First!, dominate media attention with dramatic, publicity-grabbing actions, while mainstream conservation organizations, such as The Nature Conservancy and the World Wildlife Fund, follow behind to negotiate a compromise.

5.11   Demonstrations, such as this protest against the extensive logging of old-growth forests in the Pacific Northwest, can focus media attention on environmental problems that the society needs to deal with. (Photograph by Michael Graybill and Jan Hodder/Biological Photo Service.)

The role of conservation biologists in achieving the agenda

Conservation biology differs from many other scientific disciplines in that it plays an active role in the preservation of biological diversity in all forms: species, genetic variability, biological communities, and ecosystem functions. Members of the diverse disciplines that contribute to conservation biology share the common goal of protecting biological diversity (Norton 1991). The ideas and theories of conservation biology are increasingly being incorporated into political debate, and the preservation of biological diversity has been targeted as a priority for new government programs.

A broad, thoughtful perspective is necessary to create and continue the most effective conservation programs. In many cases, species are driven to extinction by combinations of factors acting simultaneously or sequentially. Blaming a group of poor, rural people or a certain industry for the destruction of biological diversity is a simplistic and usually ineffective strategy. The challenge is to understand the national and international linkages that promote the destruction and to find viable alternatives. These alternatives must involve stabilizing the size of the human population, finding a livelihood for rural people in developing countries that does not damage the environment, providing incentives and penalties that will convince industries to value the environment, and restricting international trade in products that are obtained by damaging the environment. Also important is a willingness on the part of people in developed countries to reduce their consumption of the world's resources and pay fair prices for products that are produced in a sustainable, nondestructive manner.

If global biological diversity is to be preserved, conservation biologists must take on several active roles. First, they must become more effective as educators, in the public forum as well as in the classroom. Conservation biologists need to educate as broad a range of people as possible about the problems that stem from the loss of biological diversity.

Second, conservation biologists must become politically active. Involvement in the political process allows conservation biologists to influence the passage of new laws to support the preservation of biological diversity, or, alternatively, to argue against legislation that would prove harmful to species or ecosystems (Caldwell 1985). The current difficulties in getting the U.S. Congress to reauthorize the U.S. Endangered Species Act dramatically illustrate the need for greater political activism.

Third, conservation biologists need to become organizers within the biological community. By stimulating interest in conservation biology among their colleagues, conservation biologists can increase the ranks of trained professional advocates fighting the destruction of natural resources.

Fourth, conservation biologists need to become motivators, convincing a range of people to support conservation efforts. At a local level, conservation programs have to be created and presented in ways that provide incentives for local people to support them. Public discussion, educational efforts, and publicity need to be a major part of any such program. Careful attention must be devoted in particular to convincing business leaders and politicians to support conservation efforts. Many of these people will support conservation efforts when they are presented in the right way; sometimes conservation is perceived to have good publicity value, or supporting it is perceived to be better than a confrontation that may otherwise result.

Finally, and most importantly, conservation biologists need to become effective managers and practitioners of conservation projects. They must be willing to walk on the ground to find out what is really happening, to get dirty, to talk and work with local people, to knock on doors, and to take risks. Conservation biologists must learn everything they can about the species and communities that they are trying to protect, and then make that knowledge available to others. If conservation biologists are willing to put their ideas into practice, and to work with park managers, land use planners, politicians, and local people, then progress will follow. In many cases, bringing together all of the stakeholders for discussions and planning is one of the most important steps in building a consensus for action. Getting the right mixture of models, new theories, innovative approaches, and practical examples will be the key to the success of the discipline. Once this balance is found, conservation biologists working with an energized citizenry will be in a position to protect the world's biological diversity during this unprecedented era of change.

Summary

1. Sustainable development has become an important concept in guiding human activities, but it has not often been easy to find the right balance between the protection of biological diversity and the use of natural resources.

2. Local and national governments protect biological diversity through the passage of laws that regulate such activities as fishing, hunting, land use, and industrial pollution, and through the establishment of protected areas.

3. Many traditional societies have strong conservation ethics and management practices that are compatible with the protection of biological diversity, and these people need to be supported in their efforts.

4. Five major environmental documents were signed at the 1992 Earth Summit, attended by over 100 heads of state. Implementing and funding these new treaties could prove vital to international conservation efforts.

5. Conservation groups and governments in developed countries are increasing funding to protect biological diversity in developing tropical countries. While the increased levels of funding are welcome, the amount of money is still inadequate to deal with the loss of biological diversity that is taking place. Additional, innovative mechanisms, such as national environmental funds and debt-for-nature swaps, are being developed to fund conservation activities.

6. International aid agencies and development banks, including the World Bank, have often funded massive projects that cause widespread environmental damage. These funding bodies are now attempting to be more environmentally responsible in their lending policies.

7. Conservation biologists must demonstrate the validity of the theories and approaches of their new discipline, and must actively work with all components of society to protect biological diversity and to restore the degraded elements of the environment.

Suggested Readings

Abramovitz, J. N. 1994. *Trends in Biodiversity Investments: U.S.-Based Funding for Research and Conservation in Developing Countries, 1987–1991.* World Resources Institute, Washington, D.C. Unique presentation of biodiversity funding, with a list of projects, research institutions, and sources of funding; see 1991 report also.

Alcorn, J. B. 1993. Indigenous peoples and conservation. *Conservation Biology* 7: 424–426. This article and others in the same issue explore different perceptions of indigenous people.

Gomez-Pompa, A. and A. Kaus. 1992. Taming the wilderness myth. *BioScience* 42: 271–279. Traditional people often have their own approaches to preserving biodiversity.

Grumbine, R. E. 1993. *Ghost Bears: Exploring the Biodiversity Crisis.* Island Press, Washington, D.C. This popular book weaves together elements of conservation biology, law, policy, and activism.

Holloway, M. 1993. Sustaining the Amazon. *Scientific American* 269 (1): 90–99. Superb overview of the issues confronting development and conservation in the Amazon.

Redford, K. and C. Padoch (eds.). 1992. *Conservation of Neotropical Rainforests: Working from Traditional Resource Use.* Columbia University Press, New York. Case studies in which traditional resource use patterns also protect biodiversity.

Wells, M. and K. Brandon. 1992. *People and Parks: Linking Protected Area Management with Local Communities.* World Bank, WWF, U.S. Agency for International Development, Washington, D.C. Integrated conservation–development projects associated with protected areas, with numerous case studies.

Western, D., R. M. Wright and S. C. Strum (eds.). 1994. *Natural Connections: Perspectives in Community-Based Conservation.* Island Press, Washington, D.C. Strong collection of case studies focusing on rural communities.

Willers, B. 1994. Sustainable development: A new world deception. *Conservation Biology* 8: 1146–1148. Short, effective critique of the concept and its proponents.

WRI/IUCN/UNEP. 1992. *Global Biodiversity Strategy: Guidelines for Action to Save, Study, and Use Earth's Biotic Wealth Sustainably and Equitably.* World Resources Institute, Washington, D.C. Current views on needed policy changes, with a long list of key people in the field.

Selected Environmental Organizations and Sources of Information

The best single reference on conservation activities is the *Conservation Directory*, updated each year by the National Wildlife Federation, 1400 Sixteenth Street N.W., Washington, D.C. 20036. This directory lists thousands of local, national, and international conservation organizations, conservation publications, and leaders in the field of conservation. Other publications of interest include *The New Complete Guide to Environmental Careers* (1993), published by Island Press, 1718 Connecticut Avenue N.W., Washington, D.C. 20009, and *Environmental Profiles: A Global Guide to Projects and People* (1993), published by Garland Publishing, 717 Fifth Avenue, New York, N.Y. 10022.

The following lists some major organizations and resources.

American Association of Zoological Parks and Aquariums
Oglebay Park
Wheeling, W.V. 26003 U.S.A.
    Preservation and propagation of captive wildlife.

Center for Marine Conservation
1725 De Sales St. N.W., Suite 500
Washington, D.C. 20036 U.S.A.
    Focus on marine wildlife and ocean and coastal habitats.

Center for Plant Conservation and Missouri Botanical Garden
P.O. Box 299
St. Louis, MO 63166 U.S.A.
    Major centers for worldwide plant conservation activities.

CITES Secretariat, UNEP
15 Chemin des Anemones
Case Postale 356
1219 Chatelaine
Geneva, Switzerland
    Regulates trade in endangered species.

Conservation International
1015 18th St. N.W., Suite 100
Washington, D.C. 20036 U.S.A.
    Active in conservation efforts and working for sustainable development.

Earthwatch
P.O. Box 403N
Mt. Auburn Street
Watertown, MA 02272 U.S.A.
    Clearinghouse for international projects in which volunteers can work with scientists.

Environmental Defense Fund
257 Park Avenue South
New York, N.Y. 10010 U.S.A.
Involved in scientific, legal, and economic issues.

Friends of the Earth
218 "D" St. S.E.
Washington, D.C. 20003 U.S.A.
International environmental organization working to improve public policy.

Greenpeace, U.S.A., Inc.
1436 "U" St. N.W.
Washington, D.C. 20009 U.S.A.
Activist organization, known for grassroots efforts and dramatic protests against environmental damage.

Institute for Economic Botany and New York Botanical Gardens
Bronx, N.Y. 10458 U.S.A.
Research and conservation programs involving plants that are useful to people.

International Council for Bird Preservation
32 Cambridge Road, Girton
Cambridge CB3 0PJ, United Kingdom
Determines conservation status and priorities for birds throughout the world.

International Union for the Conservation of Nature and Natural Resources (IUCN)
Avenue de Mont Blanc
CH-1196 Gland, Switzerland
Also known as the World Conservation Union (WCU). This is the premier coordinating body for international conservation efforts. Produces directories of specialists who are knowledgable about captive breeding programs and other aspects of conservation.

National Audubon Society
950 Third Avenue
New York, N.Y. 10022 U.S.A.
Extensive program, including wildlife conservation, public education, research, and political lobbying.

National Wildlife Federation
1400 Sixteenth St. N.W.
Washington, D.C. 20036 U.S.A.
Advocates for wildlife conservation. Publishes the *Conservation Directory*, as well as the outstanding children's publications *Ranger Rick* and *Your Big Backyard*.

Natural Resources Defense Council, Inc.
40 West Twentieth St.
New York, N.Y. 10011 U.S.A.
Uses legal and scientific methods to monitor and influence government actions and legislation.

The Nature Conservancy
1815 North Lynn St.
Arlington, VA 22209 U.S.A.
Emphasis on land preservation. Maintains extensive records on rare species distribution in the Americas, particularly North America.

Rain Forest Action Network
301 Broadway, Suite "A"
San Francisco, CA 94133 U.S.A.
Works actively for rain forest conservation.

Royal Botanical Garden, Kew
Richmond
Surrey TW9 3AE, United Kingdom
The famous "Kew Gardens" are home to a leading botanical research institute.

Sierra Club
730 Polk St.
San Francisco, CA 94109 U.S.A.
Leading advocate for the preservation of wilderness and open space.

Smithsonian Institution and National Zoological Park
1000 Jefferson Drive S.W.
Washington, D.C. 20560 U.S.A.
The National Zoo and the nearby U.S. National Museum of Natural History represent a vast resource of literature, biological materials, and skilled people.

Society for Conservation Biology
c/o Blackwell Scientific Publications, Inc.
238 Main St.
Cambridge, MA 02142 U.S.A.
Leading scientific society for the field. Develops and publicizes new ideas and scientific results through the journal *Conservation Biology*.

United Nations Development Programme (UNDP)
U.N. Plaza
New York, N.Y. 10017 U.S.A.
Funds and coordinates international economic development activities, particularly those that use natural resources in a responsible way.

United Nations Environment Programme (UNEP)
P.O. Box 30552
Nairobi, Kenya
or
1899 "F" St. N.W.
Washington, D.C. 20006 U.S.A.
International program of research and management relating to major environmental problems.

United States Fish and Wildlife Service

Washington, D.C. 20240 U.S.A.

The leading U.S. government agency in the conservation of endangered species, with a vast research and management network. Major activities also take place within other federal government units, such as the National Marine Fisheries Service and the U.S. Forest Service. The Agency for International Development is active in many developing nations. Individual state governments have comparable units, with National Heritage programs being especially relevant. The *Conservation Directory* shows how these units are organized.

**Wildlife Conservation International
and New York Zoological Society**

Bronx Zoo

185th St. & Southern Blvd.

Bronx, N.Y. 10460 U.S.A.

Leaders in wildlife conservation and research.

World Bank

1818 "H" St. N.W.

Washington, D.C. 20433 U.S.A.

A multinational bank involved in economic development; increasingly concerned with environmental issues.

World Conservation Monitoring Centre

219 Huntingdon Road

Cambridge CB3 0DL, United Kingdom

Monitors global wildlife trade, the status of endangered species, natural resource use, and protected areas.

World Resources Institute (WRI)

1709 New York Ave. N.W.

Washington, D.C. 20006 U.S.A.

Research center producing excellent papers on environmental, conservation, and development topics.

World Wildlife Fund (WWF)

1250 24th St. N.W.

Washington, D.C. 20037 U.S.A.

Also known as the Worldwide Fund for Nature. Major conservation organization, with branches throughout the world. Active in both research and in the management of national parks.

Xerces Society

10 Ash St. S.W.

Portland, OR 97204 U.S.A.

Focuses on the conservation of insects and other invertebrates.

Zoological Society of London

Regents Park

London NW1 4RY, United Kingdom

Center for worldwide activities to preserve nature.

Bibliography

Abramovitz, J. N. 1991. *Investing in Biological Diversity: U.S. Research and Conservation Efforts in Developing Countries.* World Resources Institute, Washington, D.C.

Abramovitz, J. N. 1994. *Trends in Biodiversity Investments: U.S.-Based Funding for Research and Conservation in Developing Countries, 1987–1991.* World Resources Institute, Washington, D.C.

Ackerman, D. 1992. Last refuge of the monk seal. *National Geographic* 181 (January): 128–144.

Aguirre, A. A. and E. E. Starkey. 1994. Wildlife disease in U.S. National Parks: Historical and coevolutionary perspectives. *Conservation Biology* 8: 654–661.

Alcock, J. 1993. *Animal Behavior: An Evolutionary Approach,* 5th ed. Sinauer Associates, Sunderland, MA.

Alcorn, J. B. 1984. Development policy, forests, and peasant farms: Reflections on Huastec-managed forests' contributions to commercial production and resource conservation. *Economic Botany* 38: 389–406.

Alcorn, J. B. 1991. Ethics, economies, and conservation. *In* M. L. Oldfield and J. B. Alcorn (eds.), *Biodiversity: Culture, Conservation, and Ecodevelopment,* pp. 317–349. Westview Press, Boulder, CO.

Alcorn, J. B. 1993. Indigenous peoples and conservation. *Conservation Biology* 7: 424–426.

Allan, T. and A. Warren (eds.). 1993. *Deserts: The Encroaching Wilderness. A World Conservation Atlas.* Oxford University Press, Oxford.

Allen, W. H. 1988. Biocultural restoration of a tropical forest: Architects of Costa Rica's emerging Guanacaste National Park plan to make it an integral part of local culture. *BioScience* 38: 156–161.

Allen, W. H. 1994. Reintroduction of endangered plants. *BioScience* 44: 65–68.

Allendorf, F. W. and R. F. Leary. 1986. Heterozygosity and fitness in natural populations of animals. *In* M. E. Soulé (ed.), *Conservation Biology: The Science of Scarcity and Diversity,* pp. 57–76. Sinauer Associates, Sunderland, MA.

Altieri, M. A. and M. K. Anderson. 1992. Peasant farming systems, agricultural modernization, and the conservation of crop genetic resources in Latin America. *In* P.

L. Fiedler and S. K. Jain (eds.), *Conservation Biology: The Theory and Practice of Nature Conservation, Preservation and Management,* pp. 49–64. Chapman and Hall, New York.

Anderson, A. B. (ed.). 1990. *Alternatives to Deforestation.* Columbia University Press, New York.

Angel, M. V. 1993. Biodiversity of the pelagic ocean. *Conservation Biology* 7: 760–772.

Armbruster, P. and R. Lande. 1993. A population viability analysis for African elephant (*Loxodonta africana*): How big should reserves be? *Conservation Biology* 7: 602–610.

Balmford, A. and A. Long. 1994. Avian endemism and forest loss. *Nature* 372: 623–624.

Baltz, D. M. 1991. Introduced fishes in marine systems and inland seas. *Biological Conservation* 56: 151–177.

Barbier, E. B., J. C. Burgess and C. Folke. 1994. *Paradise Lost? The Ecological Economics of Biodiversity.* Earthscan Publications, London.

Barrett, S. C. H. and J. R. Kohn. 1991. Genetic and evolutionary consequences of small population size in plants: Implications for conservation. *In* D. A. Falk and K. E. Holsinger (eds.), *Genetics and Conservation of Rare Plants,* pp. 3–30. Oxford University Press, New York.

Bartley, D., M. Bagley, G. Gall and B. Bentley. 1992. Use of linkage disequilibrium data to estimate effective size of hatchery and natural fish populations. *Conservation Biology* 6: 365–375.

Baskin, Y. 1994a. Ecologists dare to ask: How much does diversity matter? *Science* 264: 202–203.

Baskin, Y. 1994b. There's a new wildlife policy in Kenya: Use it or lose it. *Science* 265: 733–734.

Bawa, K. S. 1990. Plant–pollinator interactions in tropical rainforests. *Annual Review of Ecology and Systematics* 21: 399–422.

Bazzaz, F. A. and E. D. Fajer. 1992. Plant life in a CO_2-rich world. *Scientific American* (January): 68–74.

BGCS (Botanic Gardens Conservation Secretariat). 1987. *The International Transfer Format for Botanic Gardens Plant Records.* Hunt Institute for Botanical Documentation, Carnegie Mellon University, Pittsburgh, PA.

Bean, M. J. 1983. *The Evolution of National Wildlife Law,* 2nd ed. Praeger, New York.

Beck, B. B., L. G. Rapport, M. R. Stanley Price and A. C. Wilson. 1994. Reintroduction of captive-born animals. *In* P. J. Olney, G. M. Mace and A. T. C. Feistner (eds.), *Creative Conservation: Interactive Management of Wild and Captive Animals,* pp. 265–286. Chapman and Hall, London.

Beebee, T. J. C. et al. 1990. Decline of the natterjack toad *Bufo calamita* in Britain: Palaeoecological, documentary, and experimental evidence for breeding site acidification. *Biological Conservation* 53: 1–20.

Benz, B. F., L. R. Sánchez-Velásquez and F. J. Santana Michel. 1990. Ecology and ethnobotany of *Zea diploperennis:* Preliminary investigations. *Maydica* 35: 85–98.

Berger, J. 1990. Persistence of different-sized populations: An empirical assessment of rapid extinctions in bighorn sheep. *Conservation Biology* 4: 91–98.

Best, P. B. 1988. Right whales *Eubalaena australis* at Tristan da Cunha—a clue to the "non-recovery" of depleted stocks? *Biological Conservation* 46: 23–51.

Bibby, C. J. et al. 1992. *Putting Biodiversity on the Map: Priority Areas for Global Conservation.* International Council for Bird Preservation, Cambridge, U.K.

Bierregaard, R. O., T. E. Lovejoy, V. Kapos, A. A. Dos Santos and R. W. Hutchings. 1992. The biological dynamics of tropical rainforest fragments. *BioScience* 42: 859–866.

Billington, H. L. 1991. Effect of population size on genetic variation in a dioecious conifer. *Conservation Biology* 5: 115–119.

Blaustein, A. R. and D. B. Wake. 1995. The puzzle of declining amphibian populations. *Scientific American* 272 (April): 52–57.

Bleich, V. C., J. D. Wehausen and S. A. Holl. 1990. Desert-dwelling mountain sheep: Conservation implications of a naturally fragmented distribution. *Conservation Biology* 4: 383–389.

Blockhus, J. M., M. Dillenbeck, J. A. Sayer and P. Wegge (eds.). 1992. *Conserving Biological Diversity in Managed Tropical Forests.* IUCN, Gland, Switzerland.

Bormann, F. H. 1976. An inseparable linkage: Conservation of natural ecosystems and conservation of fossil energy. *BioScience* 26: 759.

Bowles, I. A. and G. T. Prickett. 1994. *Reframing the Green Window: An Analysis of the GEF Pilot Phase Approach to Biodiversity and Global Warming and Recommendations for the Operational Phase.* Conservation International/National Resources Defense Council, Washington, D.C.

Bowles, M. L. and C. J. Whelan. 1994. *Restoration of Endangered Species: Conceptual Issues, Planning, and Implementation.* Cambridge University Press, Cambridge.

Boyce, M. S. 1992. Population viability analysis. *Annual Review of Ecology and Systematics* 23: 481–506.

Bradshaw, A. D. 1990. The reclamation of derelict land and the ecology of ecosystems. *In* W. R. Jordan III, M. E. Gilpin and J. D. Aber (eds.), *Restoration Ecology: A Synthetic Approach to Ecological Research,* pp. 53–74. Cambridge University Press, Cambridge.

Bradshaw, A. D. and M. J. Chadwick. 1980. *The Restoration of Land.* Blackwell Scientific Publications, Oxford.

Breman, H. 1992. Desertification control, the West African case: Prevention is better than cure. *Biotropica* (special issue) 24: 328–334.

Brown, B. E. and J. C. Ogden. 1993. Coral bleaching. *Scientific American* 268: 64–70.

Browning, J. A. 1991. Conserving crop plant–pathogen coevolutionary processes in situ. *In* M. L. Oldfield and J. B. Alcorn (eds.), *Biodiversity: Culture, Conservation and Ecodevelopment,* pp. 59–85. Westview Press, Boulder, CO.

Brush, S. B. 1989. Rethinking crop genetic resource conservation. *Conservation Biology* 3: 19–29.

Burbidge, A. A. and N. L. McKenzie. 1989. Patterns in the modern decline of western Australia's vertebrate fauna: Causes and conservation implications. *Biological Conservation* 50: 143–198.

Burgman, M. A., S. Ferson and H. R. Ackçakaya. 1993. *Risk Assessment in Conservation Biology.* Chapman and Hall, London.

Cade, T. J., J. H. Enderson, C. G. Thelander and C. M. White. 1988. *Peregrine Falcon Populations: Their Management and Recovery.* The Peregrine Fund, Boise, ID.

Cahn, R. and P. Cahn. 1985. Saved but threatened. *Audubon* 87: 48–51.

Cairns, J. Jr. 1986. Restoration, reclamation, and regeneration of degraded or destroyed ecosystems. *In* M. E. Soulé (ed.), *Conservation Biology: The Science of Scarcity and Diversity,* pp. 153–181. Sinauer Associates, Sunderland, MA.

Caldecott, J. 1988. *Hunting and Wildlife Management in Sarawak.* IUCN, Gland, Switzerland.

Caldwell, L. 1985. Science will not save the Biosphere but politics might. *Environmental Conservation* 12: 195–197.

Callicott, J. B. 1990. Whither conservation ethics? *Conservation Biology* 4: 15–20.

Callicott, J. B. 1994. *Earth's Insights: A Multicultural Survey of Ecological Ethics from the Mediterranean Basin to the Australian Outback.* University of California Press, Berkeley.

Campbell, S. 1980. Is reintroduction a realistic goal? *In* M. E. Soulé and B. A. Wilcox (eds.), *Conservation Biology: An Evolutionary–Ecological Perspective,* pp. 263–269. Sinauer Associates, Sunderland, MA.

Carlton, J. T. and J. B. Geller. 1993. Ecological roulette: The global transport of nonindigenous marine organisms. *Science* 261: 78–82.

Carroll, C. R. 1992. Ecological management of sensitive natural areas. *In* P. L. Fiedler and S. K. Jain (eds.), *Conservation Biology: The Theory and Practice of Nature Conservation, Preservation and Management,* pp. 347–372. Chapman and Hall, New York.

Carson, H. L. 1983. The genetics of the founder effect. *In* C. M. Schonewald-Cox, S. M. Chambers, B. MacBryde and L. Thomas (eds.), *Genetics and Conservation: A Reference for Managing Wild Animal and Plant Populations,* pp. 189–200. Benjamin/Cummings, Menlo Park, CA.

Carson, R. 1962. *Silent Spring.* Reprinted 1982 by Penguin, Harmondsworth, U.K.

Caswell, H. 1989. *Matrix Population Models: Construction, Analysis, and Interpretation.* Sinauer Associates, Sunderland, MA.

Ceballos-Lascuráin, H. (ed.). 1993. *Tourism and Protected Areas.* IUCN, Gland, Switzerland.

Center for Plant Conservation. 1991. Genetic sampling guidelines for conservation collections of endangered plants. *In* D. A. Falk and K. E. Holsinger (eds.), *Genetics and Conservation of Rare Plants,* pp. 224–238. Oxford University Press, New York.

Chadwick, D. H. 1993. The American prairie: Roots of the sky. *National Geographic* 184 (October): 90–119.

Chadwick, D. H. 1995. Dead or alive: The Endangered Species Act. *National Geographic* 187 (March): 2–41.

Charlesworth, D. and B. Charlesworth. 1987. Inbreeding depression and its evolutionary consequences. *Annual Review of Ecology and Systematics* 18: 237–268.

Chase, A. 1986. *Playing God in Yellowstone: The Destruction of America's First National Park.* Atlantic Monthly Press, Boston.

Cherfas, J. 1991. Disappearing mushrooms: Another mass extinction? *Science* 254: 1458.

Chernela, J. 1987. Endangered ideologies: Tukano fishing taboos. *Cultural Survival Quarterly* 11: 50–52.

Clark, C. 1992. Empirical evidence for the effect of tropical deforestation on climatic change. *Environmental Conservation* 19: 39–47.

Clark, T. W., R. P. Reading and A. L. Clark (eds.). 1994. *Endangered Species Recovery: Finding the Lessons, Improving the Process.* Island Press, Washington, D.C.

Clay, J. 1991. Cultural survival and conservation: Lessons from the past twenty years. *In* M. L. Oldfield and J. B. Alcorn (eds.), *Biodiversity: Culture, Conservation and Ecodevelopment,* pp. 248–273. Westview Press, Boulder, CO.

Cleveland, D. A., D. Soleri and S. E. Smith. 1994. Do folk crop varieties have a role in sustainable agriculture? *BioScience* 44: 740–751.

Coblentz, B. E. 1990. Exotic organisms: A dilemma for conservation biology. *Conservation Biology* 4: 261–265.

Cody, M. L. 1986. Diversity, rarity, and conservation in Mediterranean-climate regions. *In* M. Soulé (eds.), *Conservation Biology: The Science of Scarcity and Diversity,* pp. 123–152. Sinauer Associates, Sunderland, MA.

Cohn, J. P. 1994. Salamanders: Slip-sliding away or too surreptitious to count? *BioScience* 44: 219–223.

Colwell, R. K. 1986. Community biology and sexual selection: Lessons from hummingbird flower mites. *In* T. J. Case and J. Diamond (eds.), *Ecological Communities,* pp. 406–424. Harper and Row, New York.

Conant, S. 1988. Saving endangered species by translocation. *BioScience* 38: 254–257.

Condit, R., S. P. Hubbel and R. B. Foster. 1992. Short-term dynamics of a Neotropical forest. *BioScience* 42: 822–828.

Conservation International. 1990. *The Rain Forest Imperative.* Conservation International, Washington, D.C.

Conway, W. G. 1980. An overview of captive propagation. *In* M. E. Soulé and B. A. Wilcox (eds.), *Conservation Biology: An Evolutionary–Ecological Perspective,* pp. 199–208. Sinauer Associates, Sunderland, MA.

Conway, W. G. 1988. Can technology aid species preservation? *In* E. O. Wilson and F. M. Peter (eds.), *Biodiversity,* pp. 263–268. National Academy Press, Washington, D.C.

Costanza, R. (ed.). 1991. *Ecological Economics: The Science and Management of Sustainability.* Columbia University Press, New York.

Costanza, R. and H. E. Daly. 1992. Natural capital and sustainable development. *Conservation Biology* 6: 37–46.

Cottam, G. 1990. Community dynamics on an artificial prairie. *In* W. R. Jordan III, M. E. Gilpin and J. D. Aber (eds.), *Restoration Ecology: A Synthetic Approach to Ecological Research,* pp. 257–270. Cambridge University Press, Cambridge.

Cox, G. W. 1993. *Conservation Ecology.* W. C. Brown, Dubuque, IA.

Cox, P. A. and M. J. Balick. 1994. The ethnobotanical approach to drug discovery. *Scientific American* 270: 82–87.

Cox, P. A. and T. Elmqvist. 1991. Indigenous control of tropical rainforest reserves: An alternative strategy for conservation. *Ambio* 20: 317–321.

Cox, P. A. and T. Elmqvist. 1993. Ecocolonialism and indigenous knowledge systems: Village controlled rainforest preserves in Samoa. *Pacific Conservation Biology* 1: 6–13.

Cox, P. A., T. Elmqvist, E. D. Pierson and W. E. Rainey. 1991. Flying foxes as strong interactors in South Pacific island ecosystems: A conservation hypothesis. *Conservation Biology* 5: 448–454.

Crow, J. F. and N. E. Morton. 1955. Measurement of gene frequency drift in small populations. *Evolution* 9: 202–214.

Crumpacker, D. W., S. W. Hodge, D. Friedley and W. P. Gregg Jr. 1988. A preliminary assessment of the status of major terrestrial and wetland ecosystems on federal and Indian lands in the United States. *Conservation Biology* 2: 103–115.

Currie, D. J. 1991. Energy and large-scale patterns of animal- and plant-species richness. *American Naturalist* 137: 27–49.

Dallmeier, F. (ed.). 1992. *Long-term Monitoring of Biological Diversity in Tropical Forest Areas.* MAB Digest no. 11. UNESCO, Paris.

Daly, H. E. and J. B. Cobb Jr. 1989. *For the Common Good: Redirecting the Economy Toward Community, the Environment, and a Sustainable Future.* Beacon Press, Boston MA

Dasgupta, P. S. 1995. Population, poverty, and the local environment. *Scientific American* 272: 40–45.

Dasmann, R. F. 1991. The importance of cultural and biological diversity. *In* M. L. Oldfield and J. B. Alcorn (eds.), *Biodiversity: Culture, Conservation and Ecodevelopment,* pp. 7–15. Westview Press, Boulder, CO.

Dasmann, R. F., J. P. Milton and P. H. Freeman. 1973. *Ecological Principles for Economic Development.* John Wiley & Sons, London.

Davis, M. B. and C. Zabinski. 1992. Changes in geographical range resulting from greenhouse warming: Effects on biodiversity in forests. *In* R. Peters and T. E. Lovejoy (eds.), *Global Warming and Biological Diversity,* pp. 297–308. Yale University Press, New Haven, CT.

Davis, S. D. et al. 1986. *Plants In Danger: What Do We Know?* IUCN, Gland, Switzerland.

Davis, S. H. and A. Wali. 1994. Indigenous land tenure and tropical forest management in Latin America. *Ambio* 23: 485–490.

Del Tredici, P. 1991. Ginkgos and people: A thousand years of interaction. *Arnoldia* 51: 2–15.

De Mauro, M. M. 1993. Relationship of breeding system to rarity in the lakeside daisy (*Hymenoxys acaulis* var. *glabra*). *Conservation Biology* 7: 542–550.

Denslow, J. S. and C. Padoch (eds.). 1988. *People of the Tropical Rain Forest.* University of California Press, Berkeley.

Devall, B. and G. Sessions. 1985. *Deep Ecology: Living as if Nature Mattered.* Gibbs Smith, Salt Lake City, UT.

Diamond, A. W. 1985. The selection of critical areas and current conservation efforts in tropical forest birds. *In* A. W. Diamond and T. E. Lovejoy (eds.), *Conservation of Tropical Forest Birds,* pp. 33–48. Technical Publication no. 4. International Council for Bird Preservation, Cambridge, U.K.

Diamond, J. M. 1975. The island dilemma: Lessons of modern biogeographic studies for the design of natural reserves. *Biological Conservation* 7: 129–146.

Diamond, J. M. 1987. Extant unless proven extinct? Or, extinct unless proven extant? *Conservation Biology* 1: 77–81.

Diamond, J. M. 1988a. Factors controlling species diversity: Overview and synthesis. *Annals of the Missouri Botanical Gardens* 75: 117–129.

Diamond, J. M. 1988b. Red books or green lists? *Nature* 332: 304–305.

Diamond, J. M. 1990. Reflections on goals and on the relationship between theory and practice. *In* W. R. Jordan III, M. E. Gilpin and J. D. Aber (eds.), *Restoration Ecology: A Synthetic Approach to Ecological Research,* pp. 329–336. Cambridge University Press, Cambridge.

Dinerstein, E. and G. F. McCracken. 1990. Endangered greater one-horned rhinoceros carry high levels of genetic variation. *Conservation Biology* 4: 417–422.

Dingwall, P., J. Harrison and J. A. McNeely (eds.). 1994. *Protecting Nature: Regional Reviews of Protected Areas.* IUCN Publications, Gland, Switzerland.

Dogsé, P. and B. von Droste. 1990. *Debt-for-Nature Exchanges and Biosphere Reserves.* UNESCO, Paris.

Dowling, T. E. and M. R. Childs. 1992. Impact of hybridization on a threatened trout of the south-western United States. *Conservation Biology* 6: 355–364.

Drake, J. A. et al. (eds.). 1989. *Biological Invasions: A Global Perspective.* SCOPE Report no. 37. John Wiley, New York.

Drayton, B. and R. Primack. 1995. Plant species loss from 1894 to 1993 in an isolated conservation area in metropolitan Boston. *Conservation Biology.* In press.

Dregné, H. E. 1983. *Desertification of Arid Lands.* Academic Press, New York.

Dresser, B. L. 1988. Cryobiology, embryo transfer, and artificial insemination in ex situ animal conservation programs. *In* E. O. Wilson and F. M. Peter (eds.), *Biodiversity,* pp. 296–308. National Academy Press, Washington, D.C.

Duffey, E. and A. S. Watt (eds.). 1971. *The Scientific Management of Animal and Plant Communities for Conservation.* Blackwell Scientific Publications, Oxford.

Duffus, D. A. and P. Dearden. 1990. Non-consumptive wildlife-oriented recreation: A conceptual framework. *Biological Conservation* 53: 213–231.

Dufour, D. L. 1990. Use of tropical rainforest by native Amazonians. *BioScience* 40: 652–659.

Dugan, P. (ed.). 1993. *Wetlands in Danger: A World Conservation Atlas.* Oxford University Press, New York.

Dyer, M. I. and M. M. Holland. 1991. The biosphere-reserve concept: Needs for a network design. *BioScience* 41: 319–325.

Eales, S. 1992. *Earthtoons: The First Book of Ecohumor.* Warner Books, New York.

Edwards, P. J., R. M. May and N. R. Webb (eds.). 1994. *Large-Scale Ecology and Conservation Biology.* Blackwell Scientific Publications, Oxford.

Ehrenfeld, D. W. 1970. *Biological Conservation.* Holt, Rinehart and Winston, New York.

Ehrenfeld, D. W. 1989. Hard times for diversity. *In* D. Western and M. Pearl (eds.), *Conservation for the Twenty-first Century,* pp. 247–250. Oxford University Press, New York.

Ehrlich, P. R. and H. A. Mooney. 1983. Extinction, substitution, and ecosystem services. *BioScience* 33: 248–254.

Ehrlich, P. R. and D. D. Murphy. 1987. Conservation lessons from long-term studies of checkerspot butterflies. *Conservation Biology* 1: 122–131.

Eisner, T. 1991. Chemical prospecting: A proposal for action. *In* F. H. Bormann and S. R. Kellert (eds.), *Ecology, Economics, Ethics: The Broken Circle,* pp. 196–202. Yale University Press, New Haven, CT.

Eisner, T. and E. A. Beiring. 1994. Biotic exploration fund: Protecting biodiversity through chemical prospecting. *BioScience* 44: 95–98.

Elfring, C. 1989. Preserving land through local land trusts. *BioScience* 39: 71–74.

Ellis, R. 1992. Whale kill begins anew. *Audubon* 94: 20–22.

Ellstrand, N. C. 1992. Gene flow by pollen: Implications for plant conservation genetics. *Oikos* 63: 77–86.

Ellstrand, N. C. and D. R. Elam. 1993. Population genetic consequences of small population size: Implications for plant conservation. *Annual Review of Ecology and Systematics* 24: 217–242.

Endangered Species Coalition. 1992. *The Endangered Species Act: A Commitment Worth Keeping.* The Wilderness Society, Washington, D.C.

Erdelen, W. 1988. Forest ecosystems and nature conservation in Sri Lanka. *Biological Conservation* 43: 115–135.

Erwin, W. L. 1991. An evolutionary basis for conservation strategies. *Science* 253: 750–753.

ESCAP (Economic and Social Commission for Asia and the Pacific). 1985. *Marine Environmental Problems and Issues in the ESCAP Region.* United Nations, ESCAP, Bangkok, Thailand.

Etter, R. J. and J. F. Grassle. 1992. Patterns of species diversity in the deep sea as a function of sediment particle size diversity. *Nature* 360: 575–578.

Eudey, A. A. 1987. *Action Plan for Asian Primate Conservation: 1987–1991.* IUCN Species Survival Commission Primate Specialist Group, Gland, Switzerland.

Faith, D. P. 1994. Phylogenetic diversity: A general framework for the prediction of feature diversity. *In* P. L. Forey, C. J. Humphries and R. I. Vane-Wright (eds.), *Systematics and Conservation Evaluation,* pp. 25–268. Oxford University Press, New York.

Falk, D. A. 1991. Joining biological and economic models for conserving plant genetic diversity. *In* D. A. Falk and K. E. Holsinger (eds.), *Genetics and Conservation of Rare Plants,* pp. 209–224. Oxford University Press, New York.

Falk, D. A. and P. Olwell. 1992. Scientific and policy considerations in restoration and reintroduction of endangered species. *Rhodora* 94: 287–315.

Farnsworth, E. J. and J. Rosovsky. 1993. The ethics of ecological field experimentation. *Conservation Biology* 74: 463–472.

Farnsworth, N. R. 1988. Screening plants for new medicines. *In* E. O. Wilson and F. M. Peter (eds.), *Biodiversity,* pp. 83–97. National Academy Press, Washington, D.C.

Fearnside, P. M. 1987. Deforestation and international economic development projects in Brazilian Amazonia. *Conservation Biology* 1: 214–221.

Fearnside, P. M. 1989. Extractive reserves in Brazilian Amazonia. *BioScience* 39: 387–393.

Fearnside, P. M. 1990. Predominant land uses in Brazilian Amazonia. *In* A. Anderson (ed.), *Alternatives to Deforestation: Steps toward Sustainable Use of the Amazon Rain Forest,* pp. 233–251. Columbia University Press, Irvington, NY.

Fillon, F. L., A. Jacquemot and R. Reid. 1985. *The Importance of Wildlife to Canadians.* Canadian Wildlife Service, Ottawa.

Fitter, R. and M. Fitter. 1987. *The Road to Extinction.* IUCN, Gland, Switzerland.

Fitzgerald, S. 1989. *International Wildlife Trade: Whose Business Is It?* World Wildlife Fund, Washington, D.C.

Fleischner, T. L. 1994. Ecological costs of livestock grazing in western North America. *Conservation Biology* 8: 629–644.

Foose, T. J. 1983. The relevance of captive populations to the conservation of biotic diversity. *In* C. M. Schonewald-Cox, S. M. Chambers, B. MacBryde and L. Thomas (eds.), *Genetics and Conservation,* pp. 374–401. Benjamin/Cummings, Menlo Park, CA.

Forman, R. T. and M. Godron. 1981. Patches and structural components for a landscape ecology. *BioScience* 31: 733–740.

Forman, R. T. and M. Godron. 1986. *Landscape Ecology.* John Wiley and Sons, New York.

Franklin, I. R. 1980. Evolutionary change in small populations. *In* M. E. Soulé and B. A. Wilcox (eds.), *Conservation Biology: An Evolutionary–Ecological Perspective,* pp. 135–149. Sinauer Associates, Sunderland, MA.

Frederick, R. J. and M. Egan. 1994. Environmentally compatible applications of biotechnology. *BioScience* 44: 529–535.

French, H. F. 1994. Making environmental treaties work. *Scientific American* 271: 94–97.

Fujita, M. S. and M. D. Tuttle. 1991. Flying foxes (Chiroptera: Pteropodidae): Threatened animals of key ecological and economic importance. *Conservation Biology* 5: 455–463.

Futuyma, D. J. 1986. *Evolutionary Biology,* 2nd ed. Sinauer Associates, Sunderland, MA.

Gadgil, M. and R. Guha. 1992. *This Fissured Land: An Ecological History of India.* Oxford University Press, Oxford.

Gagné, W. C. 1988. Conservation priorities in Hawaiian natural systems. *BioScience* 38: 264–271.

Gates, D. M. 1993. *Climate Change and Its Biological Consequences.* Sinauer Associates, Sunderland, MA.

Gentry, A. H. 1986. Endemism in tropical versus temperate plant communities. *In* M. E. Soulé (ed.), *Conservation Biology: The Science of Scarcity and Diversity,* pp. 153–181. Sinauer Associates, Sunderland, MA.

Gerrodette, T. and W. G. Gilmartin. 1990. Demographic consequences of changing pupping and hauling sites of the Hawaiian monk seal. *Conservation Biology* 4: 423–430.

Gersh, J. and R. Pickert. 1991. Land-use modeling: Accommodating growth while conserving biological resources in Dutchess County, New York. *In* D. J. Decker, M. E. Krasnyk, G. R. Goff, C. R. Smith and D. W. Gross (eds.), *Challenges in the Conservation of Biological Resources: A Practitioner's Guide,* pp. 233–242. Westview Press, Boulder, CO.

Getz, W. M. and R. G. Haight. 1989. *Population Harvesting: Demographic Models of Fish, Forest, and Animal Resources.* Princeton University Press, Princeton, NJ.

Gillis, A. M. 1990. The new forestry. *BioScience* 40: 558–562.

Gilpin, M. E. 1990. Experimental community assembly: Competition, community structure, and the order of species introductions. *In* W. R. Jordan III, M. E. Gilpin and J. D. Aber (eds.), *Restoration Ecology: A Synthetic Approach to Ecological Research,* pp. 151–161. Cambridge University Press, Cambridge.

Gilpin, M. E. and M. E. Soulé. 1986. Minimum viable populations: Processes of species extinction. *In* M. E. Soulé (ed.). *Conservation Biology: The Science of Scarcity and Diversity,* pp. 19–34. Sinauer Associates, Sunderland, MA.

Giovannoni, S. J., T. B. Britschgi, C. L. Moyer and K. G. Field. 1990. Genetic diversity in Sargasso Sea bacterioplankton. *Nature* 345: 60–63.

Gipps, J. H. W. (ed.). 1991. *Beyond Captive Breeding: Reintroducing Endangered Species Through Captive Breeding.* Zoological Society of London Symposia, no. 62. Clarendon Press, Oxford.

Gittleman, J. L. 1994. Are the pandas successful specialists or evolutionary failures? *BioScience* 44: 456–464.

Gliessman, S. R. 1991. Ecological basis of traditional management of wetlands in tropical Mexico: Learning from agroecosystem models. *In* M. L. Oldfield and J. B. Alcorn (eds.), *Biodiversity: Culture, Conservation, and Ecodevelopment,* pp. 211–229. Westview Press, Boulder, CO.

Given, D. R. 1994. *Principles and Practice of Plant Conservation.* Timber Press, Portland, OR.

Godoy, R. A., R. Lubowski and A. Markandya. 1993. A method for the economic valuation of non-timber tropical forest products. *Economic Botany* 47: 220–233.

Gold, T. 1992. The deep, hot biosphere. *Proceedings of the National Academy of Science* 89: 6045–6049.

Goldman, B. and F. H. Talbot. 1976. Aspects of the ecology of coral reef fishes. *In* O. A. Jones and R. Endean (eds.), *Biology and Geology of Coral Reefs,* vol. 3, pp. 125–154. Academic Press, New York.

Goldsmith, B. (ed.). 1991. *Monitoring for Conservation and Ecology.* Chapman and Hall, New York.

Gomez-Pompa, A. and A. Kaus. 1992. Taming the wilderness myth. *BioScience* 42: 271–279.

Goodland, R. J. A. 1990. The World Bank's new environmental policy for dams and reservoirs. *Water Resources Development* 6: 226–239.

Goodland, R. J. A. 1992. Environmental priorities for financing institutions. *Environmental Conservation* 19: 9–22.

Grabherr, G., M. Dottfried and H. Pauli. 1994. Climate effects on mountain plants. *Nature* 369: 448.

Graedel, T. E. and P. J. Crutzen. 1989. The changing atmosphere. *Scientific American* 261: 58–68.

Grant, P. R. and B. R. Grant. 1992. Darwin's finches: Genetically effective population sizes. *Ecology* 73: 766–784.

Grassle, J. F., P. Lasserre, A. D. McIntyre and G. C. Ray. 1991. Marine biodiversity and ecosystem function. *Biology International.* Special Issue 23: i–iv, 1–19.

Green, G. N. and R. W. Sussman. 1990. Deforestation history of the eastern rain forests of Madagascar from satellite images. *Science* 248: 212–215.

Greeson, P. E., J. R. Clark and J. E. Clark (eds.). 1979. *Wetland Functions and Values: The State of Our Understanding.* American Water Resources Association, Minneapolis.

Gregg, W. P. Jr. 1991. MAB Biosphere Reserves and conservation of traditional land use systems. *In* M. L. Oldfield and J. B. Alcorn (eds.), *Biodiversity: Culture, Conservation and Ecodevelopment,* pp. 274–294. Westview Press, Boulder, CO.

Griffith, B., J. M. Scott, J. W. Carpenter and C. Reed. 1989. Translocation as a species conservation tool: Status and strategy. *Science* 245: 477–480.

Grigg, R. W. and D. Epp. 1989. Critical depth for the survival of coral islands: Effects on the Hawaiian archipelago. *Science* 243: 638–641.

Groombridge, B. (ed.). 1992. *Global Biodiversity: Status of the Earth's Living Resources.* Compiled by the World Conservation Monitoring Centre, Cambridge, U.K. Chapman and Hall, London.

Gross, D. W., B. T. Wilkins, R. R. Quinn and A. E. Zepp. 1991. Local land protection and planning efforts. *In* D. J. Decker, M. E. Krasny, G. R. Goff, C. R. Smith and D. W. Gross (eds.), *Challenges in the Conservation of Biological Resources: A Practitioner's Guide,* pp. 355–366. Westview Press, Boulder, CO.

Grove, N. 1988. Quietly conserving nature. *National Geographic* 174 (January): 818–844.

Grove, R. H. and J. J. Burdon (eds.). 1986. *Ecology of Biological Invasions.* Cambridge University Press, Cambridge.

Grumbine, E. R. 1994. What is ecosystem management? *Conservation Biology* 8: 27–38.

Grumbine, E. R. (ed.). 1994. *Environmental Policy and Biodiversity.* Island Press, Washington, D.C.

Guerrant, E. O. 1992. Genetic and demographic considerations in the sampling and reintroduction of rare plants. *In* P. L. Fiedler and S. K. Jain (eds.), *Conservation Biology: The Theory and Practice of Nature Conservation, Preservation and Management,* pp. 321–344. Chapman and Hall, New York.

Gullison, R. E. and E. C. Losos. 1993. The role of foreign debt in deforestation in Latin America. *Conservation Biology* 7: 140–147.

Gupta, T. A. and A. Guleria. 1982. *Non-wood Forest Products from India.* IBH Publishing Co., New Delhi.

Haas, P. M., M. A. Levy and E. A. Parson. 1992. Appraising the Earth Summit: How should we judge UNCED's success? *Environment* 34 (8): 7–35.

Hair, J. D. 1988. The economics of conserving wetlands: A widening circle. Paper presented at Workshop in Economics, IUCN General Assembly, 4–5 February 1988, Costa Rica.

Hair, J. D. and G. A. Pomerantz. 1987. The educational value of wildlife. *In* D. J. Decker and G. R. Goff (eds.), *Valuing Wildlife: Economic and Social Perspectives,* pp. 197–207. Westview Press, Boulder, CO.

Hamrick, J. L. and M. J. W. Godt. 1989. Allozyme diversity in plant species. *In* A. H. D. Brown, M. T. Clegg, A. L. Kahler and B. S. Weir (eds.), *Plant Population Genetics, Breeding, and Genetic Resources,* pp. 43–63. Sinauer Associates, Sunderland, MA.

Hansen, A. J., T. A. Spies, F. J. Swanson and J. L. Ohmann. 1991. Conserving biodiversity in managed forests. *BioScience* 41: 382–392.

Hansen, S. 1989. Debt for nature swaps—overview and discussion of key issues. *Ecological Economics* 1: 77–93.

Hanski, I. 1989. Metapopulation dynamics: Does it help to have more of the same? *Trends in Ecology and Evolution* 4: 113–114.

Hansson, L., L. Fahrig and G. Merriam (eds.). 1995. *Mosaic Landscapes and Ecological Processes*. Chapman and Hall, London.

Harcourt, A. H. 1995. Population viability estimates: Theory and practice for a wild gorilla population. *Conservation Biology* 9:134–142.

Hardin, G. 1968. The tragedy of the commons. *Science* 162: 1243–1248.

Hardin, G. 1985. *Filters Against Folly: How to Survive Despite Economists, Ecologists, and the Merely Eloquent*. Viking Press, New York.

Hardin, G. 1993. *Living within Limits: Ecology, Economics, and Population Taboos*. Oxford University Press, New York.

Hargrove, E. C. (ed.). 1986. *Religion and Environmental Crisis*. University of Georgia Press, Athens.

Hargrove, E. C. 1989. *Foundations of Environmental Ethics*. Prentice-Hall, Englewood Cliffs, NJ.

Harrison, J. L. 1968. The effect of forest clearance on small mammals. *In Conservation in Tropical Southeast Asia*. IUCN, Morges, Switzerland.

Harrison, S. 1994. Metapopulations and conservation. *In* P. J. Edwards, R. M. May and N. R. Webb (eds.), *Large-Scale Ecology and Conservation Biology,* pp. 111–128. Blackwell Scientific Publications, Oxford.

Hartell, K. E. 1992. Non-native fishes known from Massachusetts fresh waters. *Occasional Reports of the Museum of Comparative Zoology Fish Department* 2: 1–9.

Hawkins, J. P. and C. M. Roberts. 1994. The growth of coastal tourism in the Red Sea: Present and future effects on coral reefs. *Ambio* 23: 503–508.

Hawksworth, D. L. 1990. The long-term effects of air pollutants on lichen communities in Europe and North America. *In* G. M. Woodwell (ed.), *The Earth in Transition: Patterns and Processes of Biotic Impoverishment,* pp. 45–64. Cambridge University Press, Cambridge.

Hawksworth, D. L. 1992. Biodiversity in microorganisms and its role in ecosystem function. *In* O. T. Solbrig, H. M. van Emden and P. G. W. J. van Oordt (eds.), *Biodiversity and Global Change,* pp. 83–94. International Union of Biological Sciences, Paris.

Hedgpeth, J. W. 1993. Foreign invaders. *Science* 261: 34–35.

Hellawell, J. M. 1986. *Biological Indicators of Freshwater Pollution and Environmental Management*. Elsevier Applied Science Publishers, London.

Hemley, G. (ed.). 1994. *International Wildlife Trade: A CITES Sourcebook*. Island Press, Washington, D.C.

Heschel, M. S. and K. N. Paige. 1995. Inbreeding depression, environmental stress and population size variation in Scarlet Gilia (*Ipomopsis aggregata*). *Conservation Biology* 9: 126–133.

Heyer, W. R., M. A. Donnelly, R. W. McDiarmid, L.-A. C. Hayek and M. S. Foster (eds.). 1994. *Measuring and Monitoring Biological Diversity: Standard Methods for Amphibians*. Smithsonian Institution Press, Washington, D.C.

Heywood, V. H., G. M. Mace, R. M. May and S. N. Stuart. 1994. Uncertainties in extinction rates. *Nature* 368: 105.

Hinrichsen, D. 1987. The forest decline enigma. *BioScience* 37: 542–546.

Hladick, C. M. et al. (eds.). 1993. *Tropical Forests, People, and Food*. Parthenon Publishing and UNESCO, Paris.

Holloway, M. 1993. Sustaining the Amazon. *Scientific American* 269: 90–99.

Holloway, M. 1994. Nurturing nature. *Scientific American* 270: 98–108.

Horton, T. 1992. The Endangered Species Act: Too tough, too weak, or too late? *Audubon* (March/April): 68–74.

Horwich, R. H., D. Murray, E. Saqui, J. Lyon and D. Godfrey. 1993. Ecotourism and community development: A view from Belize. *In* K. Lindberg and D. E. Hawkins (eds.), *Ecotourism: A Guide for Planners and Managers*. The Ecotourism Society, North Bennington, VT.

Howe, H. F. 1984. Implications of seed dispersal by animals for tropical reserve management. *Biological Conservation* 30: 261–281.

Hoyt, E. 1988. *Conserving the Wild Relatives of Crops*. IBPGR, IUCN, WWF, Rome.

Hughes, T. P. 1994. Catastrophes, phase shifts, and large-scale degradation of a Caribbean coral reef. *Science* 265: 1547–1551.

Huston, M. A. 1994. *Biological Diversity: The Coexistence of Species on Changing Landscapes*. Cambridge University Press, Cambridge.

Hutchings, M. J. 1987. The population biology of the early spider orchid, *Ophrys sphegodes* Mill. I. A demographic study from 1975–1984. *Journal of Ecology* 75: 711–727.

Iltis, H. H. 1988. Serendipity in the exploration of biodiversity: What good are weedy tomatoes? *In* E. O. Wilson and F. M. Peter (eds.), *Biodiversity,* pp. 98–105. National Academy Press, Washington, D.C.

IUCN (IUCN–The World Conservation Union). 1984. Categories, objectives and criteria for protected areas. *In* J. A. McNeely and K. R. Miller (eds.), *National Parks, Conservation, and Development,* pp. 47–53. Smithsonian Institution Press, Washington, D.C.

IUCN. 1985. *United Nations List of National Parks and Protected Areas*. IUCN, Gland, Switzerland.

IUCN. 1988. *1988 IUCN Red List of Threatened Animals*. IUCN, Gland, Switzerland.

IUCN. 1990. *The IUCN Red Data Book*. IUCN, Gland, Switzerland.

IUCN/TNC (The Nature Conservancy)/WWF (World Wildlife Fund). 1994. *Report of the First Global Forum on Environmental Funds*. IUCN, Washington, D.C.

IUCN/UNEP (United Nations Environment Programme). 1986. *Review of the Protected Areas System in the Indo-Malayan Realm*. IUCN, Gland, Switzerland.

IUCN/UNEP. 1988. *Coral Reefs of the World*. 3 vols. IUCN, Gland, Switzerland.

IUCN/UNEP/WWF. 1991. *Caring for the Earth: A Strategy for Sustainable Living*. Gland, Switzerland.

IUCN/WWF. 1989. *The Botanic Gardens Conservation Strategy*. IUCN, Gland, Switzerland.

Jacobson, G. L. Jr., H. Almquist-Jacobson and J. C. Winne. 1991. Conservation of rare plant habitat: Insights from the recent history of vegetation and fire at Crystal Fen, northern Maine, USA. *Biological Conservation* 57: 287–314.

Jacobson, S. K., E. Vaughan and S. W. Miller. 1995. New directions in conservation biology: Graduate programs. *Conservation Biology* 9:5–17.

James, F. C., C. E. McCulloch and D. A. Wiedenfeld. In press. New approaches to the analysis of population trends in land birds. *Ecology.*

Janzen, D. H. 1986a. Keystone plant resources in the tropical forest. *In* M. E. Soulé (ed.), *Conservation Biology: The Science of Scarcity and Diversity,* pp. 330–344. Sinauer Associates, Sunderland, MA.

Janzen, D. H. 1986b. The eternal external threat. *In* M. Soulé (ed.), *Conservation Biology: The Science of Scarcity and Diversity,* pp. 286–303. Sinauer Associates, Sunderland, MA.

Janzen, D. H. 1988a. Tropical dry forests: The most endangered major tropical ecosystem. *In* E. O. Wilson and F. M. Peter (eds.), *Biodiversity,* pp. 130–137. National Academy Press, Washington, D.C.

Janzen, D. H. 1988b. Tropical ecological and biocultural restoration. *Science* 239: 243–244.

Jiménez, J. A., K. A. Hughes, G. Alaks, L. Graham and R. C. Lacy. 1994. An experimental study of inbreeding depression in a natural habitat. *Science* 266: 271–273.

Johns, A. D. 1987. The use of primary and selectively logged rainforest by Malaysian Hornbills (Bucerotidae) and implications for their conservation. *Biological Conservation* 40: 179–190.

Johnson, N. In press. *What to Save First? Setting Biodiversity Conservation Priorities in a Crowded World.* World Resources Institute.

Johnson, N. and B. Cabarale. 1993. *Surviving the Cut: Natural Forest Management in the Humid Tropics.* WRI, Washington, D.C.

Jones, H. L. and J. M. Diamond. 1976. Short-time-base studies of turnover in breeding birds of the California Channel Islands. *Condor* 76: 526–549.

Jones, P. D. and T. M. L. Wigley. 1990. Global warming trends. *Scientific American* 263: 84–91.

Jordan, W. R. III, M. E. Gilpin and J. D. Aber (eds.). 1990. *Restoration Ecology: A Synthetic Approach to Ecological Research.* Cambridge University Press, Cambridge.

Julien, M. H. (ed.). 1987. *Biological Control of Weeds: A World Catalog of Agents and Their Target Weeds.* CAB CIB Contr., Slough, London.

Kapos, V. 1989. Effects of isolation on the water status of forest patches in the Brazilian Amazon. *Journal of Tropical Ecology* 5: 173–185.

Karron, J. D. 1987. A comparison of levels of genetic polymorphisms and self-compatibility in geographically restricted and widespread plant congeners. *Evolutionary Ecology* 1: 47–58.

Kaufman, L. 1988. Caught between a reef and a hard place: Why aquariums must invest in the propagation of endangered species. *Proceedings of the Annual Meet*

ing of the American Association of Zoological Parks and Aquariums, pp. 365–382.

Kaufman, L. 1992. Catastrophic change in a species-rich freshwater ecosystem: Lessons from Lake Victoria. *BioScience* 42: 846–858.

Kaufman, L. and A. S. Cohen. 1993. The great lakes of Africa. *Conservation Biology* 7: 632–633.

Keller, L. F. et al. 1994. Selection against inbred song sparrows during a natural population bottleneck. *Nature* 372: 356–357.

Kellert, S. R. and E. O. Wilson (eds.). 1993. *The Biophilia Hypothesis.* Island Press, Washington, D.C.

Kenchington, R. A. and M. T. Agardy. 1990. Achieving marine conservation through biosphere reserve planning and management. *Environmental Conservation* 17: 39–44.

Kennedy, D. M. 1987. What's new at the zoo? *Technology Review* 90: 66–73.

Keyfitz, N. 1989. The growing human population. *Scientific American* 261: 119–126.

Kiew, R. 1991. *The State of Nature Conservation in Malaysia.* Malayan Nature Society, Kuala Lumpur.

Kimura, M. and J. F. Crow. 1963. The measurement of effective population numbers. *Evolution* 17: 279–288.

King, W. B. 1985. Island birds: Will the future repeat the past? *In* P. J. Moors (ed.), *Conservation of Island Birds,* pp. 3–15. International Council for Bird Preservation, Cambridge, U.K.

Kinnaird, M. F. and T. G. O'Brien. 1991. Viable populations for an endangered forest primate, the Tana River Crested Mangabey (*Cercocebus galeritus galeritus*). *Conservation Biology* 5: 203–213.

Kleiman, D. G. 1989. Reintroduction of captive mammals for conservation. *BioScience* 39: 152–161.

Kline, V. M. and E. A. Howell. 1990. Prairies. *In* W. R. Jordan III, M. E. Gilpin and J. D. Aber (eds.), *Restoration Ecology: A Synthetic Approach to Ecological Research,* pp. 75–84. Cambridge University Press, Cambridge.

Koopowitz, H., A. D. Thornhill and M. Andersen. 1994. A general stochastic model for the prediction of biodiversity losses based on habitat conversion. *Conservation Biology* 8: 425–438.

Kozol, A. J., J. F. A. Traniello and S. M. Williams. 1994. Genetic variation in the endangered burying beetle *Nicrophorus americanus* (Coleoptera: Silphidae). *Annals of the Entomological Society of America* 87: 928–935.

Kraus, S. D. 1990. Rates and potential cause of mortality in North Atlantic right whales (*Eubalaena glacialis*). *Marine Mammal Science* 6: 278–291.

Kremen, C., A. M. Merenlender and D. D. Murphy. 1994. Ecological monitoring: A vital need for integrated conservation and development programs in the tropics. *Conservation Biology* 8: 388–397.

Kristensen, R. M. 1983. Loricifera, a new phylum with Aschelminthes characters from the meiobenthos. *Zeitschrift für Zoologische Systematik* 21: 163–180.

Küchler, A. W. 1964. Potential natural vegetation of the conterminous United States. Special Publication no. 36. American Geographical Society, New York. (Map of the conterminous 48 states, scale = 1:3,168,000, and manual.)

Kummer, D. M. and B. L. Turner II. 1994. The human causes of deforestation in Southeast Asia. *BioScience* 44: 323.

Kusler, J. A. and M. E. Kentula (eds.). 1990. *Wetland Creation and Restoration: The Status of the Science.* Island Press, Washington, D.C.

Lacey, R. C. 1987. Loss of genetic diversity from managed populations: Interacting effects of drift, mutation, immigration, selection, and population subdivision. *Conservation Biology* 1: 143–158.

Lamberson, R. H., R. McElvey, B. R. Noon and C. Voss. 1992. A dynamic analysis of Northern Spotted Owl viability in a fragmented forest landscape. *Conservation Biology* 6: 505–512.

Land Trust Exchange. 1988. *Land Trust Standard Practices.* Land Trust Exchange, Alexandria, VA.

Lande, R. 1988. Genetics and demography in biological conservation. *Science* 241: 1455–1460.

Lande, R. and G. F. Barrowclough. 1987. Effective population size, genetic variation, and their use in population management. *In* M. E. Soulé (ed.), *Viable Populations for Conservation,* pp. 87–124. Cambridge University Press, Cambridge.

Lasiak, T. 1991. The susceptibility and/or resilience of rocky littoral molluscs to stock depletion by the indigenous coastal people of Transkei, southern Africa. *Biological Conservation* 56: 245–264.

Laurance, W. F. 1991. Edge effects in tropical forest fragments: Application of a model for the design of nature reserves. *Biological Conservation* 57: 205–219.

Leader-Williams, N. 1990. Black rhinos and African elephants: Lessons for conservation funding. *Oryx* 24:23–29.

Ledig, F. T. 1988. The conservation of diversity in forest trees. *BioScience* 38: 471–479.

Lehmkuhl, J. F., R. K. Upreti and U. R. Sharma. 1988. National parks and local development: Grasses and people in Royal Chitwan National Park, Nepal. *Environmental Conservation* 15: 143–148.

Leigh, J. H., J. D. Briggs and W. Hartley. 1982. The conservation status of Australian plants. *In* R. H. Groves and W. D. L. Ride (eds.), *Species at Risk: Research in Australia,* pp. 13–25. Springer-Verlag, New York.

Leighton, M. and N. Wirawan. 1986. Catastrophic drought and fire in Borneo tropical rain forest associated with the 1982–1983 El Niño southern oscillation event. *In* G. T. Prance (ed.). *Tropical Rain Forests and World Atmosphere,* pp. 75–102. Westview Press, Boulder, CO.

Lesica, P. and F. W. Allendorf. 1992. Are small populations of plants worth preserving? *Conservation Biology* 6: 135–139.

Lewis, D., G. B. Kaweche and A. Mwenya. 1990. Wildlife conservation outside protected areas: Lessons from an experiment in Zambia. *Conservation Biology* 4: 171–180.

Lieth, H. and M. Lohmann (eds.). 1993. *Restoration of Tropical Rainforest Ecosystems.* Kluwer Academic Publishers, Dordrecht.

Likens, G. E. 1991. Toxic winds: Whose responsibility? *In* F. Herbert Bormann and S. R. Kellert (eds.), *Ecology, Economics, Ethics: The Broken Circle,* pp. 136–152. Yale University Press, New Haven, CT.

Lindberg, K. 1991. *Policies for Maximizing Nature Tourism's Ecological and Economic Benefits.* World Resources Institute, Washington, D.C.

Linden, Eugene. 1994. Ancient creatures. *Time* 143: 52–54.

Lipske, M. 1991. Big hopes for bold beasts: Can grizzlies and wolves be reintroduced safely into old haunts? *National Wildlife* 29: 44–53.

Loeschcke, V., J. Tomiuk and S. K. Jain (eds.). 1994. *Conservation Genetics.* Birkhauser Verlag, Basel, Switzerland.

Loope, L. L., O. Hamann and C. P. Stone. 1988. Comparative conservation biology of oceanic archipelagoes: Hawaii and the Galápagos. *BioScience* 38: 272–282.

Lovejoy, T. E. et al. 1986. Edge and other effects of isolation on Amazon forest fragments. *In* M. E. Soulé (ed.), *Conservation Biology: The Science of Scarcity and Diversity,* pp. 257–285. Sinauer Associates, Sunderland, MA.

Lovelock, J. 1988. *The Ages of Gaia.* W. W. Norton, New York.

Lubchenco, J. et al. 1991. The sustainable biosphere initiative: An ecological research agenda. *Ecology* 72: 371–412.

Ludwig, D. 1993. Environmental sustainability: Magic, science, and religion in natural resource management. *Ecological Applications* 3: 555–558.

Ludwig, D., R. Hilborn and C. Walters. 1993. Uncertainty, resource exploitation, and conservation: Lessons from history. *Science* 260: 17, 36.

Luoma, J. R. 1992. Born to be wild. *Audubon* 94: 50–61.

Lutz, R. A. 1991. The biology of deep-sea vents and seeps. *Oceanus* 34: 75–83.

MacArthur, R. H. and E. O. Wilson. 1967. *The Theory of Island Biogeography.* Princeton University Press, Princeton, NJ.

Mace, G. M. 1994. An investigation into methods for categorizing the conservation status of species. *In* P. J. Edwards, R. M. May and N. R. Webb (eds.), *Large-Scale Ecology and Conservation Biology,* pp. 293–312. Blackwell Scientific Publications, Oxford.

Mace, G. M. and R. Lande. 1991. Assessing extinction threats: Towards a reevaluation of IUCN threatened species categories. *Conservation Biology* 5: 148–157.

Machlis, G. and K. Johnson. 1987. Panda outposts. *National Parks* 61(9–10): 14–16.

Machlis, G. E. and D. L. Tichnell. 1985. *The State of the World's Parks: An International Assessment of Resource Management, Policy, and Research.* Westview Press, Boulder, CO.

MacKenzie, J. J. and M. T. El-Ashry. 1988. *Ill Winds: Airborne Pollution's Toll on Trees and Crops.* World Resources Institute, Washington, D.C.

MacKinnon, J. 1983. Irrigation and watershed protection in Indonesia. Report to IBRD Regional Office, Jakarta.

MacKinnon, J., K. MacKinnon, G. Child and J. Thorsell. 1992. *Managing Protected Areas in the Tropics.* IUCN, Gland, Switzerland.

Maehr, D. S. 1990. The Florida panther and private lands. *Conservation Biology* 4: 167–170.

Magnuson, J. J. 1990. Long-term ecological research and the invisible present. *BioScience* 40: 495–501.

Makarewicz, J. C. and P. Bertram. 1991. Evidence for the restoration of the Lake Erie ecosystem. *BioScience* 41: 216–223.

Maltby, E. 1988. Wetland resources and future prospects: An international perspective. *In* J. Zelazny and J. Scott Feierabend (eds.), *Wetlands: Increasing Our Wetland Resources,* pp. 3–14. National Wildlife Federation, Washington, D.C.

Mangel, M. and C. Tier. 1994. Four facts every conservation biologist should know about persistence. *Ecology* 75: 607–614.

Mann, C. C. and M. L. Plummer. 1993. The high cost of biodiversity. *Science* 260: 1868–1871.

Mares, M. A. 1992. Neotropical mammals and the myth of Amazonian biodiversity. *Science* 255: 976–979.

Martin, P. S. and R. G. Klein (eds.). 1984. *Quaternary Extinctions: A Prehistoric Revolution.* University of Arizona Press, Tucson.

Master, L. L. 1991. Assessing threats and setting priorities for conservation. *Conservation Biology* 5: 559–563.

Mathews, A. 1992. *Where the Buffalo Roam.* Grove Weidenfeld, New York.

May, R. M. 1988. Conservation and disease. *Conservation Biology* 2: 28–30.

May, R. M. 1992. How many species inhabit the Earth? *Scientific American* 267: 42–48.

McCloskey, J. M. and H. Spalding. 1989. A reconnaissance-level inventory of the amount of wilderness remaining in the world. *Ambio* 18: 221–227.

McLaren, B. E. and R. O. Peterson. 1994. Wolves, moose, and tree rings on Isle Royale. *Science* 266: 1555–1558.

McNaughton, S. J. 1989. Ecosystems and conservation in the twenty-first century. *In* D. Western and M. Pearl (eds.), *Conservation for the Twenty-First Century,* pp. 109–120. Oxford University Press, New York.

McNeely, J. A. 1987. How dams and wildlife can coexist: Natural habitats, agriculture, and major water resource development projects in tropical Asia. *Conservation Biology* 1: 228–238.

McNeely, J. A. 1988. *Economics and Biological Diversity: Developing and Using Economic Incentives to Conserve Biological Resources.* IUCN, Gland, Switzerland.

McNeely, J. A. (ed.). 1993a. *Protected Areas and Modern Societies: Regional Reviews of Conservation Issues.* IUCN, Gland, Switzerland.

McNeely, J. A. (ed.). 1993b. *Building Partnerships for Conservation.* IUCN, Gland, Switzerland.

McNeely, J. A. et al. 1990. *Conserving the World's Biological Diversity.* IUCN, World Resources Institute, Conservation International, WWF-US, and the World Bank, Gland, Switzerland and Washington, D.C.

McNeely, J. A., J. Harrison and P. Dingwall (eds.). 1994. *Protecting Nature: Regional Reviews of Protected Areas.* IUCN, Gland, Switzerland.

Meffe, G. K. and C. R. Carroll. 1994. *Principles of Conservation Biology.* Sinauer Associates, Sunderland, MA.

Meffe, G. K., A. H. Ehrlich and D. Ehrenfeld. 1993. Human population control: The missing agenda. *Conservation Biology* 7: 1–3.

Menges, E. S. 1986. Predicting the future of rare plant populations: Demographic monitoring and modeling. *Natural Areas Journal* 6: 13–25.

Menges, E. S. 1990. Population viability analysis for an endangered plant. *Conservation Biology* 4: 52–62.

Menges, E. S. 1991. The application of minimum viable population theory to plants. *In* D. A. Falk and K. E. Holsinger (eds.), *Genetics and Conservation of Rare Plants,* pp. 45–61. Oxford University Press, New York.

Menges, E. S. 1992. Stochastic modeling of extinction in plant populations. *In* P. L. Fiedler and S. K. Jain (eds.), *Conservation Biology: The Theory and Practice of Nature Conservation, Preservation, and Management,* pp. 253–275. Chapman and Hall, New York.

Merola, M. 1994. A reassessment of homozygosity and the case for inbreeding depression in the cheetah, *Acinonyx jubatus:* Implications for conservation. *Conservation Biology* 8 (4): 961–971.

Meyer, W. B. and B. L. Turner II. 1994. *Changes in Land Use and Land Cover: A Global Perspective.* Cambridge University Press, New York.

Miller, R. M. 1990. Mycorrhizae and succession. *In* W. R. Jordan III, M. E. Gilpin and J. D. Aber (eds.), *Restoration Ecology: A Synthetic Approach to Ecological Research,* pp. 205–220. Cambridge University Press, Cambridge.

Mills, E. L., J. H. Leach, J. T. Carlton and C. L. Secor. 1994. Exotic species and the integrity of the Great Lakes. *BioScience* 44: 666–676.

Milton, S. J., W. R. J. Dean, M. A. du Plessis and W. R. Siegfried. 1994. A conceptual model of arid rangeland degradation. *BioScience* 44: 70–76.

Mikitin, K. and D. Osgood. 1994. *Issues and Options in the Design of Global Environment Facility-Supported Trust Funds for Biodiversity Conservation.* World Bank, Washington, D.C.

Mitchell, J. G. 1992. Our disappearing wetlands. *National Geographic* 182 (October): 3–45.

Mittermeier, R. A. 1988. Primate diversity and the tropical forest: Case studies from Brazil and Madagascar and the importance of the megadiversity countries. *In* E. O. Wilson and F. M. Peter (eds.), *Biodiversity,* pp. 145–154. National Academy Press, Washington, D.C.

Mittermeier, R. A. and T. B. Werner. 1990. Wealth of plants and animals unites "megadiversity" countries. *Tropicus* 4: 1, 4–5.

Mlot, C. 1992. Botanists sue Forest Service to preserve biodiversity. *Science* 257: 1618–1619.

Moffat, M. W. 1994. *The High Frontier: Exploring the Tropical Rainforest Canopy.* Harvard University Press, Cambridge, MA.

Mohsin, A. K. M. and M. A. Ambak. 1983. *Freshwater Fishes of Peninsular Malaysia.* University Pertanian Malaysia Press, Kuala Lumpur.

Moiseenko, T. 1994. Acidification and critical loads for surface waters: Kola, northern Russia. *Ambio* 23: 418–424.

Morell, V. 1994. Serengeti's big cats going to the dogs. *Science* 264: 1664.

Moyle, P. B. and R. A. Leidy. 1992. Loss of biodiversity in aquatic ecosystems: Evidence from fish faunas. *In* P. L. Fiedler and S. K. Jain (eds.), *Conservation Biology: The Theory and Practice of Nature Conservation, Preservation, and Management,* pp. 127–169. Chapman and Hall, New York.

Munn, C. A. 1992. Macaw biology and ecotourism or "when a bird in the bush is worth two in the hand." *In* S. R. Beissinger and N. F. R. Snyder (eds.), *New World Parrots in Crisis,* pp. 47–72. Smithsonian Institution Press, Washington, D.C.

Munn, C. A. 1994. Macaws: Winged rainbows. *National Geographic* 185 (January): 118–140.

Murphy, D. D., K. E. Freas and S. B. Weiss. 1990. An environment-metapopulation approach to population viability analysis for a threatened invertebrate. *Conservation Biology* 4: 41–51.

Murphy, D. D. and B. R. Noon. 1992. Integrating scientific methods with habitat conservation planning: Reserve design for northern spotted owls. *Ecological Applications* 2: 3–17.

Murphy, P. G. and A. E. Lugo. 1986. Ecology of tropical dry forest. *Annual Review of Ecology and Systematics* 17: 67–88.

Mwalyosi, R. B. B. 1991. Ecological evaluation for wildlife corridors and buffer zones for Lake Manyara National Park, Tanzania, and its immediate environment. *Biological Conservation* 57: 171–186.

Myers, N. 1980. *Conversion of Tropical Moist Forests.* National Academy of Sciences, Washington, D.C.

Myers, N. 1984. *The Primary Source: Tropical Forests and Our Future.* W. W. Norton, New York.

Myers, N. 1986. Tropical deforestation and a mega-extinction spasm. *In* M. E. Soulé (ed.), *Conservation Biology: The Science of Scarcity and Diversity,* pp. 394–409. Sinauer Associates, Sunderland, MA.

Myers, N. 1987. The extinction spasm impending: Synergisms at work. *Conservation Biology* 1: 14–21.

Myers, N. 1988a. Threatened biotas: "Hotspots" in tropical forests. *Environmentalist* 8: 1–20.

Myers, N. 1988b. Tropical forests: Much more than stocks of wood. *Journal of Tropical Ecology* 4: 209–221.

Myers, N. 1991a. The biodiversity challenge: Expanded "hotspots" analysis. *Environmentalist* 10: 243–256.

Myers, N. 1991b. Tropical deforestation: The latest situation. *BioScience* 41: 282.

Myers, N. 1993. Sharing the earth with whales. *In* L. Kaufman and K. Mallory (eds.), *The Last Extinction,* pp. 179–194. MIT Press, Cambridge, MA.

Nabhan, G. P. 1985. Native crop diversity in Aridoamerica: Conservation of regional gene pools. *Economic Botany* 39: 387–399.

Naess, A. 1986. Intrinsic value: Will the defenders of nature please rise? *In* M. E. Soulé (ed.), *Conservation Biology: The Science of Scarcity and Diversity,* pp. 153–181. Sinauer Associates, Sunderland, MA.

Naess, A. 1989. *Ecology, Community, and Lifestyle.* Cambridge University Press, Cambridge.

NAS/NRC (National Academy of Sciences/National Research Council. 1972. *Genetic Vulnerability of Major Crop Plants.* NAS/NRC, Washington, D.C.

Nei, M., T. Maruyama and R. Chakraborty. 1975. The bottleneck effect and genetic variability in populations. *Evolution* 29: 1–10.

Nepstad, D. C., F. Brown, L. Luz, A. Alechandra and V. Viana. 1992. Biotic impoverishment of Amazonian forests by rubber tappers and cattle ranchers. *In* D. C. Nepstad and S. Schwartzman (eds.), *Non-Timber Products from Tropical Forests: Evaluation of a Conservation and Development Strategy.* The New York Botanical Garden, Bronx, NY.

Nepstad, D. C. and S. Schwartzman (eds.). 1992. *Non-Timber Products from Tropical Forests: Evaluation of a Conservation and Development Strategy.* The New York Botanical Garden, Bronx, NY.

New England Wild Flower Society. 1992. New England plant conservation program. *Wild Flower Notes* 7.

Niemelä, J., D. Langor and J. R. Spence. 1993. Effects of clear-cut harvesting on boreal ground-beetle assemblages (Coleoptera: Carabidae) in Western Canada. *Conservation Biology* 7: 551–561.

Nilsson, G. 1983. *The Endangered Species Handbook.* Animal Welfare Institute, Washington, D.C.

Nobre, C. A., P. J. Sellers and J. Shukla. 1991. Amazonian deforestation and regional climate change. *Journal of Climate* 4: 957–988.

Norse, E. A. (ed.). 1993. *Global Marine Biological Diversity: A Strategy for Building Conservation into Decision Making.* Island Press, Washington, D.C.

Norse, E. A. et al. 1986. *Conserving Biological Diversity in Our National Forests.* The Wilderness Society, Washington, D.C.

Norton, B. G. 1988. Commodity, amenity, and morality: The limits of quantification in valuing biodiversity. *In* E. O. Wilson and F. M. Peter (eds.), *Biodiversity,* pp. 200–205. National Academy Press, Washington, D.C.

Norton, B. G. 1991. *Toward Unity Among Environmentalists.* Oxford University Press, New York.

Noss, R. F. 1992. Essay: Issues of scale in conservation biology. *In* P. L. Fiedler and S. K. Jain (eds.), *Conservation Biology: The Theory and Practice of Nature Conservation, Preservation, and Management,* pp. 239–250. Chapman and Hall, New York.

Noss, R. F. and A. Y. Cooperrider. 1994. *Saving Nature's Legacy: Protecting and Restoring Biodiversity.* Island Press, Washington, D.C.

Nunney, L. and D. R. Elam. 1994. Estimating the effective population size of conserved populations. *Conservation Biology* 8: 175–184.

O'Brien, S. J. and J. F. Evermann. 1988. Interactive influence of infectious disease and genetic diversity in natural populations. *Trends in Ecology and Evolution* 3: 254–259.

Odum, E. P. 1993. *Ecology and Our Endangered Life-Support Systems,* 2nd ed. Sinauer Associates, Sunderland, MA.

Oldfield, M. L. and Alcorn, J. B. (eds.). 1991. *Biodiversity: Culture, Conservation, and Ecodevelopment.* Westview Press, Boulder, CO.

Olivieri, I., D. Couvet and P. H. Gouyon. 1990. The genetics of transient populations: Research at the metapopulation level. *Trends in Ecology and Evolution* 5: 207–210.

Olney, P. J. S. and P. Ellis (eds.). 1991. *1990 International Zoo Yearbook,* vol. 30. Zoological Society of London, London.

Olson, S. L. 1989. Extinction on islands: Man as a catastrophe. *In* M. Pearl and D. Western (eds.), *Conservation Biology for the Twenty-first Century,* pp. 50–53. Oxford University Press, Oxford.

Orians, G. H. 1993. Endangered at what level? *Ecological Applications* 3: 206–208.

OTA (Office of Technology Assessment of the U.S. Congress.) 1987. *Technologies to Maintain Biological Diversity.* OTA-F-330. U.S. Government Printing Office, Washington, D.C.

Packer, C. 1992. Captives in the wild. *National Geographic* 181 (April): 122–136.

Packer, C., A. E. Pusey, H. Rowley, D. A. Gilbert, J. Martenson and S. J. O'Brien. 1991. Case study of a population bottleneck: Lions of the Ngorongoro Crater. *Conservation Biology* 5: 219–230.

Palmer, M. E. 1987. A critical look at rare plant monitoring in the United States. *Biological Conservation* 39: 113–127.

Pandit, A. K. 1991. Conservation of wildlife resources in wetland ecosystems of Kashmir, India. *Journal of Environmental Management* 33: 143–154.

Panwar, H. S. 1987. Project Tiger: The reserves, the tigers, and their future. *In* R. L. Tilson and U. S. Seal (eds.), *Tigers of the World: The Biology, Biopolitics, Management, and Conservation of an Endangered Species,* pp. 100–117. Noyes Publications, Park Ridge, NJ.

Parikh, J. and K. Parikh. 1991. *Consumption Patterns: The Driving Force of Environmental Stress.* UNCED, Geneva, Switzerland.

Parkes, R. J., B. A. Cragg, S. J. Bale, J. M. Getliff, K. Goodman, P. A. Rochelle, J. C. Fry, A. J. Weightman and S. M. Harvey. 1994. Deep bacterial biosphere in Pacific Ocean sediments. *Nature* 371: 410–413.

Paton, P. W. C. 1994. The effect of edge on avian nest success: How strong is the evidence? *Conservation Biology* 8: 17–26.

Patterson, A. 1990. Debt for nature swaps and the need for alternatives. *Environment* 32: 5–32.

Pavlik, B. M., D. L. Nickrent and A. M. Howald. 1993. The recovery of an endangered plant. I. Creating a new population of *Amsinckia grandiflora*. *Conservation Biology* 7: 510–526.

Pearson, D. L. and F. Cassola. 1992. World-wide species richness patterns of tiger beetles (Coleoptera: Cicindelidae): Indicator taxon for biodiversity and conservation studies. *Conservation Biology* 6: 376–391.

Pechmann, J. H. K., D. E. Scott, R. D. Semlitsch, J. P. Caldwell, L. J. Vitt and J. W. Gibbons. 1991. Declining amphibian populations: The problems of separating human impacts from natural fluctuations. *Science* 253: 825–940.

Peres, C. A. and J. W. Terborgh. 1995. Amazonian nature reserves: An analysis of the defensibility status of existing conservation units and design criteria for the future. *Conservation Biology* 9: 34–46.

Peterken, G. F. 1994. *Woodland Conservation and Management,* 2nd ed. Chapman and Hall, London.

Peters, C. M., A. H. Gentry and R. Mendelsohn. 1989. Valuation of a tropical forest in Peruvian Amazonia. *Nature* 339: 655–656.

Phillips, O. L. and A. H. Gentry. 1994. Increasing turnover through time in tropical forests. *Science* 263: 954–958.

Pianka, E. 1966. Latitudinal gradients in species diversity: A review of the concepts. *American Naturalist* 100: 33–46.

Pimm, S. L. 1991. *The Balance of Nature? Ecological Issues in the Conservation of Species and Communities.* University of Chicago Press, Chicago.

Pimm, S. L., H. L. Jones and J. Diamond. 1988. On the risk of extinction. *American Naturalist* 132: 757–785.

Plotkin, M. J. 1988. The outlook for new agricultural and industrial products from the tropics. *In* E. O. Wilson and F. M. Peter (eds.), *Biodiversity,* pp. 106–116. National Academy Press, Washington, D.C.

Plotkin, M. J. 1993. *Tales of a Shaman's Apprentice.* Viking/Penguin, New York.

Plucknett, D. L., N. J. H. Smith, J. T. Williams and N. M. Anishetty. 1987. *Gene Banks and the World's Food.* Princeton University Press, Princeton, NJ.

Poffenberger, M. (ed.). 1990. *Keepers of the Forest.* Kumarian, West Hartford, CT.

Popper, F. J. and D. E. Popper. 1991. The reinvention of the American frontier. *Amicus Journal* (Summer): 4–7.

Porteous, P. L. 1992. Eagles on the rise. *National Geographic* 182 (November): 42–55.

Porter, S. D. and D. A. Savignano. 1990. Invasion of polygyne fire ants decimates native ants and disrupts arthropod communities. *Ecology* 71: 2095–2106.

Posey, D. A. 1992. Traditional knowledge, conservation, and "the rain forest harvest." *In* M. Plotkin and L. Famolare (eds.), *Sustainable Harvest and Marketing of Rain Forest Products,* pp. 46–50. Island Press, Washington, D.C.

Poten, C. J. 1991. A shameful harvest: America's illegal wildlife trade. *National Geographic* 180 (September): 106–132.

Power, T. M. 1991. Ecosystem preservation and the economy in the Greater Yellowstone area. *Conservation Biology* 5: 395–404.

Prescott-Allen, C. and R. Prescott-Allen. 1986. *The First Resource: Wild Species in the North American Economy.* Yale University Press, New Haven, Ct.

Prescott-Allen, R. 1986. *National Conservation Strategies and Biological Diversity.* Report to the IUCN, Gland, Switzerland.

Prescott-Allen, R. and C. Prescott-Allen. 1982. *What's Wildlife Worth? Economic Contributions of Wild Plants and Animals to Developing Countries.* International Institute for Environment and Development (Earthscan), London.

Pressey, R. L. 1994. Ad hoc reservations: Forward or backward steps in developing representative reserve systems? *Conservation Biology* 8: 662–668.

Primack, R. B. 1992. Tropical community dynamics and conservation biology. *BioScience* 42: 818–820.

Primack, R. B. 1995. Dispersal, establishment and population structure: Lessons from ecological theory for rare plant reintroduction. *In* P. Olwell, C. Millar and D. Falk (eds.), *Ecological Restorations and Endangered Species.* Island Press, Washington, D.C. In press.

Primack, R. B. and P. Hall. 1992. Biodiversity and forest change in Malaysian Borneo. *BioScience* 42: 829–837.

Primack, R. B. and S. L. Miao. 1992. Dispersal can limit local plant distribution. *Conservation Biology* 6: 513–519.

Pritchard, P. C. 1991. "The best idea America ever had": The National Parks service turns 75. *National Geographic* 180: 36–59.

Rabinowitz, A. 1993. *Wildlife Field Research and Conservation Training Manual.* International Wildlife Conservation Park, New York.

Ralls, K. and J. Ballou. 1983. Extinction: Lessons from zoos. *In* C. M. Schonewald-Cox, S. M. Chambers, B. MacBryde and L. Thomas (eds.), *Genetics and Conservation: A Reference for Managing Wild Animal and Plant Populations,* pp. 164–184. Benjamin/Cummings, Menlo Park, CA.

Ralls, K., J. D. Ballou and A. Templeton. 1988. Estimates of lethal equivalents and the cost of inbreeding in mammals. *Conservation Biology* 2: 185–193.

Ralls, K. and R. L. Brownell. 1989. Protected species: Research permits and the value of basic research. *BioScience* 39: 394–396.

Randall, A. 1987. *Resource Economics,* 2nd ed. John Wiley, New York.

Raup, D. M. 1979. Size of the Permo-Triassic bottleneck and its evolutionary implications. *Science* 206: 217–218.

Raup, D. M. and S. M. Stanley. 1978. *Principles of Paleontology,* 2nd ed. W. H. Freeman, San Francisco.

Raven, P. H. and E. O. Wilson. 1992. A fifty-year plan for biodiversity surveys. *Science* 258: 1099–1100.

Ravenscroft, N. O. M. 1990. The ecology and conservation of the silver-studded blue butterfly *Plejebus argus* L. on the sandlings of East Anglia, England. *Biological Conservation* 53: 21–36.

Ray, G. C. and W. P. Gregg Jr. 1991. Establishing biosphere reserves for coastal barrier ecosystems. *BioScience* 41: 301–309.

Reading, R. P. and S. R. Kellert. 1993. Attitudes toward a proposed reintroduction of black-footed ferrets (*Mustela nigripes*). *Conservation Biology* 7: 569–580.

Redford, K. H. 1992. The empty forest. *BioScience* 42: 412–422.

Redford, K. H. and C. Padoch (eds.). 1992. *Conservation of Neotropical Rainforests: Working from Traditional Resource Use.* Columbia University Press, Irvington, NY.

Reid, W. V. 1992. *The United States Needs a National Biodiversity Policy.* Issues and Ideas Brief. World Resources Institute, Washington, D.C.

Reid, W. V. and K. R. Miller. 1989. *Keeping Options Alive: The Scientific Basis for Conserving Biodiversity.* World Resources Institute, Washington, D.C.

Repetto, R. 1990a. Deforestation in the tropics. *Scientific American* 262: 36–42.

Repetto, R. 1990b. *Promoting Environmentally Sound Economic Progress: What the North Can Do.* World Resources Institute, Washington, D.C.

Repetto, R. 1992. Accounting for environmental assets. *Scientific American* 266 (June): 94–100.

Repetto, R. et al. 1989. *Wasting Assets: Natural Resources in the National Income Accounts.* World Resources Institute, Washington, D.C.

Rhoades, R. E. 1991. World's food supply at risk. *National Geographic* 179 (April): 74–105.

Rich, B. 1990. Multilateral development banks and tropical deforestation. *In* S. Head and R. Heinzman (eds.), *Lessons from the Rainforest,* pp. 118–130. Sierra Club Books, San Francisco.

Richter-Dyn, N. and N. S. Goel. 1972. On the extinction of a colonizing species. *Population Biology* 3: 406–433.

Ricklefs, R. E. 1993. *The Economy of Nature.* W. H. Freeman and Co., New York.

Robinson, M. H. 1992. Global change, the future of biodiversity, and the future of zoos. *Biotropica* (Special Issue) 24: 345–352.

Rohlf, D. L. 1989. *The Endangered Species Act: A Guide to Its Protections and Implementation.* Stanford Environmental Law Society, Stanford, CA.

Rohlf, D. L. 1991. Six biological reasons why the Endangered Species Act doesn't work—and what to do about it. *Conservation Biology* 5: 273–282.

Rojas, M. 1992. The species problem and conservation: What are we protecting? *Conservation Biology* 6: 170–178.

Rolston, H. III. 1985. Duties to endangered species. *BioScience* 35: 718–726.

Rolston, H. III. 1988. *Environmental Ethics: Values in and Duties to the Natural World.* Temple University Press, Philadelphia.

Rolston, H. III. 1989. *Philosophy Gone Wild: Essays on Environmental Ethics.* Prometheus Books, Buffalo, NY.

Ruggiero, L. F., G. D. Hayward and J. R. Squires. 1994. Viability analysis in biological evaluations: Concepts of population viability analysis, biological population, and ecological scale. *Conservation Biology* 8: 364–368.

Runte, A. 1979. *National Parks: The American Experience.* University of Nebraska Press, Lincoln.

Safina, C. 1993. Bluefin tuna in the West Atlantic: Negligent management and the making of an endangered species. *Conservation Biology* 7:229–234.

Salm, R. and J. Clark. 1984. *Marine and Coastal Protected Areas: A Guide for Planners and Managers.* IUCN, Gland, Switzerland.

Salwasser, H., C. M. Schonewald-Cox and R. Baker. 1987. The role of interagency cooperation in managing for viable populations. *In* M. E. Soulé, ed., *Viable Populations for Conservation,* pp. 159–173. Cambridge University Press, Cambridge.

Sample, V. A. 1994. *Remote Sensing and GIS in Ecosystem Management.* Island Press, Washington, D.C.

Samways, M. J. 1994. *Insect Conservation Biology.* Chapman and Hall, London.

Savidge, J. A. 1987. Extinction of an island forest avifauna by an introduced snake. *Ecology* 68: 660–668.

Sayer, J. A. and S. Stuart. 1988. Biological diversity and tropical forests. *Environmental Conservation* 15: 193–194.

Sayer, J. A. and T. C. Whitmore. 1991. Tropical moist forests: Destruction and species extinction. *Biological Conservation* 55: 199–213.

Schemske, D. W., B. C. Husband, M. H. Ruckelshaus, C. Goodwillie, I. M. Parker and J. G. Bishop. 1994. Evaluating approaches to the conservation of rare and endangered plants. *Ecology* 75: 584–606.

Scheiner, S. M. and J. M. Rey-Benayas. 1994. Global patterns of plant diversity. *Evolutionary Ecology* 8: 331–347.

Schonewald-Cox, C. M. 1983. Conclusions: Guidelines to management: A beginning attempt. *In* C. M. Schonewald-Cox, S. M. Chambers, B. MacBryde and L. Thomas (eds.), *Genetics and Conservation: A Reference for Managing Wild Animal and Plant Populations,* pp. 414–445. Benjamin/Cummings, Menlo Park, CA.

Schonewald-Cox, C. M. and M. Buechner. 1992. Park protection and public roads. *In* P. L. Fiedler and S. K. Jain (eds.), *Conservation Biology: The Theory and Practice of Nature Conservation, Preservation, and Management,* pp. 373–396. Chapman and Hall, New York.

Schonewald-Cox, C. M., S. M. Chambers, B. MacBryde and L. Thomas (eds.). 1983. *Genetics and Conservation: A Reference for Managing Wild Animal and Plant Populations.* Benjamin/Cummings, Menlo Park, CA.

Schultes, R. E. and R. F. Raffauf. 1990. *The Healing Forest: Medicinal and Toxic Plants of the Northwest Amazonia.* Dioscorides Press, Portland, OR.

Schulze, E. D. and H. A. Mooney (eds.). 1993. *Biodiversity and Ecosystem Function.* Springer-Verlag, Berlin and New York.

Scott, J. M., B. Csuti and F. Davis. 1991. Gap analysis: An application of Geographic Information Systems for wildlife species. *In* D. J. Decker, M. E. Krasny, G. R. Goff, C. R. Smith and D. W. Gross (eds.), *Challenges in the Conservation of Biological Resources: A Practitioner's Guide,* pp. 167–179. Westview Press, Boulder, CO.

Scott, M. E. 1988. The impact of infection and disease on animal populations: Implications for conservation biology. *Conservation Biology* 2: 40–56.

Seal, U. S. 1988. Intensive technology in the care of ex situ populations of vanishing species. *In* E. O. Wilson and F. M. Peter (eds.), *Biodiversity,* pp. 289–295. National Academy Press, Washington, D.C.

Sepkoski, J. J. Jr. and D. M. Raup. 1986. Periodicity in marine extinction events. *In* D. K. Elliott (ed.), *Dynamics of Extinction,* pp. 3–36. John Wiley, New York.

Sessions, G. 1987. The deep ecology movement: A review. *Environmental Review* 11: 105–125.

Shafer, C. L. 1990. *Nature Reserves: Island Theory and Conservation Practice.* Smithsonian Institution Press, Washington, D.C.

Shaffer, M. L. 1981. Minimum population sizes for species conservation. *BioScience* 31: 131–134.

Shaffer, M. L. 1990. Population viability analysis. *Conservation Biology* 4: 39–40.

Shaffer, M. L. 1991. Population viability analysis. *In* D. J. Decker, M. E. Krasny, G. R. Goff, C. R. Smith and D. W. Gross (eds.), *Challenges in the Conservation of Biological Resources: A Practitioner's Guide,* pp. 107–118. Westview Press, Boulder, CO.

Shaw, W. W. and W. R. Mangun. 1984. *Nonconsumptive use of wildlife in the United States.* Resource Publication 154. U.S. Fish and Wildlife Service, Washington, D.C.

Shulman, S. 1986. Seeds of controversy. *BioScience* 36: 647–651.

Simberloff, D. S. 1986. Are we on the verge of a mass extinction in tropical rainforests? *In* D. K. Elliott (ed.), *Dynamics of Extinction,* pp. 165–180. John Wiley & Sons, New York.

Simberloff, D. S. 1988. The contribution of population and community biology to conservation science. *Annual Review of Ecology and Systematics* 19: 473–511.

Simberloff, D. S. and L. G. Abele. 1976. Island biogeography theory and conservation practice. *Science* 191: 285–286.

Simberloff, D. S. and L. G. Abele. 1982. Refuge design and island biogeographic theory: Effects of fragmentation. *American Naturalist* 120: 41–50.

Simberloff, D. S. and N. Gotelli. 1984. Effects of insularization on plant species richness in the prairie-forest ecotone. *Biological Conservation* 29: 27–46.

Simberloff, D. S., J. A. Farr, J. Cox and D. W. Mehlman. 1992. Movement corridors: Conservation bargains or poor investments? *Conservation Biology* 6: 493–505.

Skole, D. L., W. H. Chomentowski, W. A. Salas and A. D. Nobre. 1994. Physical and human dimensions of deforestation in Amazonia. *BioScience* 44: 314–322.

Smith, F. D. M., R. M. May, R. Pellew, T. H. Johnson and K. R. Walter. 1993. How much do we know about the current extinction rate? *Trends in Ecology and Evolution* 8: 375–378.

Smith, J. B. and D. A. Tirpak (eds.). 1988. *The Potential Effects of Global Climate Changes on the United States,* vol. 2. U.S. Environmental Protection Agency, Washington, D.C. Society for Ecological Restoration. 1991. Program and abstracts, 3rd Annual Conference, Orlando, FL, 18–23 May 1991.

Soulé, M. 1985. What is conservation biology? *BioScience* 35: 727–734.

Soulé, M. (ed.). 1987. *Viable Populations for Conservation.* Cambridge University Press, Cambridge.

Soulé, M. 1990. The onslaught of alien species, and other challenges in the coming decades. *Conservation Biology* 4: 233–239.

Soulé, M. E. and D. Simberloff. 1986. What do genetics and ecology tell us about the design of nature reserves? *Biological Conservation* 35: 19–40.

Sparrow, H. R., T. D. Sisk, P. R. Ehrlich and D. D. Murphy. 1994. Techniques and guidelines for monitoring neotropical butterflies. *Conservation Biology* 8: 800–809.

Species Survival Commission. 1990. *Membership Directory.* IUCN, Gland, Switzerland.

Spellerberg, I. F. 1994. *Evaluation and Assessment for Conservation: Ecological Guidelines for Determining Priorities for Nature Conservation.* Chapman and Hall, London.

Stacey, P. B. and M. Taper. 1992. Environmental variation and the persistence of small populations. *Ecological Applications* 2: 18–29.

Standley, L. A. 1992. Taxonomic issues in rare species protection. *Rhodora* 94: 218–242.

Stanley Price, M. R. 1989. *Animal Re-introductions: The Arabian Oryx in Oman.* Cambridge University Press, Cambridge.

Stanley, T. R. 1995. Ecosystem management and the arrogance of humanism. *Conservation Biology* 9:255–262.

Stehli, F. G. and J. W. Wells. 1971. Diversity and age patterns in hermatypic corals. *Systematic Zoology* 20: 115–125.

Stevens, T. P. 1988. *California State Mussel Watch Marine Water Quality Monitoring Program 1986–87.* California State Water Resource Control Board, Sacramento.

Stiassny, M. L. J. and Mário C. C. de Pinna. 1994. Basal taxa and the role of cladistic patterns in the evaluation of conservation priorities: A view from freshwater. *In* P. L. Forey, C. J. Humphries and R. I. Vane-Wright (eds.), *Systematics and Conservation Evaluation.* Oxford University Press, New York.

St. John, H. 1973. *List and Summary of the Flowering Plants in the Hawaiian Islands.* Pacific Tropical Botanical Garden Memoir no. 1. Cathay Press, Hong Kong.

Stolzenburg, W. 1992. The mussels' message. *Nature Conservancy* 42: 16–23.

Stuart, S. N. 1987. Why we need Action Plans. *Species: Newsletter 8 of the IUCN Species Survival Commission,* February, 1987. Gland, Switzerland.

Swanson, F. J. and R. E. Sparks. 1990. Long-term ecological research and the invisible place. *BioScience* 40: 502–508.

Tangley, L. 1986. Saving tropical forests. *BioScience* 36: 4–15.

Tear, T. H., J. M. Scott, P. H. Hayward and B. Griffith. 1993. Status and prospects for success of the Endangered Species Act: A look at recovery plans. *Science* 262: 976–977.

Temple, S. A. 1990. The nasty necessity: Eradicating exotics. *Conservation Biology* 4: 113–115.

Temple, S. A. 1991. Conservation biology: New goals and new partners for managers of biological resources. *In* D. J. Decker et al. (eds.), *Challenges in the Conservation of Biological Resources: A Practitioner's Guide,* pp. 45–54. Westview Press, Boulder, CO.

Templeton, A. R. 1986. Coadaptation and outbreeding depression. *In* M. E. Soulé (ed.). *Conservation Biology: The Science of Scarcity and Diversity,* pp. 105–116. Sinauer Associates, Sunderland, MA.

Terborgh, J. 1974. Preservation of natural diversity: The problem of extinction prone species. *BioScience* 24: 715–722.

Terborgh, J. 1976. Island biogeography and conservation: Strategy and limitations. *Science* 193: 1029–1030.

Terborgh, J. 1989. *Where Have All the Birds Gone? Essays on the Biology and Conservation of Birds that Migrate to the American Tropics.* Princeton University Press, Princeton, NJ.

Terborgh, J. 1992a. Maintenance of diversity in tropical forests. *Biotropica* (Special Issue) 24: 283–292.

Terborgh, J. 1992b. Why American songbirds are vanishing. *Scientific American* 264: 98–104.

Thiollay, J. M. 1989. Area requirements for the conservation of rainforest raptors and game birds in French Guiana. *Conservation Biology* 3: 128–137.

Thiollay, J. M. 1992. Influence of selective logging on bird species diversity in a Guianan rain forest. *Conservation Biology* 6: 47–63.

Thomas, C. D. 1990. What do real population dynamics tell us about minimum viable population sizes? *Conservation Biology* 4: 324–327.

Thorne, E. T. and E. S. Williams. 1988. Disease and endangered species: The black-footed ferret as a recent example. *Conservation Biology* 2: 66–74.

Thorne, R. F. 1967. A flora of Santa Catalina Island, California. *Aliso* 6: 1–77.

Thornhill, N. W. (ed.). 1993. *The Natural History of Inbreeding and Outbreeding.* University of Chicago Press, Chicago, IL.

Thorsell, J. and J. Sawyer. 1992. *World Heritage: The First Twenty Years.* IUCN, Gland, Switzerland.

Tilman, D. and J. A. Downing. 1994. Biodiversity and stability in grasslands. *Nature* 367: 363–365.

Tobin, R. 1990. *The Expendable Future: U.S. Politics and the Protection of Biological Diversity.* Duke University Press, Durham, NC.

Toledo, V. M. 1988. La diversidad biológica de México. *Ciencia y Desarollo.* Conacyt, México City.

Toledo, V. M. 1991. Patzcuaro's lesson: Nature, production, and culture in an indigenous region of Mexico. *In* M. L. Oldfield and J. B. Alcorn (eds.), *Biodiversity: Culture, Conservation, and Ecodevelopment,* pp. 147–171. Westview Press, Boulder, CO.

Tunnicliffe, V. 1992. Hydrothermal vent communities of the deep sea. *American Scientist* 80: 336–349.

UNDP (United Nations Development Programme)/UNEP/World Bank. 1994. *Global Environment Facility: Independent Evaluation of the Pilot Phase.* World Bank, Washington, D.C.

UNESCO (United Nations Educational, Scientific, and Cultural Organization). 1985. Action plan for biosphere reserves. *Environmental Conservation* 12: 17–27.

United Nations. 1993a. *Agenda 21: Rio Declaration and Forest Principles.* Post-Rio Edition. United Nations Publications, New York.

United Nations. 1993b. *The Global Partnership for Environment and Development.* United Nations Publications, New York.

Urban, D. L., R. V. O'Neill and H. H. Shugart Jr. 1987. Landscape ecology. *BioScience* 37: 119–127.

U.S. Congress. 1973. Sec. 2(a) in Endangered Species Act 87 STAT. 884 (Public Law 93-205).

Usher, M. B. 1975. *Biological Management and Conservation: Ecological Theory, Application, and Planning.* Chapman and Hall, London.

Vane-Wright, R. I., C. R. Smith and I. J. Kitching. 1994. A scientific basis for establishing networks of protected areas. *In* P. L. Forey, C. J. Humphries and R. I. Vane-Wright (eds.), *Systematics and Conservation Evaluation.* Oxford University Press, New York.

Vedder, A. 1989. In the hall of the mountain king. *Animal Kingdom* 92: 31–43.

Vitousek, P. M. 1994. Beyond global warming: Ecology and global change. *Ecology* 75: 1861–1876.

Vogel, J. H. 1994. *Genes for Sale: Privatization as a Conservation Policy.* Oxford University Press, New York.

Ward, D. M., R. Weller and M. M. Bateson. 1990. 16 rRNA sequences reveal numerous uncultured microorganisms in a natural community. *Nature* 345: 63–65.

Ward, G. C. 1992. India's wildlife dilemma. *National Geographic* 181: 2–29.

Waser, N. M. and M. V. Price. 1989. Optimal outcrossing in *Ipomopsis aggregata:* Seed set and offspring fitness. *Evolution* 43: 1097–1109.

WCED (World Commission on Environment and Development). 1987. *Our Common Future.* Oxford University Press, Oxford.

Welch, E. B. and G. D. Cooke. 1990. Lakes. *In* W. R. Jordan III, M. E. Gilpin and J. D. Aber (eds.). *Restoration Ecology: A Synthetic Approach to Ecological Research,* pp. 109–129. Cambridge University Press, Cambridge.

Wells, M. and K. Brandon. 1992. *People and Parks: Linking Protected Area Management with Local Communities.* The World Bank/WWF/USAID, Washington, D.C.

Western, D. 1989. Conservation without parks: Wildlife in the rural landscape. *In* D. Western and M. Pearl (eds.), *Conservation for the Twenty-first Century,* pp. 158–165. Oxford University Press, New York.

Western, D. and W. Henry. 1979. Economics and conservation in Third World national parks. *BioScience* 29: 414–418.

Western, D. and J. Ssemakula. 1981. The future of the savannah ecosystem: Ecological islands or faunal enclaves? *African Journal of Ecology* 19: 7–19.

Western, D. and R. M. Wright (eds.). 1994. *Natural Connections: Perspectives in Community-Based Conservation.* Island Press, Washington, D.C.

Whitmore, T. C. 1990. *An Introduction to Tropical Rain Forests.* Clarendon Press, Oxford.

Whitten, A. J. 1987. Indonesia's transmigration program and its role in the loss of tropical rain forests. *Conservation Biology* 1: 239–246.

Whitten, A. J., K. D. Bishop, S. V. Nash and L. Clayton. 1987. One or more extinctions from Sulawesi, Indonesia? *Conservation Biology* 1: 42–48.

Wijnstekers, W. 1992. *The Evolution of CITES.* CITES Secretariat, Geneva, Switzerland.

Wilcove, D. S. and R. M. May. 1986. National park boundaries and ecological realities. *Nature* 324: 206–207.

Wilcove, D. S., C. H. McLellan and A. P. Dobson. 1986. Habitat fragmentation in the temperate zone. *In* M. E. Soulé (ed.). *Conservation Biology: The Science of Scarcity and Diversity,* pp. 237–256. Sinauer Associates, Sunderland, MA.

Wilcove, D. S., M. McMillan and K. C. Winston. 1993. What exactly is an endangered species? An analysis of the U.S. Endangered Species List: 1985–1991. *Conservation Biology* 7: 87–93.

Wilkes, G. 1991. *In situ* conservation of agricultural systems. *In* M. L. Oldfield and J. B. Alcorn (eds.), *Biodiversity: Culture, Conservation, and Ecodevelopment,* pp. 86–101. Westview Press, Boulder, CO.

Wilkie, D. S., J. G. Sidle and G. C. Boundzanga. 1992. Mechanized logging, market hunting, and a bank loan in the Congo. *Conservation Biology* 5: 570–580.

Willers, B. 1994. Sustainable development: A New World deception. *Conservation Biology* 8: 1146–1148.

Williams, J. D. and R. M. Nowak. 1993. Vanishing species in our own backyard: Extinct fish and wildlife of the United States and Canada. *In* L. Kaufman and K. Mallory (eds.), *The Last Extinction,* pp. 107–140. MIT Press, Cambridge, MA.

Wilson, E. O. 1984. *Biophilia.* Harvard University Press, Cambridge, MA.

Wilson, E. O. 1989. Threats to biodiversity. *Scientific American* 261: 108–116.

Wilson, E. O. 1991. Rain forest canopy: The high frontier. *National Geographic* 180: 78–107.

Wilson, E. O. 1992. *The Diversity of Life.* The Belknap Press of Harvard University Press, Cambridge, MA.

Wong, M 1985. Understory birds as indicators of regeneration in a patch of selectively logged west Malaysian rainforest. *In* J. W. Diamond and T. E. Lovejoy (eds.), *Conservation of Tropical Forest Birds,* pp. 249–263. Technical Publication no. 4. International Council for Bird Preservation, Cambridge, U.K.

World Wide Fund for Nature. 1989. *The Importance of Biological Diversity.* WWF, Gland, Switzerland.

WRI/IIED (World Resources Institute/International Institute for Environment and Development). 1986. *World Resources 1986.* Basic Books, New York.

WRI/IIED. 1988. *World Resources 1988.* Basic Books, New York.

WRI/IUCN/UNEP. 1992. *Global Biodiversity Strategy: Guidelines for Action to Save, Study, and Use Earth's Biotic Wealth Sustainably and Equitably.* World Resources Institute/IUCN/UNEP.

WRI/UNEP/UNDP. 1992. *World Resources 1992–93.* Oxford University Press, New York.

WRI/UNEP/UNDP. 1994. *World Resources 1994–95.* Oxford University Press, New York.

Wright, R. G., J. G. MacCracken and J. Hall. 1994. An ecological evaluation of proposed new conservation areas in Idaho: Evaluating proposed Idaho national parks. *Conservation Biology* 8: 207–216

Wright, S. 1931. Evolution in Mendelian populations. *Genetics* 16: 97–159.

Yahner, R. H. 1988. Changes in wildlife communities near edges. *Conservation Biology* 2: 333–339.

Yoakum, J. and W. P. Dasmann. 1971. Habitat manipulation practices. *In* R. H. Giles (ed.). *Wildlife Management Techniques,* pp. 173–231. The Wildlife Society, Washington, D.C.

Young, R. A., D. J. P. Swift, T. L. Clarke, G. R. Harvey and P. R. Betzer. 1985. Dispersal pathways for particle-associated pollutants. *Science* 229: 431–435.

Young, T. P. 1994. Natural die-offs of large mammals: Implications for conservation. *Conservation Biology* 8: 410–418.

Zonneveld, I. S. and R. T. Forman (eds.). 1990. *Changing Landscapes: An Ecological Perspective.* Springer-Verlag, New York.

Index

ABOUT THE AUTHOR

Richard B. Primack is Professor of Plant Ecology at Boston University. He received his B.A. from Harvard University and his Ph.D. from Duke University. His main research deals with the conservation biology of rare plants in Massachusetts and the ecology of tree communities in Malaysia. Dr. Primack also is involved in conservation and policy issues relating to the use of tropical forests in Malaysia, India, and Central America and is currently editing a book on the ecology, conservation, and management of Asian rain forests. He is the author of the textbook *Essentials of Conservation Biology* (1993), and serves as book review editor for the journal *Conservation Biology*. He is active in the Tropical Forest Foundation and the Tropical Ecosystems Directorate of the U.S. Man and the Biosphere Program.

ABOUT THE BOOK

Editor: Andrew D. Sinauer

Project Editor: Carol J. Wigg

Copy Editor: Norma Roche

Production Manager: Christopher Small

Book and Cover Design: Christopher Small

Book Production in QuarkXpress: Janice Holabird

Cover Manufacture: Henry N. Sawyer Company, Inc.

Book Manufacture: Courier Companies